Faith of Our Fathers

Faith of Our Fathers:
Popular Culture and Belief in Post-Reformation England, Ireland and Wales

Edited by

Joan Allen and Richard C. Allen

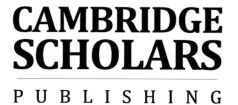

CAMBRIDGE
SCHOLARS

P U B L I S H I N G

Faith of Our Fathers: Popular Culture and Belief in Post-Reformation England, Ireland and Wales,
Edited by Joan Allen and Richard C. Allen

This book first published 2009

Cambridge Scholars Publishing

12 Back Chapman Street, Newcastle upon Tyne, NE6 2XX, UK

British Library Cataloguing in Publication Data
A catalogue record for this book is available from the British Library

ISBN (10): 1-4438-0487-8, ISBN (13): 978-1-4438-0487-5

THE FAITH OF OUR FATHERS:

THIS BOOK IS DEDICATED TO ALFRED ALLEN AND JAMES STRINGER

TABLE OF CONTENTS

Chapter Seven 118
'The Most Singular and Eccentric Sect of this Generation': The White
Quakers of Ireland, *c.*1840–1854
JAMES GREGORY

Chapter Eight 137
'High days and Holy days': St Patrick's Day in the North East of
England, *c.*1850–1900
JOAN ALLEN

Chapter Nine 157
'Exploited with fury on a thousand platforms': Women, Unionism and
the *Ne Temere* Decree in Ireland, 1908–1913
D.A.J. MACPHERSON

Chapter Ten 176
'What has been started in the cinema has ended in Maternity Homes for
single girls': The Church of England and popular culture in the industrial
diocese, Durham *c.*1860 – *c.*1930
ROBERT LEE

Contributors 198

Index 201

ACKNOWLEDGMENTS

First and foremost we would like to pay tribute to our contributors who have written such stimulating essays, and for responding generously and with remarkable patience to our editorial queries and suggestions. Their skilful analyses of popular culture and religion have given dynamic shape to this thematic volume and we hope that collectively and individually they are pleased with the final result.

We would like to record our thanks to the University of Northumbria who hosted the Popular Culture and Religion conference in July 2001 and to all those who took part, as speakers, rapporteurs or conferees. Although not all of the speakers were able to contribute to this collection their input at the conference has informed the intellectual debates with which we have wrestled.

Some of these chapters have been aired at other conferences too, and the editors would like to register their particular gratitude to the organisers of the North American Association for the Study of Welsh Culture and History Conference (Bryn Mawr, Pennsylvania, 2002); Harvard University Celtic Colloquium (October 2006) and the St Patrick's Day conference (Queens University, Belfast, March 2006) for providing an opportunity to disseminate their research and secure feedback.

We are grateful to Cambridge Scholars Press for providing a home for the collection and to Kate Legon who has, once again, produced an excellent index. Finally we would like to thank the following friends and colleagues for their support and encouragement: Rob Colls, Martin Farr, Allan Fear, Ray Howell, John Graham Jones, Tim Kirk, Roger Newbrook, Stephen Regan, Jennie Sparks and Rosie White.

INTRODUCTION

The study of popular culture has been an abiding preoccupation of historians and literary critics for many decades, not just in the British Isles but elsewhere too.[1] New perspectives and interpretations continue to be advanced, not least by those who have extended the earlier historiography to encompass a better understanding of gender and patriarchy.[2] In 2001 Northumbria University hosted an international conference on Popular Culture and Religion which brought together scholars from as far afield as the Americas and Australia as well as from various parts of Europe.[3] Then and since, historians have wrestled with the problems of definition and the difficulty of charting changes in popular culture over time. It was Peter Burke who first mapped the popular culture of pre-industrial European society by using broadsides and chapbooks to uncover the rituals and attitudes of ordinary people, and attempts by elites to modify behavioural patterns in line with their own view of the world. His work set the tone of the historiographical debate and prompted new lines of enquiry.[4] Barry Reay's edited collection on English seventeenth-century popular culture centred largely upon the attitudes of the middling sorts and complemented Burke's European survey.[5] Notwithstanding the expansive remit of Burke

---

[1] In 1978 Peter Burke's work on European popular culture drew upon the groundbreaking studies by Natalie Zemon Davis, Carlo Ginzburg, Keith Thomas and others. See P. Burke, *Popular Culture in Early Modern Europe* (Aldershot, 1978; revised edn. Cambridge, 1994).

[2] Morag Shiach, *Discourse on Popular Culture: class, gender and history in cultural analysis, 1730 to present* (Cambridge, 1989); T. Harris, 'Problematising Popular Culture', in T. Harris (ed.), *Popular Culture in England c.1500–1850* (Basingstoke, 1995), p. 13.

[3] Popular Culture and Religion Conference, Northumbria University, Newcastle, 12–14 July 2001. A follow-up conference was held at Northumbria in June 2002.

[4] Burke, *Popular Culture in Early Modern Europe*. See also Susan Karant-Nunn, *The Reformation of Ritual: an interpretation of early modern Germany* (London and New York, 1997); Martin Ingram, 'Reformation of Manners in Early Modern England', in Paul Griffiths, Adam Fox and Steve Hindle (eds), *The Experience of Authority in Early Modern England* (London, 1996), pp. 47–88.

[5] B. Reay (ed.), *Popular Culture in the Seventeenth Century England* (London, 1985, 1988).

and Reay's studies, and those which followed, much remained to be uncovered. In the mid-1990s Tim Harris drew attention to the need to find new and more appropriate sources for exploring a culture that was inadequately documented and frequently privatised.[6] His collection of essays set a new agenda that was more concerned with issues such as gender, religion and literacy which he believed had either been 'insufficiently explored or were in need of fresh examination'.[7] Recent commentators have agreed that the binary model, which distinguished between elite and popular culture, was a crude and unhelpful distortion, and have elected to stress the diversity and richness of popular cultures.[8] This has been a valuable development which has enabled scholars to acknowledge the control often exercised by ordinary people and to correct earlier misconceptions that cultural values were imposed unproblematically from above.

Religious beliefs largely shaped popular cultures and rituals, and this has impacted in varying degrees on the historiography.[9] For Christianity to retain its hold over the faithful the 'Godly community' had to be preserved at all costs.[10] The pressure to control popular customs was increasingly heightened in the post-Reformation period as puritan ideals took centre stage.[11] Even after Puritanism was displaced by a new religious ethos,

---

[6] Harris, 'Problematising Popular Culture', pp. 3, 6.

[7] Harris (ed.), *Popular Culture in England*, p. x.

[8] Barry Reay, *Popular Cultures in England, 1550–1750* (London and New York, 1998); J. M. Golby and A. W. Purdue, *The Civilisation of the Crowd: popular culture in England 1750–1900* (revised pbk edn. Stroud, 1999).

[9] For examples, see R. Hutton, *The Rise and Fall of Merry England: the ritual year 1400–1700* (Oxford, 1994); Anthony Fletcher and Peter Roberts (eds), *Religion, Culture and Society in Early Modern Britain: essays in honour of Patrick Collinson* (Cambridge, 1994), particularly ch. 3; M. Ingram, 'From Reformation to Toleration: popular religious cultures in England 1540–1690', in Harris (ed.), *Popular Culture in England*, ch. 5; K. Wrightson and D. Levine, *Poverty and Piety in an English Village: Terling 1525–1700* (Oxford, 1995); David Cressy, *Birth, Marriage and Death: ritual, religion and the life-cycle in Tudor and Stuart England* (Oxford, 1997); S. Williams, *Religious Belief and Popular Culture in Southwark c.1880–1939* (Oxford, 1999).

[10] Euan Cameron, 'The "Godly Community" in the Theory and Practice of the European Reformation', in W. J. Sheils and D. Wood (eds), *Studies in Church History, 23: voluntary religion* (Oxford, 1986), pp. 131–53.

[11] For example, see P. Collinson, *Godly People: essays on English Protestantism and Puritanism* (London, 1983) and his *The Birthpangs of Protestant England: religious and cultural change in the sixteenth and seventeenth centuries* (London, 1988); John Spurr, *English Puritanism, 1603–1689* (Basingstoke, 1998); J. Gwynfor Jones, 'Some Puritan influences on the Anglican Church in Wales in the

which gave rise to a plethora of nonconformist movements, godliness still secured the individual's place in respectable society. As the eighteenth century progressed religious belief was challenged by the rise of anticlericalism and, according to Jose Harris, by 'creeping secularisation' in the nineteenth century.[12] Nevertheless earlier belief systems proved remarkably resilient; many people clung more fiercely to their old religious practices as they were buffeted by the dislocating effects of economic and social change. In some parts of Britain and Ireland these insecurities occasionally spilled over into sectarianism, largely in response to the perceived threat of migrant cultures.[13]

This collection is an attempt to illuminate the nexus between religion and popular cultures after the Reformation. It makes no claim to be exhaustive for the chronological remit would render this impracticable. Rather, it offers new insights thematically via a selection of diverse contributions. These are differentiated by period and geography with a view to encouraging, as others have done before, an understanding of the complexity of popular cultures and the array of factors which determined how they were expressed over time.

The Reformation has to be considered a defining moment, not only for its long-term impact on the religious confession of the people but also in terms of its cultural manifestations. As already noted, Reformation historians have been at pains to complicate an earlier model which emphasised an absolute separation between elite and popular religious beliefs.[14] What Ethan Shagan and others have shown is that there were

---

early seventeenth century', *Journal of Welsh Religious History*, new series, 2 (2002), 19–50; James Innell Packer, *The Redemption and Restoration of Man in the Thought of Richard Baxter: a study in Puritan theology* (Carlisle, 2003).
[12] Jose Harris, *Private Lives, Public Spirit: a social history of Britain, 1870–1914* (Oxford, 1993), pp. 150–79. See also Callum Brown, *The Death of Christian Britain: understanding secularisation, 1800–2000* (London, 2000).
[13] For examples of sectarian divisions see John Walsh, 'Methodism and the Mob in the Eighteenth Century', in G. J. Cuming and D. Baker (eds), *Studies in Church History, 8: popular belief and practice* (Cambridge, 1972), pp. 213–27; P. J. Waller, *Sectarianism and Democracy: a political and social history of Liverpool, 1868–1939* (Liverpool, 1981); Graham Davis, *The Irish in Britain, 1815–1914* (Dublin, 1991); Steven Fielding, *Class and Ethnicity: Irish Catholics in England, 1880–1939* (Buckingham, 1993); Donald M. MacRaild, *Faith, Fraternity and Fighting: the Orange Order and Irish migrants in northern England, c.1850–1920* (Liverpool, 2005); Terence McBride, *The Experience of Irish Migrants to Glasgow, Scotland, 1863–1891* (Lampeter, Queenston and Lewiston, 2006).
[14] Burke, *Popular Culture in Early Modern Europe*; Christopher Haigh, *Reformation and Resistance in Tudor Lancashire* (London, 1975); Patrick

greater levels of accommodation and compromise on both sides of the divide.[15] Even those who believed religion had little to offer them were reluctant to cut themselves off from the 'ritual community'. Rites of passage were community events as much as religious ceremonies. While the clergy were accorded an official role in managing the ceremonial aspects of baptisms, marriages and burials, the presence of the wider community also served to legitimise the process. Inevitably changes in ritual practice following the Reformation were highly contested, especially where the Church actively sought to exclude from the rites of passage those who had been excommunicated. The clergy, however, did not always succeed in exerting their authority, particularly over cultural practice.

Maddy Gray's study of ritual space highlights the inherent contradictions between post-Reformation dogma and its practical implementation by individual ministers, serving in isolated parishes such as Bedwellty in seventeenth century south-east Wales. Her chapter explores popular attitudes towards Christian baptism and burial. Wales, Gray informs us, was 'notorious in this period for its religious conservatism' and the clergy struggled to persuade parishioners to give up their attachment to the 'hen ffydd' (old religion). The continued use of relics, candles and rosaries, as well as the practice of 'churching' women, were viewed as particularly problematic. The Rev. Lewis James who took up his appointment in Bedwellty in 1633 emerges as a man torn between a changing belief system and the unchanging needs of a community which looked to him to provide not only spiritual leadership but the certainty of salvation in an uncertain world. Economic constraints played a significant part in determining what he could and, more importantly, could not do. With a stipend of just £10 per annum and a family to support he needed to retain his position, and he could not do that without the backing of his parishioners.

Eryn White's chapter on the Welsh Church in eighteenth-century Wales also reflects upon the importance of rites of passage which held both 'a traditional and superstitious meaning for many people'. Most of all, however, she highlights the multi-functional role of the clergy and the

Collinson, *The Religion of Protestants: the Church in English society 1559–1625* (Oxford, 1982); Eamon Duffy, *The Stripping of the Altars: traditional religion in England, c.1400–c.1580* (New Haven and London, 1992), and his 'The Long Reformation: Catholicism, Protestantism and the multitude', in Nicholas Tyacke (ed.), *England's Long Reformation 1500-1800* (London, 1998), pp. 33–70.
[15] Ethan H. Shagan, *Popular Politics and the English Reformation* (Cambridge and New York, 2002).

church in the community. While parishioners were quick to criticise those clergymen who neglected their duties, whether in failing to officiate at baptisms and burials, or denying spiritual support to the dying, they appreciated the way that ministers and curates provided charitable relief to the poor and education for the young. Even when challenged by dissenters from the seventeenth century onwards, 'y fam eglwys' (the mother church), as White infers, 'remained one of the central institutions in Welsh communities'. Parish churches and churchyards were not just sacred space, but the ideal place for the community to assemble, celebrate and play. To a large extent the immediate community assumed ownership of their parish church and accessed it on their own terms, without necessarily feeling obligated to attend divine service on a regular basis. White notes that the clergy were increasingly less than assiduous about pursuing non-attenders or insisting upon churching women, suggesting that the old relationship between minister and congregation had been recalibrated. She illustrates this by recounting an assault in 1756 on the curate of Coedcernyw in Monmouthshire by the churchwarden and clerk who objected strongly to his interference in the financial management of the parish. If this seems to indicate that the old hierarchy was being breached, it is also worth noting that the seating arrangements inside the church, whereby social status was visibly and emphatically displayed, were always robustly defended, if necessary by resort to consistory courts. Opponents of the Established Church would later argue that these ambiguities represented a genuine dissatisfaction with the modes of religious worship, but as White demonstrates this is far from the truth. Rather it reflected the easy familiarity between church and people.

Few would argue that securing a good death, via the ministrations of a caring clergy whose job it was to help the individual to find their way to salvation, lay at the heart of the relationship between church and people. As the concept of purgatory and prayerful intercessions on behalf of the departed were no longer acceptable, devout Protestants were presented with a stark choice between heaven or hell. Inevitably, in this climate of uncertainty, the people set greater store by the pronouncements of Divines and other educated commentators. Clark Lawlor's contribution uses the example of Dudley Ryder, a nonconformist, to explore changing ideas about Christian death in the early modern period. His interdisciplinary work draws from religious, literary and medical sources in order to elucidate popular and elite views on the *Ars Moriendi* – the art of dying well – which first appeared at the end of the fifteenth century. There were competing Protestant discourses concerning whether consumption was 'a good or bad disease for the devout Christian'. In the eyes of popular divines, such as the seventeenth-century physician Thomas Fuller, a slow wasting disease or consumption provided the invalid with time to prepare for death and to reconcile themselves with God and their families. Not everyone agreed. Lawlor singles out Jeremy Taylor and his 1651 text *Holy Living and Holy Dying* which 'exposed the foolishness of desiring a consumptive death'. Taylor considered these popular attitudes undesirable. He brought much needed 'medical realism' to a discourse strongly influenced by romantic ideas and acute anxieties about eternal salvation. Ryder's positive response to his consumptive illness was strongly informed by the writings of Fuller and Sir Thomas Browne, as well as seventeenth-century poets which led him to believe that dying would be a 'soft' and easy transition, rather like going to sleep. Lawlor envisages Ryder as imagining himself 'making a dramatic exit to everlasting glory'. These popular and elite engagements with death and disease did not disappear, and were revisited during the evangelical revival.

The religious revival which encompassed Europe and north America in the eighteenth century can be attributed in part to the impact of charismatic preaching by individuals, such as John and Charles Wesley, George Whitefield, Howel Harris and Daniel Rowland. It also drew strength from post-Reformation anxieties, which destabilised the old relationships at the heart of orthodoxy and encouraged the spread of alternative religious movements. As David Ceri Jones and Edward Royle have shown the evangelical revival quickly took root in Wales and England as part of the 'trend towards the democratisation of Christianity'. Although there was much that was distinctive about revival in these two countries, both authors stress that these shifts need to be viewed in their trans-national and trans-Atlantic contexts. Jones' study of Welsh Methodism focuses upon Whitefield, 'the first evangelical celebrity', who made the most of improvements in communications and travel. Whitefield and Harris first met in Cardiff in March 1739 and thereafter collaborated closely on the alignment of English and Welsh Calvinistic Methodism. Harnessing print culture they launched a periodical, *The Weekly History*. This created 'a public space' in which conversion narratives and testimonies of faith could be shared by the international Methodist community. Women particularly benefited from access to the journal and used the letters page as a forum for self-help. These early Methodists made many personal sacrifices and suffered hostility for their religious beliefs and their attacks on popular pastimes. Yet during the political instability of the mid-1740s they became model subjects of the British state. Thereafter, as Linda Colley claims,

Protestantism is held to have been a unifying force in the wake of the wars with France and Spain.[16]

Both Jones and Royle emphasise the fellowship network between Methodists in Britain and elsewhere in the world. Royle seeks to establish the importance of regional studies, 'not to test a generalisation . . . but, rather, to contribute an interpretation rooted in a specific and limited geographical context, which can then form a part of the mosaic which makes up the national picture'. He posits that while religious revival in the early eighteenth century swept the western world from Moravia to Massachusetts, an explanation is to be found in the interaction of general factors with local circumstances. By 1800 Yorkshire was one of the strongest centres of the Evangelical revival, and Royle offers this as a good case study to illuminate the social, economic and religious context in which dynamic personalities were able to effect a religious transformation. Key factors in the revival were the widespread dissatisfaction with existing religious provision, the considerable support advanced by some wealthy and influential members of eighteenth-century society, and the impact of charismatic preaching on scattered rural communities. In the Vale of York some of the livings were so impoverished that the clergy were unable to provide both morning and afternoon services. Parishioners who wished could easily find an additional Sunday service, but this 'did not build up parochial loyalty'. In the event the 'less formal and restrained services' of Methodist meetings proved an attractive alternative.

Methodism may well have been the most popular form of nonconformity in the eighteenth century, but it was not the only choice available to those who were disaffected with the Established Church. The Religious Society of Friends (Quakers) which emerged in the aftermath of the mid-seventeenth century civil wars in the British Isles attracted many adherents, particularly in the north of England but with communities throughout Britain, Ireland and the Americas. An important distinguishing feature of Quakerism was that the Friends abjured *all* notion of a paid ministry, insisting that there was no need for an intermediary between God and the people. Richard Allen and James Gregory examine different aspects of Quakerism and the attitudes to popular culture. Both stress the importance of print culture to the Society as it developed and changed. The recourse to print was not simply a propagandist strategy. For a religious group, which set so much store upon private contemplation and exposition of belief, testimonies and diaries assumed particular

---

[16] L. Colley, *Britons: Forging the Nation 1707–1837* (New Haven and London, 1992).

significance. It is fortunate that a considerable percentage of these private and public documents survive for they enable us to access a hidden world of religious struggle and revivalism.

Allen's study throws the spotlight on the intransigent views of John Kelsall jnr, an eighteenth-century diarist and clerk of the Dolobran meeting in Montgomeryshire. Kelsall scorned the rise of popular consumerism in Britain and sought to persuade the wider community of the spiritual and moral benefits of the simple life. Yet, as Allen observes, even Kelsall was unable to distance himself completely from what he regarded as a decadent society. As an intellectual he frequently courted the attentions of the affluent elite in his desire for cultured conversation. This did not prevent him from exposing the superficial values of the world about him and promoting a moral reformation.

As with other religious groups generalisations often mask important differences. Gregory's study of the White Quakers in Ireland is a case in point for this small but vocal mid-nineteenth century sect in Dublin, Waterford, Clonmel and Mountmellick exhibited characteristics that bore little resemblance to mainstream Quakerism elsewhere. He breaks new ground for this group has been little studied. Their origins can be located in the erosion of the Quaker code of discipline and tendency towards worldliness. A handful of leading Irish Quakers, such as Joshua Jacob and Abigail Beale, set out to provide an alternative vision notably in their journal *The Progress of Truth*. This schismatic group proved to be highly controversial not least because they embraced 'communism in property, and the alleged abandonment of marriage'. Gregory explores the way their ideas were rejected by Friends and the wider population, and concludes that 'resistance to constructive change and the fear of open discussion remained a feature of the Society'.

The desire to publicly proclaim and celebrate religious belief was a common impulse, both before and after the Reformation, but such displays could be a source of conflict as well as community solidarity. Joan Allen's analysis of the St Patrick's Day festival in north-east England considers the way that the event was politicised in the second half of the nineteenth century as the campaign for Home Rule gathered momentum. The overwhelmingly Catholic confession of the region's Irish migrant population meant that there was rather less sectarian conflict and little friction associated with high days and holy days. The political overtones of the St Patrick Day festival was challenged by the Catholic clergy who were anxious to distance themselves and their congregations from Fenianism. But nationalist politics was not the only source of friction between the Catholic Church and the festival's organisers. In many areas of major Irish settlement the Catholic hierarchy sought to counter the claim that the Saint's day was just an excuse for excessive drinking and immoral behaviour. More focus was placed on attendance at special masses and on the *Corpus Christi* procession as a way of demonstrating the respectability and religiosity of the faithful. Although the temperance lobby achieved some success in providing an effective counter culture the propagandist opportunities of the festival were too important to be denied. The indoor meeting, which was the centrepiece of the Tyneside celebrations, was dominated by political speeches and fundraising for the nationalist cause.

The political and religious life of Ulster is the focus of James MacPherson's study. He examines the impact of the 1908 Papal decree *Ne Temere*, which insisted that children born of a mixed marriage should be brought up as Catholics, during the crisis over the third Home Rule bill. He anchors his analysis around a particular piece of evidence, the extraordinary McCann marriage case *c.*1909 which ruled that the children should be removed in accordance with the decree. This controversial judgement is held to explain why women were subsequently drawn into Unionist politics in order to preserve their domestic safety and autonomy. The Protestant community of Belfast were demographically dominant, and yet still insecure about their position and the threat that Home Rule represented. This emotive case appeared to suggest that their fears were not ill-founded and Protestant women were galvanised into direct action. This chapter demonstrates the interaction of gender and popular belief at a time of great political change in Ireland.

The problems encountered by Church of England clergymen appointed to serve the hitherto neglected coal communities of County Durham is the focus of Robert Lee's study. This new mission presented significant challenges as the incumbent minister struggled both to settle into an unfamiliar environment and to liberate 'the uneducated mind from the fallacies of popular culture'. The responsibilities of 'parochial leadership' were substantial for the popular literature of the time attested to the rowdy, rough culture of northern coalfield communities. As it turned out, the capitalist culture which defined British society in the nineteenth and twentieth centuries was viewed as a much greater threat than the old semi-pagan pastimes of old. These difficulties were compounded by endemic migration which undermined the clergy's desire to inculcate bonds of religious and social solidarity. While the popularity of 'parish entertainments' seemed to suggest that a reformation of manners had been wrought, such improvement was far from uniform or stable. During the miner's strike of 1892 Lord Londonderry's bank inspector was 'rough musicked' as he returned home and Lee provides plenty of evidence that a popular culture 'red in tooth and claw' continued into the early decades of the twentieth century. Inevitably, church attendance suffered as leisure opportunities proved more attractive to those who worked hard all week, and while the clergy railed against the dangers of alcohol they were also wary of the fanaticism of the teetotallers.

As this collection of essays has shown in other periods and for many diverse communities, conflict not harmony typifies the transitions in popular culture and religion. If a reformation of manners was detectable the evidence suggests that the people exercised their own free will in accepting or rejecting changes to their cultural and religious life.

CHAPTER ONE

RITUAL SPACE AND RITUAL BURIAL IN THE EARLY MODERN CHRISTIAN TRADITION

MADELEINE GRAY

The Civil War and Commonwealth registers of the parish of Bedwellty, in the hills of south Wales, contain several entries for the burials of children described as *filii abortivi*. The word *abortivi* is possibly being used here to mean 'premature': this is the sense in which it was used in the Latin translation of the Bible, when St Paul was said to have described himself as *abortivum*, 'one untimely born'.[1] Equally, the word has also been used to denote a still-birth. An entry in the Bedwellty registers in 1650 refers to twins, one of whom was born alive and baptized, while the other was described as *abortivus* and buried.[2] These infants were, therefore, unbaptized but were still recorded in the burial registers and were presumably buried in consecrated ground with at least some of the rituals of the church. The same register of burials also contains occasional entries for children explicitly categorised as unbaptized. Such descriptions are rare in the extreme.[3] The right of the unbaptized to burial was one of the

---

[1] I Cor. 15:8.

[2] Gwent County Record Office (hereafter GCRO), Cwmbrân, D/Pa.14.104.

[3] Will Coster, 'Tokens of innocence: infant baptism, death and burial in early modern England', in Bruce Gordon and Peter Marshall (eds), *The Place of the Dead: death and remembrance in late medieval and early modern Europe* (Cambridge, 2000), pp. 266–87 suggests that the term 'chrisom child' changed its significance in sixteenth-century England from 'child dying between baptism and churching of the mother' to 'child dying before baptism'. The evidence is based on correlation of births and burials in one English parish and though fascinating is probably inconclusive. Nevertheless it suggests an ambiguity of approach to the

bones of contention in the Church of England between the Elizabethan Settlement in 1559 and the Restoration of 1660. The elucidation of these entries in the Bedwellty registers can therefore tell us a great deal about the renegot-iation of admission to, and exclusion from, the ritual community in the early modern period. From an anomaly in one parish register, the burial rituals offered to these children unfold into a consideration of the meaning of the sacraments in the post-Reformation Anglican Church, changing concepts and perceptions of ritual space, and the complex and often contested relationship between 'official' and 'popular' religion – two very problematic terms.

The history of parish graveyards has been studied from a number of perspectives: archaeological, demographic, literary, artistic and even ecological. Protestant reformers attempted to separate the dead from the spiritual community of the living,[4] and nineteenth-century public health reformers tried to do the same for the physical remains of the dead. Nevertheless, in many settlements, church and chapel graveyards survive as ritual spaces at the heart of the community, delimited from the space of the living by only the most permeable of boundaries, a low wall or fence over and through which the space of the dead can be seen and entered. These graveyards are one of the most distinctive ritual spaces in the western European tradition. They are in fact part of a concentric series of sacred spaces: the church enclosure of the early medieval tradition, the churchyard and the church building itself, then the chancel, the sanctuary, and finally the altar where the most holy of ritual activities took place. Each of these sacred spaces was deliberately consecrated with rituals laden with symbolic meaning. This pattern of concentric sacred spaces can be paralleled in many other traditions. The distinctive feature of Christian tradition is the location of a ritual burial space at the physical heart of the living community. This tendency is so fundamental that settlements have moved to be nearer the burial places of holy people. The ritual community of medieval Christianity was thus extended to include the dead as well as the living, an extension which was reinforced by the Catholic doctrine of Purgatory and the emphasis on the validity of prayers to saints and prayers for the dead.[5]

---

burial of the unbaptised in a large upland Yorkshire parish (Kirkburton in the West Riding) which is arguably similar to Bedwellty.
[4] Craig Koslofsky, *The Reformation of the Dead* (New York, 1999), especially pp. 46–54.
[5] An extensive literature on this topic is summarized in Eamon Duffy, *The Stripping of the Altars* (New Haven and London, 1992), pp. 327–37.

Churchyards are now used almost exclusively for burial. In many communities, separate cemeteries have been provided for this purpose, and burial in the actual churchyard is seen as a privilege, a mark of social esteem or status within a particular church. In this sense burial in the ritual space of the churchyard is an honour similar to that of burial within the church itself. The medieval churchyard had a much wider range of functions. Many churchyards contained 'crosses' in the form of pillars elaborately carved with depictions of the Crucifixion, and occasionally accompanied by the Virgin and Child, the Last Judgement, and a complex array of saints. These could be seen from outside the churchyard and linked the mysteries of the inner sacred space of the church, with its wealth of iconographic decoration, to the secular space outside. They depicted the central Christian mystery of the Crucifixion as the hinge between sacred and secular, between the ritual space of church and churchyard and the space of the world.[6] The churchyard was also host to a wide range of activities. In addition to burials, there were ritual processions, open-air sermons and meetings, as well as more secular functions such as church ales, traditional games and even commercial activities. It was in many ways the central meeting space for the community, and this could lead to disputes. The contested nature of the churchyard became paradoxically more acute in the period after the Reformation, when those reformers who challenged the fundamental concept of sacred space were also attempting to restrict the 'profane' use of the churchyard and to prohibit the entertainments which took place there.[7]

The ritual space of the graveyard is defined by the ceremonies enacted within it – the initial act of consecration and the subsequent rituals of burial according to the liturgy of the Church. There is thus a relationship between ritual space and ritual community. However, this relationship was also defined by the means used to exclude people, or to admit them only under certain proscribed circumstances. The right to burial in consecrated ground was not automatic in the medieval and early modern church, nor was it unproblematic. Restrictions on burials were the subject of conflict, and, as far as can be deduced from the records, disputes mostly arose

---

[6] M. Gray and E. Martin, 'Images of the Crucified Christ in Medieval Gwent', *Journal of Welsh Religious History*, New Series, 3 (2003), 1–22.
[7] David Dymond, 'God's Disputed Acre', *Journal of Ecclesiastical History*, 50 (1999), 464–97.

because of different folk traditions and official, orthodox perspectives.[8]
Yet it can be surprisingly difficult to establish what the official orthodoxy
was. This becomes even more complex in the post-Reformation period in
England and Wales. The incomplete nature of the English Reformation,
the many compromises and accommodations which had to be made in
order to secure a religious settlement acceptable to the majority of the
people, bred a reluctance to define legal restrictions too precisely. It is
nevertheless crucial to establish what constituted the official legal
framework. Whether or not it was accepted in every detail at parochial
level, this was the framework within which opposition and renegotiation
had to function. It is not possible to assess the significance of the entries in
the Bedwellty parish register, and the nature of any pressure which may
have been brought to bear on the incumbent, without detailed knowledge
of the constraints within which he operated.

Membership of the ritual community of the medieval church was based
on the sacraments. In one sense, the body of the individual Christian was
itself considered to be a sacred space, imbued with rituals of consecration
and differentiation. This concept of the body as sacred was reflected in the
wish of the Christian for burial in holy ground, ground which had been
consecrated by the burial of holy people. The traditional Catholic concept
of the Church as including the dead as well as the living was symbolised
by the funeral ritual; the bringing of the body to a consecrated churchyard
at the centre of the inhabited space, and the offering of prayers and masses
for the salvation of the soul.[9] As a result, there were extensive restrictions
on burials in consecrated ground. Those who died as excommunicants,
ritually cut off from the spiritual community, were denied religious burial
rites, as were those who died guilty of unabsolved mortal sin. Suicides
were also considered to have placed themselves outside of the ritual
community and its spatial equivalent because they had defied God's plan
for themselves. The church lawyer Gratian in his *Decretum*[10] stated that
'those whose sins have not been forgiven should not be assisted by the
holy place after death'; if sinners are buried in consecrated ground, 'the
holy ground will not free them but rather accuse them of the sin of

---

[8] For this and the following paragraphs I am indebted to a discussion on the
medieval-religion online discussion group in April 1998, archived at
http://www.jiscmail.ac.uk/cgi-bin/webadmin?A1= ind9804&L=medieval-religion.
[9] Duffy, *Stripping of the Altars*, pp. 368–9.
[10] Compiled in *c*.1140 and first printed in Strasbourg in 1471.

presumption' at the Last Judgement.[11] Of interest to archaeologists, who like to consider evidence for continuity of use in ritual spaces, is the fact that Gratian also instructs that the bodies of *pagani* and *infideles* be removed from a church before it is dedicated.[12] A church or churchyard which had been polluted by the burial of the body of an excommunicant had to be ritually purified with holy water.[13]

Sinners were considered to have removed themselves from the ritual community, and therefore did not qualify for burial in consecrated ground. Based on John Cassian's fourth-century prohibition, medieval canon law also excluded those who had never been ritually admitted to the community of belief, namely those who had not been baptised.[14] Folk custom went further than canon law in excluding not only the unbaptised and stillborn children but even women who died while pregnant, since the foetus within them was not baptised. The orthodox argument of the Christian Church was that as a pregnant woman had access to all the other sacraments she should be buried in consecrated ground. Nevertheless, women who had died in childbirth and even women who had died before they could be 'churched' or ritually purified after the birth process were sometimes buried in unconsecrated ground.[15]

The burial of the unbaptized is thus an example of how folk belief was less accepting than official doctrine, although, as so frequently happened, this was mediated in actual practice. For the medieval church, baptism was the one sacrament which could be administered by the unqualified and even by a woman. The traditional Catholic belief is that sacraments work *ex opere operato*, by their own inherent power, and irrespective of the limitations of the person administering them. In the case of baptism, Thomas Aquinas, whose views may be considered authoritative, went so

---

[11] *Decretum* C.13 q.2 c.16–17: I am grateful for this and the following references to Stephen Allen of the University of Notre Dame, largely drawn from his unpublished paper at the 1997 Kalamazoo conference, 'Pollution and Community: Church Burials in Later Medieval Canon Law'.

[12] *De cons.* D.1 c.27–28.

[13] According to a canon of Innocent III, in the *Liber extra*, 3.4.70. See Allen, 'Pollution and Community'.

[14] For Cassian see J. P. Migne, *Patrologiae Latinae Cursus Completus* (221 vols. Paris, 1844–55, 1862–4), XL, p. 573. I am obliged to Wyn Thomas for this reference.

[15] Burchard of Worms criticized this practice and even insisted on penance for those responsible for it, in the *Corrector* XIX: 5. I am indebted to Nancy Caciola of the University of California for this reference.

far as to claim that even an unbaptised person could legitimately baptise a child *in extremis*.[16] Midwives were therefore able to baptise the newborn by claiming that the child had been born alive and had lived long enough to be baptized, and would even baptize unborn babies whose lives were in danger. In northern France and the Channel Islands, women who had died in childbirth could be churched by proxy, a friend of the dead woman standing in for her during the ceremony.[17] Yet there was continuing unease in some folk traditions about the burial of the unbaptised. Anne O'Connor's *Child Murderess and Dead Child Traditions* records a number of European societies in which treading on the graves of unbaptised children was thought to bring disaster, from the contagion of 'grave-merels' or 'grave-scab' to the Irish tradition of the 'hungry grass' which grew on the unmarked graves of unbaptised children and caused starvation if trodden on.[18]

The Protestant Reformation heralded, among other things, a change in the concept of the ritual community. The implications of the doctrine of 'salvation by faith alone' implied the breaking of the link between the living and the dead. The intricate medieval tradition of prayers, masses and offerings for the souls of the departed was declared to be futile. Death for the Protestant was now a final separation: the living could not communicate with the dead, nor could they assist their passage to salvation. This was symbolised in Protestant Germany by a return to the practice of burials on the outskirts of larger settlements, endorsing Luther's argument that the burial ground should be a place of quiet retreat which symbolised the removal of the dead from the world of the living. This change in the location of burial grounds was regarded as highly significant. Inevitably Catholics argued against it, defending the centrality of the churchyard in the community and the importance of the place of the dead in everyday life.[19]

The Reformation also brought about changes in attitudes to the sacraments and their importance. Luther was far from clear about the meaning he attached to the sacrament of baptism. On the one hand, he

---

[16] *Summa Theologica* part 3, q 67 articuli 3–5, citing texts from Isidore of Seville, Augustine, Pope Nicholas and Pope Gregory II. I am grateful to Bill East for this reference.

[17] This is drawn from the medieval religion online discussion group. See n.8.

[18] Anne O'Connor, *Child Murderess and Dead Child Traditions* (Helsinki, 1991), pp. 37, 70.

[19] For example, the Leipzig burial controversy of 1536 is provided in Koslofsky, *Reformation of the Dead*, pp. 54–77.

viewed baptism as a physical channel through which the gift of faith could be imparted. God, he observed, had 'desired that by [baptism] little children, who were incapable of greed and superstition, might be initiated and sanctified in the simple faith of his word'.[20] He described baptism as a more important sacrament than the Eucharist. It was regarded as 'incomparably greater' because 'the Eucharist is not so necessary that salvation depends on it'.[21] On the other hand, in spite of what he maintained about the importance of baptism, Luther did not in the last analysis regard it as vital for salvation. His thoughts on this are summarized in a fascinating little pamphlet, 'Comfort for women who have had a miscarriage', which arose out of his own pastoral concerns. In this work he suggested that the mother's love for the dead child would secure all that was necessary for its salvation, without the actual rite of baptism being conducted:

> Because the mother is a believing Christian, it is to be hoped that her heartfelt cry and deep longing to bring her child to be baptized will be accepted by God as an effective prayer . . . Who can doubt that those Israelite children who died before they could be circumcized on the eighth day were yet saved by the prayers of their parents in view of the promise that God willed to be their God? God (they say) has not limited his power to the sacraments, but has made a covenant with us through his word.[22]

What Luther is saying here is not, of course, that the sacrament of baptism was meaningless. Rather, he suggests that in extreme cases the bestowal of the sacrament's blessings could be effected through prayer and faith, without the physical act of the pouring of water. The infant thus becomes an accepted member of the ritual community on the basis of the mother's love which, in such circumstances, assumes an almost sacramental quality. Reformers in the Calvinist tradition viewed baptism more as a public covenant which acknowledged the child to be a member of the Christian community of faith. Baptism could not procure salvation, but it was still a recognition of membership of the ritual community.[23]

---

[20] Jaroslav Pelikan et al (eds), *Luther's Works* (55 vols. St. Louis and Philadelphia, 1955–1986), 36, p. 57.

[21] Ibid., 40, p. 23.

[22] Ibid., 43, pp. 245–50.

[23] For example, see John Calvin, *Institutes of the Christian Religion*, IV, p. xiv, in John T. McNeill (ed.), *Calvin: Institutes of the Christian Religion* (2 vols. London, 1960), II, p. 1465.

The Protestant Reformation in England and Wales was a compromise between the ideas of the more radical reformers and the traditionalism of a large number (possibly a majority) of the population. Nevertheless, the Church of England was broadly Calvinist in its theology. According to the Thirty-Nine Articles, the basic statement of belief hammered out in 1571, sacraments were to be regarded as 'witnesses and signs of grace' which were only effective for those who received them in a proper frame of mind. The only valid baptism was public baptism 'in the face of the church', while private baptism, especially as administered by midwives, was disapproved of.[24] In practical terms, the Protestant settlement in England and Wales meant changes in the services of the Church. The earlier restriction on the burials of the unbaptised, and those who were identified as excommunicants and suicides, was temporarily removed. This has obvious implications for our understanding of the way in which the Church of England interpreted the significance of baptism and the nature of the ritual community. Notwithstanding the emergence of more tolerant attitudes, in practice new and lesser burial rites for the unbaptised were introduced. Bishop Barnes of Durham, for example, instructed his clergy to teach their parishioners that

> if any infant die without public baptism first to it ministered, that the same is not to be condemned or adjudged as a damned soul, but to be well hoped of, and the body to be interred in the churchyard, yet without ringing or any divine service or solemnity, because the same was not solemnly professed and received into the church and congregation.[25]

It ought to be remembered that Barnes was operating in a theologically conservative climate. His instructions are a delicate attempt both to negotiate the contradictions in post-Reformation thinking on the nature and privileges of the ritual community, and to reconcile the official doctrine with traditionalist thinking.

An attempt was made in the ecclesiastical legislation of 1603–4 to reintroduce some restrictions on the right to burial in consecrated ground and with the full rituals of the Church. Canon 68 stated:

---

[24] The Thirty-Nine Articles are found in a number of old editions of the *Book of Common Prayer*. A convenient modern text is reprinted in M. A. Noll, *Confessions and Catechisms of the Reformation* (Leicester, 1991).

[25] Quoted in David Cressy, *Birth, Marriage and Death: ritual, religion and the life-cycle in Tudor and Stuart England* (Oxford, 1999), p. 114.

No minister shall refuse or delay to bury any corpse that is brought to the church or churchyard (convenient warning having been given him thereof before) in such manner and form as is prescribed in the said Book of Common Prayer.[26]

It then goes on to identify the certain exceptions to ecclesiastical law. Thus, those excommunicated for serious crimes 'where no-one can testify to their repentance' and suicides were once again explicitly barred. If this was an attempt to clarify matters, it failed. At the 1604 Hampton Court Conference, Richard Bancroft, Bishop of London, defended baptism by midwives:

the state of the infant, dying unbaptised, being uncertain, and to God only known; but if he die baptised, there is an evident assurance that he is saved; who is he that having any religion in him, would not speedily, by any means, procure his child to be baptized, and rather ground his action upon Christ's promise, than his omission thereof upon God's secret judgement?[27]

The popular response to this official standpoint can be read in the records of the church courts. We cannot assume that there was any sort of homogenous or unified 'popular' belief, any more than that the official line was coherent. There is evidence of complaints in the church courts against ministers who preached that the actual ritual of baptism did not matter, who refused to baptise children privately (though there were always suspicions that this was due more to laziness than to conviction) and who would not accept baptism by midwives. On the other hand, there were just as many complaints against traditionalist ministers who preached that children who died unbaptised were damned and refused to read the burial service over them. The concerns of the ordinary members of the congregation seem to have been local, personal and essentially pastoral. The increasing emphasis which the Church placed on the sacraments in the 1630s seems mainly to have affected attitudes towards the Eucharist, but there is little evidence of any overt change in thinking about baptism, or of any change in popular attitudes towards the burial of the unbaptised.[28]

---

[26] Sir Robert Phillimore, *The Ecclesiastical Law of the Church of England* (2nd edn. London, 1895), p. 669.
[27] Cressy, *Birth, Marriage and Death*, pp. 114–15.
[28] Ibid., pp. 101–23. See also the numerous references in Judith Maltby, *Prayer Book and People in Elizabethan and Early Stuart England* (Cambridge, 1998).

One of the first decisions taken by Parliament after the outbreak of
Civil War in 1642 was to summon an assembly of suitable reformed
clergy, the Westminster Assembly (1643–1652), to debate the reform of
religious practice. This produced the Westminster Confession (1646) and
an alternative Prayer Book, the *Directory of Public Worship*, based largely
on John Knox's Genevan service book of 1556, the *Book of Common
Order*. The *Directory of Public Worship* has no order of service for the
burial of the dead:

> When any person departeth this life, let the dead body, on the day of
> burial, be decently attended from the house to the place appointed for
> public burial, *and there immediately interred, without any ceremony.*[29]

There was no need even for the presence of the minister, though Knox's
Book of Common Order did suggest he might turn up if convenient,
advising that he 'goeth to the church if he be not far off and maketh some
comfortable exhortation to the people touching death and resurrection'.[30]
This was intended as a final separation of the living from the dead.
Ironically, though, it also left space for the continued, if clandestine, use
of the rituals of the former Established Church.

It is within this context that the significance of the 1650 entry in the
Bedwellty parish register must be assessed. In order to do this the attitudes
of both the community and the incumbent clergyman, Lewis James, must
be appraised.[31] The pre-industrial parish of Bedwellty was the largest in
Monmouthshire and one of the largest in south Wales: over twenty-five
square miles of rough mountain and steep river valley, with only a little
good farmland. The parish church was centrally placed but it was still
eight or nine miles from the farms at the northern extremity of the parish.
Parishioners from the eastern part of the parish had to cross a steep valley
and the fast-flowing river Sirhowy to reach the parish church, and so far
as is known, there were no bridges there before the eighteenth century.[32]

---

[29] F. Procter and W. H. Frere, *A New History of the Book of Common Prayer*
(London, 1949), p. 161 (my italicisation added for emphasis).
[30] W. D. Maxwell, *John Knox's Genevan Service Book, 1556* (Edinburgh and
London, 1931), pp. 161, 164.
[31] For more detail of both than it has been possible to include here, see M. Gray,
'The Clergy as Remembrancers of the Community: Lewis James, Curate of
Bedwellty 1633–67, and the Civil War Clergy of Monmouthshire',
Monmouthshire Antiquary, XVI (2000), 113–20.
[32] Joseph A. Bradney, *A History of Monmouthshire* (5 vols. London, 1904–1933;
Cardiff, 1993), *V: The Hundred of Newport*, ed. M. Gray (Cardiff, 1993), p. 146.

Moreover, very little is known about the religious complexion of the parish. Wales was notorious in this period for its religious conservatism. Pilgrimages, images and candles survived at least until late into the sixteenth century, and in the 1620s Rhys Prichard, the vicar of Llandovery in Carmarthenshire, having failed to prevent his flock from using the rosary, was reduced to exhorting them to use it prayerfully.[33] The parish of Bedwellty had a number of families with Catholic sympathies and it may be significant that the parish church still retains one of its pre-Reformation treasures, a magnificent oak cupboard carved with the Five Wounds and the Instruments of the Passion. However, the parish was also near some of the focal points of Protestant nonconformity. The young Henry Walter preached in the neighbouring parish of Mynyddislwyn during the 1650s and after the Restoration founded an Independent congregation there.[34] To the west, in the adjoining parish of Gelli-gaer, a group of Baptists included the local landowner Edward Prichard of Llancaiach Fawr.

Lewis James was appointed to serve the Bedwellty parish in 1633.[35] Although little survives about his background or his religious ideas, his own statements in the parish register seems to suggest that he held strong Royalist sympathies. While he was almost certainly not a graduate, he was clearly well-educated and displayed painstaking care and respect for the written record. He went to considerable lengths to secure a proper register for his parish and kept careful records even during the catastrophic plague year of 1638. He was also meticulous in his attention to his duties. In spite of the size of his parish, he seems to have tried to attend to the needs of all his flock. The registers contain several entries for infants who were born, baptized, died and buried on the same day.[36] His failure to baptize some of the children he buried in the 1650s could not be attributed to any negligence on his part.

The victory of Parliament in the Civil Wars was followed by a determined campaign for religious reform. In 1650, when a commission was empowered to examine and evict inadequate and unworthy ministers in Wales, Lewis James was one of those ejected, possibly on account of

---

[33] Anthony Packer, 'Medieval Welsh Spirituality', *Journal of Welsh Religious History*, 4 (1996), 7.
[34] Bradney, *Hundred of Newport*, p. 144 (though Walter was curate at Mounton, not Mynyddislwyn). See J. E. Lloyd and R. T. Jenkins (eds), *The Dictionary of Welsh Biography down to 1940* (London, 1959), *sub* Henry Walter; Edmund Jones, *Account of the Parish of Aberystruth . . .* (Trefecca, 1779), p. 96.
[35] Bradney, *Hundred of Newport*, p. 150.
[36] GCRO, D/Pa.14.104.

his royalist sympathies.[37] He did not, however, leave his parish. Instead, as the register reveals, he continued to minister in Bedwellty, baptising children and recording marriages and burials. When he was reappointed at the Restoration he recorded in the register that

> all the children w'ch Lewis James, cler', christened, as also all such persons w'ch were buried (and also all those persons w'ch were married) in Bedwelltie from the said twentieth day of June untill the third day of June 1660 were recorded in this register in order as before, as you may see in the subsequent pagine, especiallie the children baptized as if they had bin christened *in facie ecclesiae*.[38]

In order to retain his place in the community, he must have been supported by his parishioners. He may have had a house and a little land in the parish, and his wife would normally have received a fifth of the income of the parish to maintain herself and her children. However, the parish was only a perpetual curacy with a minute stipend of £10 a year.[39] The implication is that his parishioners respected him and valued his ministry, but his precarious financial position would inevitably have limited his control and may have forced him to abide by the religious customs and practices of the community. Three possible interpretations of his action in publicly recording the burial of stillborn and premature babies, and of other infants who had died unbaptized, can be suggested. It may be that the Rev. James had always conducted such burials, but was only now able to record them in the register without fear of sanction. Equally his actions may have reflected the wishes of the parishioners who were in a position to exert pressure upon him to conform. It is possible that the burials were improperly conducted by a third party and James' noted commitment to the keeping of accurate records led him to insert the entries in the register. The Commission for the Propagation of the Gospel had appointed a replacement minister, Edmund Rosser, to serve the parish of Bedwellty.[40] The Commissioners had immense difficulty in finding suitably qualified, Welsh-speaking ministers to replace the ones they had ejected,[41] and Rosser was required to serve most of the parishes in the western valleys of Monmouthshire. He may either have managed to get to Bedwellty for

---

[37] Gray, 'The Clergy as Remembrancers of the Community', 119.
[38] GCRO, D/Pa.14.104.
[39] Gray, 'The Clergy as Remembrancers of the Community', 114.
[40] Thomas Richards, *Religious Developments in Wales, 1654–1662* (London, 1923), pp. 197–8, 202.
[41] Ibid., ch. VII: 'The Subsidised Propagation (1654–1660)', especially pp. 135–44.

burials, or members of the congregation may have taken advantage of the
freedom enshrined within the *Directory of Public Worship* to arrange the
funerals of their own children.[42]

This last suggestion is the least persuasive of the three, for two
reasons. The first is that, as far as is known, the *Directory of Public
Worship* was never translated into Welsh. This remarkable failing meant
that in Welsh-speaking areas the congregation were unlikely to have had
recourse to it. In addition, if Lewis James experienced any unease at the
burials of these children, it does not seem to have been very deep-seated.
He may have been persuaded by his parishioners, but whatever his
motivation he continued recording the burial of still-born babies after the
Restoration of 1660, when he was reappointed. Reading between the lines
of his register, he seems to have been a stubborn and determined man. The
most likely conclusion is that he acted from powerful religious
convictions. If this is the case, it must have been a great relief to him to be
able to keep a valid record of such events in his meticulously-kept
register. This hypothesis is further substantiated by the fact that he
continued to record these burials after 1660, when they were, in fact,
technically illegal. In 1662 the Restoration *Prayer Book* was revised under
pressure from a group in the Church who sought to privilege the status of
the sacraments. One of the changes for which they pressed was the
renewed exclusion of the unbaptised from burial with the services of the
Church.

There is some evidence of reluctance to accept this, even among the
clergy. David Cressy quotes the example of Isaac Archer, incumbent of
Feckenham in Suffolk, whose own child died unbaptised at the age of two
and a half weeks:

> I had taken a nurse into the house to suckle it because my wife was not
> able . . . the woman knew of its illness and yet told us not of it, so it died
> while she slept and unbaptised, which I could not in the least help, as
> knowing nothing of its illness. I know God is a god of the faithfull and
> their seed, and baptism is a sign of it; and I no more question the child's
> happiness (whatever St Austin thought) than that of the Jewish children
> who died before the eighth day. I take God to witness, I do not, did not,
> despise the sacrament; but now 'tis fallen out so, not through the fault of
> the infant, or our wilfull neglect, but through an unavoidable necessity . . .
> I laid it in Freckenham chancel near my seat, and I expect to meet it at the
> resurrection of the just, Amen.

---

[42] Procter and Frere, *New History of the Book of Common Prayer.*

Archer subsequently buried in the same place of highest honour, in the chancel of his church, the body of a still-born daughter who had been two months premature. These burials, of course, may not have been public ceremonies, but the disturbance to the chancel floor means they could not be described as clandestine either.[43] A similar sequence of events may explain the burials of several infants near the pulpit in the parish church of Llangan near Corwen in north Wales. Hostility to the official church policy is suggested by archaeological evidence for clandestine burials. The bodies of neonates are difficult to identify in the archaeological record, but a number of churchyard excavations have found shallow infant burials near the walls of church buildings.[44]

The case of Lewis James and the Bedwellty burials has a wider significance. It emphasises the changing nature of the Established Church of England and its basic doctrines. There are many pitfalls in assuming that the practices and beliefs of the Church of England of Edward VI and Elizabeth I were the same as those of the seventeenth-century Church. It is difficult to be precise about the nature of some theological changes for the Church was often reluctant for political reasons to install hard definitions of official belief. They can nevertheless be identified in changes that were made to the liturgy, and such changes in popular belief can be identified in the ways that burial rituals were renegotiated to respond to local needs. The Bedwellty burials are also important for the light which they cast on the identification and interpretation of ritual practices. Social anthropologists identify a number of ways in which rituals function in society: they may give cohesion to a community or social group; they may be used by those in power to impose or reinforce their authority; they may be used by the powerless to subvert authority, or they may be used as an escape from society and its power structures into a state of liminality. It is possible to see all these functions in the case study under discussion.

What is clear is that ritual practice in the early modern period was open to dispute and contestation. If ritual is treated as a 'text' to be read and analysed we must consider not just what is being said and done but by whom, and what else is being communicated by the subtext. Questions must be raised about how and by whom the ritual is being challenged, disputed, subverted or renegotiated. One framework for dealing with this proposes a model of contested discourses in which competing groups try

---

[43] Cressy, *Birth, Marriage and Death*, 116–17, 132–3.
[44] I am grateful to Felicity Taylor of CADW for this point. See also W. J. and K. A. Rodwell, *Rivenhall: investigation of a villa, church and village, 1950–1977* (London, 1986), pp. 99–100.

to impose their own perceptions on the ritual group.[45] It may be more fruitful, however, to consider rituals, such as burial rites, as a matter for negotiation and possibly even for reconciliation. It is tempting but risky to assume homogeneity in religious belief and practice in past societies. Ritual communities were not all-inclusive as there was always room for dissent. Nor should the standpoint of individuals be expected to be unchanging or even consistent. As the case of Isaac Archer demonstrates, there were occasions when even those who were responsible for leadership of the ritual community could get it wrong.

---

[45] For example, see J. Eade and M. J. Sallnow, *Contesting the Sacred: the anthropology of Christian pilgrimage* (London, 1991).

CHAPTER TWO

'THE GOOD AND EASY DEATH': EARLY MODERN RELIGION AND CONSUMPTIVE DISEASE

CLARK LAWLOR

Thought when I was alone about death, finding myself a little oppressed about my lungs. I fancied I might be in a consumption. I was almost pleased with the prospect of it. At least nothing shocking appeared in it and I thought if I was plainly in a dying condition I could with a great deal of calmness and serenity resign up my life.[1]

Dudley Ryder, a young and somewhat impressionable law student, introduces the popular religious notion of consumption as the disease for a good or easy death. In his diary entry, Ryder, later notorious for his role as Attorney General in the 1745 Jacobite rebellion, is merely confirming a cliché that had developed over a number of centuries and reached a powerful formulation in the seventeenth century. Classical physicians, like Aretaeus and the practical Hippocrates, had described the symptoms of a consumption of the lungs and distinguished this from many other types of consumption common at that time with reasonable accuracy. The major elements of consumptive disease consisted of: wasting flesh – as indicated by the root of the word *consumo*, to waste or be consumed; a chronic condition which was sometimes not even perceptible for years, unless it was a 'galloping consumption'; a 'hectic' flush of the cheeks which, ironically, often gave the false appearance of blooming health and beauty

---

[1] Dudley Ryder, *The Diary of Dudley Ryder, 1715–1716*, transcribed from shorthand and edited by William Matthews (London, 1939), p. 345. Ryder's diary is still an under-used resource. My thanks to Dr Akihito Suzuki for bringing it to my attention.

rather than illness, and lastly, a persistent cough and blood-spitting as the disease progressed. It was quite possible for people to die of consumption without really knowing they were suffering from pulmonary tuberculosis.

On the other hand, it was also possible for someone to die an agonizing death while in the final stages of the same disease: the disintegrating lung tissue not only provoked horrible coughing fits but also almost choked the sufferer. James Miller's 'Verses to the Memory of Mrs Elizabeth Frankland', published in 1741, described an heroic struggle with death by this young and beautiful woman:

> Whilst meagre *Phthisis* preys upon my Breast,
> With a dead Weight my feeble Limbs opprest,
> Whilst struggling *Coughs* my tender Bosom rend,
> And scorching *Hecticks* ev'ry Vein distend;
> Whilst Clay-cold Damps bedew my Body o'er,
> And Life steals painful out at ev'ry Pore;
> By *Patience* prop'd, the bitter Load I bear,
> Without a Sigh, a Murmur, or a Tear.[2]

This was hardly the easy death envisaged by Ryder and gives one aspect of the biological reality of the disease. 'Phthisis' was another name for a consumption, as was 'tabes'. Here the hectic fever roasts the victim alive, while the coughing fits tear Mrs Frankland's 'tender Bosom', that poignant sign of true, delicate, femininity, apart.

Nevertheless, the symptoms noted by the Classical medics were also immediately apparent to the lay public. If one were to die of a disease, why not make it consumption? In the classical period, as now, a lung consumption, with its low concentration of nerve endings in that part of the body, simply meant little or less pain than in many other diseases; in Christian times the benefits were even more apparent. To summarise briefly what will be examined in more detail later, the idea that consumption assisted in the good Christian death rested upon the following assumptions: it allowed people to prepare for death in plenty of time, to make their peace with God and man, and to settle their affairs; it provided a visual symbol of increasing spirituality as the flesh wasted away, and it kept the sufferer *compos mentis*, enabling the good Christian to face his maker, death and the Devil with fortitude. Conversely, other diseases, such as smallpox and the plague, might kill the victim both quickly and unpleasantly. In the early modern period when religious

---

[2] James Miller, 'Verses To The Memory of Mrs Elizabeth Frankland', *Miscellaneous Work in Verse and Prose. By Mr Miller: volume the first* [no further volumes published] (London, 1741), pp. 100–4, lines 132–49.

superstition was all pervasive, scarring of the face could be interpreted, like any physical 'deformity', as a sign of divine disapproval. In contrast, consumption did not destroy the victim's beauty, although in its final stages he/she could almost be transformed into a living skeleton. From the time that the tradition of the *Ars Moriendi* (the art of dying well) first appeared at the end of fifteenth century until the start of the eighteenth century, when such ideas began to lose purchase on the popular imagination, consumption infiltrated or at least insinuated itself into discussions about the nature of the Christian death.[3] In a sense it is possible to suggest that it was more or less inevitable that a Christian tradition meditating on the good death should light upon a disease that encouraged an ideal passing to occur. As will be shown later, however, there was also a certain amount of resistance to the notion of one disease being 'holier' than another, for, at a different remove, the whole thing seemed frankly absurd.

In the light of this contextual overview it is then feasible to construct an explanation for Ryder's apparent conviction that dying of a consumption of the lungs might be a positive or 'almost' pleasurable experience. How is it that a terminal and, in terms of medical realism, often agonising disease can be incorporated into an attractive day-dream? To answer this question Ryder's views need to be explored further, before relating this to Protestant discourses concerning consumption as a good or bad disease for the devout Christian. As has been shown consumption was largely represented as a positive experience of disease, but some seventeenth century theologians, such as Jeremy Taylor, disagreed.[4] The first section of this study will explain why consumption was widely judged to be the disease of the good and easy death by citing the work of popular Divines such as Thomas Fuller, well-known physicians, most notably Thomas Browne, and obscure poets, such as Christopher Wyvill. The second part appraises Jeremy Taylor's objections to this popular and elite discourse, and the way that his arguments were founded in theological reasoning.

Before this it is necessary to make a brief commentary upon the use of literary as well as religious and medical sources. Recent scholarship on the history of medicine and literature has been helped into fruitful convergence by the advent of cultural studies and cultural history. This has resulted in collaborations between medical historians, such as Roy Porter,

---

[3] For a useful selection of texts and an introduction to the subject see David William Atkinson (ed.), *The English Ars Moriendi* (New York, 1992), vol. 5: *Renaissance and Baroque*.

[4] Jeremy Taylor, *Holy Living and Holy Dying* (London, 1651).

and literary commentators, notably George Rousseau. Their book on *Gout: the patrician malady* is a prime example of the direction in which the cultural history of medicine is headed.[5] Likewise, Allan Ingram's work in the field of English literature, his re-framing and reconstruction of hitherto lost 'mad' voices and writings, has influenced historians and literary scholars alike.[6] Although there is no intention here to claim that literary texts can be used in precisely the same way as historical documents, they nevertheless fall into a reformulated concept of what constitutes culture, or, more strictly speaking, cultures. As Hayden White observed some time ago, all written documents are more or less generic, more or less metaphorical, and the researcher needs to be alive to their textuality and indeed artificiality.[7] Certainly, when assessing the representation of disease, the reader needs to be alive to literary texts and

[5] Roy Porter and George Rousseau, *Gout: the patrician malady* (New Haven, 1998).

[6] For example, see Allan Ingram, *Boswell's Creative Gloom* (London, 1982) and his *The Madhouse of Language: writing and reading madness in the eighteenth century* (London, 1991); and two of his edited collections, *Voices of Madness* (Stroud, 1997); *Patterns of Madness in the Eighteenth Century: a reader* (Liverpool, 1998). Other important interventions in the field include, Raymond Anselment, *The Realms of Apollo: literature and healing in seventeenth-century England* (Newark, 1995); Alan Bewell, *Romanticism and Colonial Disease* (Baltimore, 1999); Robert A. Erickson, *The Language of the Heart, 1600–1750* (Philadelphia, 1997); Margaret Healy, *Fictions of Disease in Early Modern England: bodies, plagues and politics* (Basingstoke, 2001); Clark Lawlor and Akihito Suzuki, 'The Disease of the Self: Representations of Consumption 1700–1830', *Bulletin of the History of Medicine*, 74 (2000), 258–94; Debbie Lee, 'Yellow Fever and the Slave Trade: Coleridge's *The Rime of the Ancient Mariner*', *English Literary History*, 65 (1998), 675–700; Peter Melville Logan, *Nerves and Narratives: a cultural history of hysteria in nineteenth-century British prose* (London, 1997), including a foreword by Roy Porter; Marie Mulvey-Roberts and Roy Porter (eds), *Literature and Medicine during the Eighteenth Century* (London, 1993); Alan Richardson, *British Romanticism and the Science of the Mind* (Cambridge, 2001); Jonathan Sawday, *The Body Emblazoned: dissection and the human body in Renaissance culture* (London, 1995); Michael C. Schoenfeldt, *Bodies and Selves in Early Modern England: physiology and inwardness in Spenser, Shakespeare, Herbert and Milton* (Cambridge, 1999); David E. Shuttleton, '"Pamela's Library": Samuel Richardson and Dr. Cheyne's "universal cure"', *Eighteenth-Century Life*, 23, 1 (1999), 59–79; Helen Small, *Love's Madness: medicine, the novel, and female insanity, 1800–1865* (Oxford, 1996); Anne C. Vila, *Enlightenment and Pathology: sensibility in the literature and medicine of eighteenth-century France* (Baltimore, 1998).

[7] Hayden White, *Metahistory. The historical imagination in nineteenth-century Europe* (Baltimore, 1973).

those documents, like diaries, that fell under the rubric of 'literature' in the early modern period. The latter is a crucial point. The divide between creative literature and 'factual' reportage is far from clear even today, and to the contemporaries of Dudley Ryder it made little sense. Historical fidelity requires an examination of literary expressions of popular opinion on consumption as well as the expert evaluations that can be drawn from medical and/or religious texts. Of course, literary and religious texts are not necessarily separable, nor is Dudley Ryder's diary without its own fantasies of disease, as has already been demonstrated.

Ryder exemplifies the complexity of attitudes to consumption because his notion of the condition was not entirely as positive as previous quotations might lead the reader to expect. His tendency towards hypochondria is much in evidence in this diary entry for Sunday, 1 April 1716: 'found my throat pretty sore. Was afraid I had got such a cold as might bring me into a consumption because I had heard of a consumption being got by such a thing.'[8] Although he used quack medicines and visited Islington Spa frequently for its restorative properties, Ryder knew that a consumptive death could be beneficial, as this description of his visit to a friend on 25 June showed:

> [William Crisp] is sick in bed of consumption and past hopes of recovery conversed with us. He is very serious and loves to talk of another world and to prepare for it. It is indeed a happy state when a man is got so far into religion and so far above the world as to think of passing out of it without terror and distraction, to be able to be calm and serene under the assured expectation of death and leaving whatever is dear and pleasant to him.[9]

Crisp seems to be neither mentally nor physically distressed by his condition, but rather he is content to be fading out of this world and into the next. This affirmative account is explicitly reinforced by Crisp's mother, who thanked God that her son had been given a chronic disease that allowed him time to repent his sins.[10] The diagnosis of consumption was often taken as a death-sentence, and the certainty that this enabled

---

[8] Ryder, *Diary*, p. 209. For Ryder's concern about his health and frequent visits to medical practitioners (both qualified and quack), see Ibid., passim, especially pp. 276–8, 295–8.

[9] Ibid., p. 263.

[10] Ibid., p. 234. The fear of sudden death, depriving the dying of the chance to prepare for one's end, was widespread in European society. See Philippe Ariès, *The Hour of our Death* (Harmondsworth, 1983), pp. 10–13: Pat Jalland, *Death in the Victorian Family* (Oxford, 1996), pp. 65–9.

paradoxically reduced anxiety about dying.[11] Crisp knew that he was dying and therefore could take appropriate spiritual and temporal action. Ryder evidently takes this scene to heart for three months later he is found to echo the 'calm and serene' ideal of consumptive death, using the same words during his pleasurable reverie quoted at the beginning of this chapter.

It is more than likely, however, that Ryder drew upon other sources of information which determined his attitude to consumption. One possible source was another account of the death of a consumptive friend by the famous physician-author Sir Thomas Browne in his 'A Letter to a Friend, upon the occasion of the Death of his Intimate Friend', published posthumously in 1690.[12] Browne's more extended musings on death by consumption were influential in this period and later on in the nineteenth century, in both Britain and America.[13] The letter, as its title suggests, provides a description of the death of a close friend, giving an exemplary account of an easy and good death from consumption. Beginning by asserting his own medical authority, Browne noted that lay persons were often not aware that consumption was fatal, partly because of the fabled *spes phthisica* or 'hope of the phthisic'. Thus, he argues that because the sick felt reasonably well and were symptomless, they harboured unrealistic hopes of recovery:

> strange it is, that the common fallacy of consumptive persons, who feel not themselves dying, and therefore still hope to live, should also reach their friends in perfect health and judgement; – that you should be so little acquainted with Plautus's sick complexion, or that almost an Hippocratical face should not alarm you to higher fears, or rather despair, of his continuation in such an emaciated state, wherein medical predictions fail not, as sometimes in acute diseases, and wherein 'tis as dangerous to be sentenced by a physician as a judge.[14]

---

[11] Thomas Sydenham reported that there were 'two Thirds dying of it who are spoiled by Chronical Diseases'. See *The whole works . . . of Dr. Thomas Sydenham* [Translated and] corrected from the original Latin by John Pechey MD (10th edn. London, 1734), p. 326.

[12] 'A Letter to a Friend, upon the occasion of the Death of his Intimate Friend', in L. C. Martin (ed.), *Sir Thomas Browne: Religio Medici and other works* (Oxford, 1964), pp. 177–96. Originally published posthumously in London, 1690.

[13] For the American reception see Katherine Ott, *Fevered Lives: tuberculosis in American culture since 1870* (Cambridge, 1996), p. 15.

[14] Martin (ed.), *Sir Thomas Browne*, pp. 179–80.

Even non-medical friends could be misled by the patient's optimism; only the physician acquainted with the precepts of classical medicine could interpret the true signs of a consumption in its late and fatal stages, even though they were powerless to cure it. The Greek physician Aretaeus expanded on the origins of the *spes phthisica* when he wrote that:

> haemorrhage from the lungs is particularly dangerous, although patients do not despair even when near their end. The insensibility of the lungs to pain appears to me to be the cause of this, for pain is more dreadful than precarious; whereas in the absence of it, even serious illness is unaccompanied by the fear of death and is more dangerous than dreadful.[15]

This peculiar characteristic of consumption, whereby the progress of the illness is not accompanied by increasing levels of pain, is clearly problematical. For although it makes death easier and removes despair, it also blinds the patient to the danger he/she faces. Browne's medical realism was soon blended with religious mythology however, when the 'soft death' of his friend was described:

> his soft departure, which was scarce an expiration; and his end not unlike his beginning . . . and his departure so like unto sleep, that he scarce needed the civil ceremony of closing his eyes; contrary unto the common way, wherein death draws up, sleep lets fall the eye-lids. With what strifes and pains we came into the world we know not; but 'tis commonly no easy matter to get out of it: yet if it could be made out, that such who have easy nativities have commonly hard deaths, and contrarily; his departure was so easy, that we might justly suspect his birth was of another nature, and that some Juno sat cross-legged at his nativity.[16]

On this evidence a consumptive end negates man's natural terror of death because it is more like going to sleep than having to overcome a final agony. The medieval perspective on Christian death was one which promoted the conquest of pain as one of the means of proving oneself to be a worthy Christian, while Browne's emphasis on a death so 'soft' that it is hardly death at all is very attractive to those who have no relish for a 'hard' last battle with pain. Even the eye-lids deny death's presence as they conveniently close rather than remain open; so natural is this process that it does not even require any official intervention. Rather than a

---

[15] Thomas Daniel, *Captain of Death: the story of tuberculosis* (New York, 1997), p. 19; B. L. Gordon, *Medieval and Renaissance Medicine* (New York, 1959), p. 476.
[16] Martin (ed.), *Sir Thomas Browne*, pp. 180–1.

traumatic and agonising jolt from life into death, it becomes a gentle transition to Heaven in much the same way as human beings move easily between the states of waking and sleeping. The other operative metaphor that rejects and indeed opposes death here is birth, or re-birth into the new spiritual world with reference to the way that his death was 'not unlike his beginning'. If the original birth was traumatic, this second one was gentle and 'easy'.

It was a lucky person who reached the end of life in this manner. Browne implies that the easy death had been earned by an exemplary life: 'in brief, his life and death were such that I could not blame them who wished the like, and almost to have been himself'.[17] It was possible to aspire to the same experience as Browne's friend who, in the style of Puritan biography, made a good end to a worthy, though short, life. Mary Fissell has also noted that for early modern Protestants, particularly Quakers and Methodists, sickness could be an 'opportunity for the sufferer to exhibit grace'. The guiding principle was that illness was God's choosing and therefore 'in some way beneficial to the sufferer'; His reasons were not to be questioned, merely accepted joyfully and enthusiastically. Indeed, 'a hallmark of the truly blessed was their early recognition of their final, fatal illness'.[18] A further, more personal motive may have influenced Browne's opinions on and representation of consumption, namely that in early manhood he had been phthisical himself.[19] It is therefore understandable that Browne should seek to construct an ideal scenario in the event of his own consumptive demise. From his Nonconformist vantage point, Dudley Ryder obviously agreed as he too fondly imagined himself making a dramatic exit to everlasting glory.

Browne was not the only likely influence on Ryder, however. In his *Life Out of Death, A Sermon preached at Chelsey, on the recovery of an honourable person* in 1655, Thomas Fuller, another popular Protestant Divine, offered various 'Motives to patience in illness', including the following:

---

[17] Ibid., p. 188.

[18] See Mary Fissell, 'The disappearance of the patient's narrative and the invention of hospital medicine', in R. French and Andrew Wear (eds), *British Medicine in an Age of Reform* (London, 1991), pp. 92–109 (97–8). See also Andrew Wear, 'Puritan perceptions of illness in seventeenth-century England', in Roy Porter (ed.), *Patients and Practitioners: lay perceptions of medicine in pre-industrial society* (Cambridge, 1985), pp. 55–100. My thanks to Dr Fissell for her comments on an early version of this research.

[19] Arthur C. Jacobson, *Genius: some revelations* (London, 1929), p. 51.

Secondly, consider that thy disease is far gentler and painless than what thou hast deserved, what is thy disease, a Consumption? Indeed a certain messenger of death; but know, that of all the Bayliffs, sent to arrest us to the debt of nature, none useth his prisoners with more civility and courtesie then the Consumption, though too often an ill-use is made thereof, for the prisoners to flatter themselves into a possibility of an escape; but what a Consumption hast thou deserved: *Correct us O Lord, and yet in thy judgement, not in thy fury, lest we be consumed and brought to nothing.* A Consumption of annihilation is our desert.[20]

Like Browne, Fuller offered consumption as the disease of the easy but certain death: a gift from God for which the victim should be extremely grateful, considering what he or she really deserved at the end of their sinful lives. Punning the root meaning of consumption, he argued that if God judged men according to their just deserts, they would be consumed and destroyed by His righteous wrath. Consumption was Death's gentlemanly bailiff who arrests the victim with civility; that is, a refined disease from which a person of honour would wish to die. Fuller added the caveat that consumption was so 'soft' an illness that some people felt that they could cheat death and God's judgement due to the *spes phthisica* mentioned by Browne, in which the sufferer deluded himself that he was not doomed after all.

This attitude to consumption was also present in literary representations, such Sir Christopher Wyvill's poem 'Mors Mea' ('My Death'), published in 1647. Here Wyvill, at best a minor poet but for that reason perhaps more representative of popular opinion, pondered how he might die and considered his preferences for the manner of his going in a religious way. A committed Protestant and MP for Richmond, Yorkshire, Wyvill had written an anti-papist pamphlet. 'Mors Mea' was a relatively short poem, appearing in the rare volume entitled *Certaine Serious Thoughts which at severall times & upon sundry Occasions have stollen themselves into Verse and now into the Publike View*, announcing the putatively introspective mode of the book.

The poem begins by observing that although death is ultimately certain, the timing and mode are not. Wyvill wonders:

whether my consumptive breath
Shall leisurely-expiring creep to death,
Or some more furious, hasty sicknesse have

[20] Thomas Fuller, *Life Out of Death. A sermon preached at Chelsey, on the recovery of an honourable person* (London, 1655), pp. 20–1.

Commission to snatch me to my grave.[21]

An almost restful consumption of the lungs certainly appeared to be a better option than a 'furious' acute malady, and not merely for the reason of enduring pain. Although Wyvill fights shy of asking for a choice of his fate, 'I dare not wish, nor were it fit, to be / A carver for my selfe, my God',[22] within a few more lines he admits his preference:

> Yet, if it stand with thy good pleasure, send
> Not suddaine death, nor sence-bereaved end.
> And if thou'st honor with white haires my dayes,
> O teach me how to spend them to thy praise,
> That when I shall forsake the sons of men,
> My better part may flye to thee, Amen.[23]

Consumption suited Wyvill better because it would not be sudden, nor did it afflict the mind. These peculiar characteristics of the disease were important for a Christian because they allowed sufferers time to put their affairs, spiritual and temporal, in order before their death. Clarity of mind was essential for this process, as well as enabling the sufferer to consciously outface death to the end, proving his worth as a good Christian. If the victim was mentally deranged there would be less chance of begging God's forgiveness, showing resignation to His will and even welcoming the suffering as an opportunity to arrive at a state of grace, as Wyvill attempts to do above.

It was also better to be taken ill and die at home surrounded by family and friends; advice and farewells could be given to each individual as part of the dying person's pious bequest. The death needed to be exemplary so that those left behind might be inspired to live and die well. A further advantage was consumption's lack of effect on the outward appearance of the body until the final stages of the disease. Smallpox, conversely, would ravage the skin and, according to popular superstition, was interpreted as a sign of divine displeasure. The prevailing view was that man's sins were made manifest in his flesh and, although the more enlightened might argue

---

[21] Sir Christopher Wyvill, 'Mors Mea', *Certaine Serious Thoughts which at severall times & upon sundry Occasions have stollen themselves into Verse and now into the Publike View from the Author: together wth a Chronologicall table denoeting the names of such Princes as ruled the neighbor States and were contemporary to our English Kings, observeing throughout ye number of yeares wch every one of them reigned* (London, 1647), pp. 22–3, lines 3–6.
[22] Ibid., lines 13–14.
[23] Ibid., lines 17–22.

against this, there was still a widespread belief that to die of a slowly
wasting consumption would be vastly better than scarification by
smallpox.[24] Hence, as described by Fuller, Browne and Wyvill,
consumption became a part of the *Ars Moriendi* tradition which had
continued from the (Catholic) Middle Ages through to the Protestant
Reformation, although Protestants diminished the role of the priest as
giver of the last rites and increased the part played by family and friends.
The removal of purgatory and prayers interceding on behalf of the dead
presented the devout Protestant with the frighteningly binary options of
heaven or hell; the moment of death therefore constituted a greater burden
than hitherto and engaged much of the time and energy of the Divines.[25]

Religious opinion was by no means in agreement that consumption
was the disease of the good and easy death. Despite the strong strain of
positive imagery popularly associated with consumption, commentators,
such as Jeremy Taylor, had forceful objections to the idea that any
particular disease might be preferable. Taylor published his influential
treatise, *Holy Living and Holy Dying*, in 1651, a text following in the *Ars
Moriendi* tradition, and arguably its apotheosis. In a section entitled 'Of
the Practise of Patience' within the *Holy Dying* volume, a subsection
entitled 'Do not choose the kind of thy sicknesse, or the manner of thy
death' exposed the foolishness of desiring a consumptive death:

> I have known some persons vehemently wish that they might die of a
> consumption, and some of these had a plot upon heaven, and hoped by that
> means to secure it after a careless life; as thinking a lingering sicknesse
> would certainly infer a lingering and protracted repentance; and by that
> means they thought they should be safest; other of them dreamed it would
> be an easier death, and have found themselves deceived, and their patience
> hath been tired with a weary spirit and a useless body, by often conversing
> with healthful persons and vigorous neighbours, by uneasiness of the flesh,
> and the sharpness of his bones, by want of spirits and a dying life; and in
> conclusion have been directly debauched by peevishness and a fretful
> sicknesse, and these men had better have left it to the *wisdom* and
> *goodnesse* of God, for they both are infinite.[26]

---

[24] See Lucinda McCray Beier, 'The Good Death in Seventeenth-Century England',
in Ralph Houlbrooke (ed.), *Death, Ritual and Bereavement* (London, 1989), pp.
43–61. For the features of the good death as they persist in the Victorian
Evangelical movement see Jalland, *Death in the Victorian Family*, pp. 17–19, 26–
8.
[25] Jalland, *Death in the Victorian Family*, p. 18; Houlbrooke (ed.), *Death, Ritual
and Bereavement*, pp. 25–42.
[26] Jeremy Taylor, 'Of the Practise of Patience', in Taylor, *Holy Living and Holy
Dying*, and reproduced in P. G. Stanwood (ed.), *Holy Living; Holy Dying* (2 vols.

In resisting the *Ars Moriendi* tradition, Taylor sheds further light on the reasons for its evidently powerful popularity. Consumption, as a mortal disease, encouraged repentance where there had been none before and, happily, its lingering duration gave people plenty of time to make restitution. This kind of self-deception anticipated Fuller's cautionary caveat four years later about those consumptives who might flatter themselves into believing that they could escape death. For Taylor then, consumption was not necessarily a malady that would secure a good death, nor was it one that would always deliver an easy death either. He injected some much needed medical realism into the discourse by observing that this outcome was far from likely, although, as we have seen, narratives by medics like Browne demonstrated that, even accounting for mythology, consumption could at least occasionally deliver a relatively easy death. Rather than minimise the unpleasant symptoms of consumption, Taylor emphasised them and their impact upon all aspects of the sufferer's life. The painful physical effects of wasting, the sharp bones and uneasy flesh, translate into mental trauma. In addition social intercourse was likely to become difficult for the consumptive as Taylor presented a stark contrast between the healthy and unhealthy. Ease becomes its opposite: *un*ease; peevishness and fretfulness dominate the 'debauched' consumptive's life and death. According to this assessment the only option to be taken, if indeed any existed in the first place, was to accept whatever God decided. Of course, the other writers on this topic agreed that God's will ought to be the primary concern, but the difference was that they viewed consumption as a good outcome if they happened to contract it, whereas Taylor absolutely disapproved of such a treacherous rationale. Men, he believed, could be deceived into thinking that consumption could effect some of the spiritual work that they should have done for themselves.

In summary, the seventeenth century saw a clash between two different and powerful discourses of death and disease, both encoded through religious belief. Consumption's peculiar symptomatology underpinned the popular perception that this was the disease of the good and easy death, but the religious mythology that built up around it did not simply turn upon that physiological ambiguity. Consumption literally embodied all those religious doubts and fears that haunted the popular imagination at the time, providing a space where people could fantasise about evading or easing the inevitable passage into the afterlife. Divines, like Taylor, however, thought it necessary to check the unquestioning acceptance of such dangerous popular assumptions in order to save the souls of those who entered too deeply into the fantasy of an easy consumptive death. In

---

Oxford, 1989), II: *Holy Dying*, pp. 123–4.

the following century, such concerns would be gradually modified: consumption would still be conceived in popular parlance as the disease of the good death, but a better understanding of the nervous system would mean an even greater elevation of its secular status.

Religion was not the only discourse which framed popular understanding of disease, as has been suggested elsewhere. The secular discourse of sexual passion also affected the way consumption was narrativized by both the elite and popular imaginations.[27] Nevertheless, it can be argued that religion was the most significant mode of constructing the consumptive experience, both written and endured, in the seventeenth century. Despite the assaults on religion by the 'New Science' and the schisms of the Civil Wars, religious discourse continued to influence popular perceptions of consumption, not only in the seventeenth century, but also into the nineteenth century, when the evangelical revival sparked off new ways of engaging with this paradoxical disease.[28]

---

[27] Lawlor and Suzuki, 'The Disease of the Self'.
[28] For the nineteenth century see Jalland, *Death in the Victorian Family*.

CHAPTER THREE

BAPTISMS, BURIALS AND BRAWLS: CHURCH AND COMMUNITY IN MID-EIGHTEENTH CENTURY WALES

ERYN WHITE

Few accounts of the eighteenth-century Welsh Church fail to refer to Erasmus Saunders, *A View of the State of Religion in the Diocese of St David's* (1721). It is commonly regarded as an accurate representation of the state of the Church throughout Wales, although it is worth noting that its depiction of an impoverished, overstretched institution relates more to the Church in its southern dioceses than to the north. In addition, it should not be forgotten that Saunders' account cannot be considered totally unbiased, embittered as he was by lack of promotion. Despite these reservations, there is surely some truth in his much-quoted description of the religious inclinations of the inhabitants of the diocese of St David's:

> There is, I believe, no part of the Nation more inclin'd to be Religious, and to be delighted with it than the poor Inhabitants of these Mountains. They don't think it too much when neither ways, nor weather are inviting, over cold and bleak Hills to travel three or four Miles, or more, on foot to attend the Publick prayers, and sometimes as many more to hear a Sermon, and they seldom grudge many times for several Hours together in their damp and cold Churches, to wait the coming of their Minister, who by Occasional Duties in his other Curacy's or by other Accidents may be oblig'd to disappoint them, and to be often variable in his Hours of Prayer.[1]

All too often it was members of the Anglican clergy, like Saunders, who voiced the fiercest criticism of the Church. The opinions of clerics such as Saunders, Moses Williams and Evan Evans are a matter of record, but

---

[1] Erasmus Saunders, *A View of the State of Religion in the Diocese of St. David's about the beginning of the 18th Century* (rept. Cardiff, 1949), p. 32.

rather less is known about the attitudes of the population in general towards the Church and towards the local parish church. Historical studies have tended to concentrate on the eighteenth-century Church in Wales as an institution, examining its administration, its poverty and the condition of its clergy. At a time when people had more choice than before about where and how to worship, and when people were choosing to attend places of worship other than the Church, was there any evidence of resentment or disrespect? This study has concentrated on the two southern dioceses of Saint David's and Llandaff, since it was within this area that the Welsh Methodist Revival originated, an event which has been attributed at least in part to the failings of the Church. These two dioceses seem a logical place to look for signs of discontent within a Church beset by poverty and hampered by an antiquated system of administration. It is generally accepted that the northern dioceses of Bangor and St Asaph were financially more sound and in a better position to fend off competition from Dissenters and Methodists.[2]

On the eve of the eighteenth century, the Anglican Church was widely regarded as 'y fam eglwys' (the mother church) and it remained one of the central institutions in Welsh communities. The Church had woven itself into the fabric of Welsh life over many generations. The radical changes to church services during the Commonwealth period in the mid-seventeenth century engendered a widespread feeling of nostalgia for the familiar Anglican order, which was welcomed back with a general sense of relief after the Restoration of the monarchy in 1660. Folk memories of the prevailing confusion felt under Oliver Cromwell's rule reinforced loyalty to the Church and hostility towards its rivals. Anti-Methodist disturbances in eighteenth-century Wales can indeed be classed among 'Church and King riots' whereby the participants felt themselves to be operating in defence of the status quo in state and religion.[3] The determination of the early Methodist leaders to remain within the compass of the Church is further proof of an abiding sense of loyalty and affection.

That affection was not necessarily directed towards the higher clergy as Anglican bishops in Wales tended to be birds of passage with no

---

[2] For example, Owain W. Jones, 'The Welsh Church in the Eighteenth Century', in David Walker (ed.), *A History of the Church in Wales* (Penarth, 1976), p. 103.
[3] See John Walsh, 'Methodism and the Mob in the Eighteenth Century', in G. J. Cuming and D. Baker (eds), *Studies in Church History, 8: popular belief and practice* (Cambridge, 1972), pp. 213–27; John Stevenson, *Popular Disturbances in England, 1700–1832* (2nd edn. Harlow, 1992), pp. 173–9; Eryn M. White, *Praidd Bach y Bugail Mawr: Seiadau Methodistaidd de-orllewin Cymru 1737–50* (Llandysul, 1995).

knowledge of the Welsh language. One of the most notorious examples was Benjamin Hoadly, Bishop of Bangor between 1716 and 1721, who never visited his diocese, pleading his lameness as an excuse. More active in his diocese, but also more hostile towards the Welsh language, was Robert Hay Drummond, Bishop of St Asaph (1748–61) who stated publicly he wished the language to be eradicated.[4] Given that the bishops were distant figures for most of their congregations, it was frequently the parish clergy who were the most crucial representatives of the Church in terms of influencing popular attitudes. Apart from the local squire, the parson was often the most significant individual in any parish. He was undoubtedly a source of general advice and gave practical assistance with such worldly affairs as the drawing up of wills.[5] In addition to their clerical duties several of the clergy operated as schoolmasters,[6] and were the most consistent subscribers to Welsh publications, both for their personal use and for the benefit of their parishioners.[7] The names of clergymen also figure in lists of patrons of charity schools during the eighteenth century. One of the most generous patrons of the schools established by the Society for the Promotion of Christian Knowledge (S.P.C.K.) in Pembrokeshire was the Rev. John Pember, who financed the education of children in Haroldstone West, Lambston, Laugharne and Prendergast, as well as Llangan in Carmarthenshire.[8] In 1731 Sylvanus Prosser, rector of Port Eynon, Glamorgan, was said to have contrived over a period of years to set aside from his annual salary of £70 a total of £700 with which he intended to found a charity school in the parish.[9] Even though it must be acknowledged that those who appear in records in this capacity are a small proportion of the Welsh clergy in this period, there were men of vision in holy orders who were aware of the importance of

---

[4] Eryn M. White, 'The Established Church, Dissent and the Welsh Language *c*.1660–1811', in Geraint H. Jenkins (ed.), *The Welsh Language before the Industrial Revolution* (Cardiff, 1997), pp. 236–9. See also Norman Sykes, *Church and State in England in the Eighteenth Century* (Cambridge, 1934), pp. 356–64; Jones, 'The Welsh Church in the Eighteenth Century', pp. 118–19.

[5] For example, Gerald Morgan, 'Ewyllysiau Cymraeg 1539–1858', in Geraint H. Jenkins (ed.), *Cof Cenedl*, XII (Llandysul, 1997), pp. 35–6.

[6] Gareth Elwyn Jones and Gordon Wynne Roderick, *A History of Education in Wales* (Cardiff, 2003), p. 36.

[7] Geraint H. Jenkins, *Literature, Religion and Society in Wales 1660–1730* (Cardiff, 1978), pp. 278–9; S. R. Thomas, 'The Diocese of St David's in the eighteenth century, the working of the diocese in a period of criticism', unpublished University of Wales, MA thesis, 1983, 7.

[8] Mary Clement, *The S.P.C.K. and Wales 1699–1740* (London, 1954), pp. 109–26.

[9] Ibid., p. 136.

the education of their parishioners. Griffith Jones, who established a system of circulating schools between 1731 and 1761 to provide free tuition in the art of reading, is the most obvious example,[10] but other clergymen also realised the value of publishing works on morality and religion through the medium of Welsh in order to improve standards of religious knowledge. There is no denying the fact that many of the most brilliant and productive Welsh scholars of the age, including Ellis Wynne, Theophilus Evans, Evan Evans and Goronwy Owen, were men in the holy orders of the Anglican Church.[11]

The Church and its clergy had an important role to play in the so-called rites of passage: birth, marriage and death. Dissenters remained in the minority at the dawn of the eighteenth century, despite the freedom granted under the Toleration Act of 1689. For much of the century, even those who dissented from the Church during their lifetime were ultimately interred within its grounds after death. The Church received new-born infants into the community of the parish through the ceremony of baptism and marked the passing of members from the community in its funeral services. These ceremonies had a traditional and superstitious meaning for many people. It is significant that a substantial number of cases of neglect of duty brought against clergymen in this period involved the failure to baptise or bury parishioners. Negligence in respect of these duties could cause real distress and possibly outrage to concerned parents and grieving relatives and, with feelings running high, was more likely to result in complaints before the ecclesiastical courts. For example, in 1740 a case of neglect of duty was brought against Nicholas Griffiths, curate of Llanycrwys in Carmarthenshire.[12] He was accused not only of general neglect of his duty to conduct services and administer sacraments, but, more specifically, of refusing to conduct the funeral service of the child of Rees Thomas David, a farmer of the parish. He was further accused of omitting the majority of the service at the baptism of the child of Griffith John, yeoman. Both fathers were among the several witnesses against the

---

[10] Geraint H. Jenkins, "'An Old and Much Honoured Soldier'': Griffith Jones, Llanddowror', *Welsh History Review*, 11 (1983), 449–68; Eryn M. White, 'Popular Schooling and the Welsh Language 1650–1800', in Jenkins (ed.), *Welsh Language before the Industrial Revolution*, pp. 324–37.

[11] For further examples see Geraint H. Jenkins, "'I will tell you a Word or Two about Cardiganshire'': Welsh Clerics and Literature in the Eighteenth Century', in R. W. Swanson (ed.), *Studies in Church History, 38: the Church and the book* (Woodbridge, 2004), pp. 303–23.

[12] National Library of Wales (NLW), Church in Wales Records, SD/CCCm(G)/ 290.

curate. Equally in 1741, the welfare of the dying seems to have prompted the accusation of neglect brought by the churchwardens of Llannon, Carmarthenshire, against their curate, William Price, in which it was noted that Price on three occasions in September of that year refused to visit gravely ill parishioners to administer the sacrament before they died.[13]

The role of the Church was not considered quite so essential when it came to the ceremony of marriage, as many preferred informal, clandestine marriages, such as besom or broomstick weddings, which were less complicated to terminate and easier to conduct if under age.[14] Evidence from oral testimony collected in the early twentieth century suggests that this was a common practice throughout Wales into the nineteenth century.[15] At the same time, officiating at clandestine marriage services was one of the most frequent charges brought against clergy in the ecclesiastical courts. They were invariably accused of holding marriage ceremonies in private houses or outside the legal hours of 8am to noon, often without licence or the reading of banns.[16] In the case of James Williams, curate of Llangatwg Lingoed, Monmouthshire, in 1743, it was suggested that his motive for conducting a clandestine marriage between James Jones and Anne Christopher was that the bride was carrying his (Williams) child. Williams was said to have performed the marriage ceremony after 8pm in Christopher's house without banns being published beforehand, having prevailed on the bridegroom to marry her in spite of her pregnancy 'by several fair promises'.[17] It was probably more common for clandestine marriages to involve an under-age couple who did not have parental consent. All those under the age of twenty-one were technically regarded as minors in need of their parents' approval to marry. Although the parties involved might be grateful for the clergyman's compliance at the time, parents of under-age couples were likely to be incensed by the flouting of ecclesiastical law, and the implications for the clerics

---

[13] NLW, Church in Wales Records, SD/CCCm(G)/296.

[14] T. Gwynn Jones, *Welsh Folklore and Folk Custom* (London, 1930), p. 185; David W. Howell, *The Rural Poor in Eighteenth-Century Wales* (Cardiff, 2000), pp. 147–8.

[15] W. Rhys Jones (Gwenith Gwynn), 'Besom Wedding in the Ceiriog Valley', *Folk Lore*, 39 (1928), 149–66.

[16] Roger L. Brown, 'Clandestine Marriages in Wales', *Transactions of the Cymmrodorion* (1982), 74–85; R. B. Outhwaite, *Clandestine Marriages in England 1500–1850* (London, 1995), pp. 1–49; David Cressy, *Birth, Marriage and Death: ritual, religion and the life-cycle in Tudor and Stuart England* (Oxford, 1997), pp. 317–19.

[17] NLW, Church in Wales Records, LL/CC/G/956.

concerned could be extremely serious. In 1738 David Jones, curate of St Ishmael, Carmarthenshire, was suspended from his duties for three years as a penalty for conducting a clandestine marriage between William David and Sarah Thomas, both of Meidrim.[18]

In addition to the ceremonies of baptism, marriage and burial, a wide range of popular customs and superstitions also centred on the parish church. Erasmus Saunders noted that in the more remote parts of the diocese of St David's superstition and religion were 'very oddly mixed', mainly, he believed, because Catholic practices lingered where Protestant beliefs and habits had still not been thoroughly embedded in the religious beliefs of the populace at large.[19] Such lingering Catholic practices included the 'churching' of women. In south-west Wales, for instance, it was believed that the grass would not grow where new mothers walked until they had been churched.[20] Moreover, a number of popular customs concerned with finding a marriage partner still accorded a central role to the parish church. Lewis Morris of Anglesey, writing in the mid-eighteenth century, commented on the widespread belief that it was possible to determine the initial of the name of one's true love by collecting three snails from the church wall at Hallowe'en, taking them home and placing them on the kitchen table overnight. In the morning the tracks they had made on the table would spell the first letter of the name of the prospective spouse.[21] Another popular means of discovering a sweetheart's identity also associated with Hallowe'en involved walking nine times around the church, at the end of which one's true love would miraculously appear.[22]

The churchyard was not infrequently the location for numerous sports and pastimes in an age before public parks and playing fields, particularly on the occasion of the parish wake or gŵyl mabsant, which commemorated the church's patron saint. A religious service might be

---

[18] NLW, Church in Wales Records, SD/CCCm(G)/279.

[19] Saunders, *A View*, pp. 36–7; Geraint H. Jenkins, 'Popular Beliefs in Wales from the Restoration to Methodism', *Bulletin of the Board of Celtic Studies*, 27 (1977), 440–3; Howell, *Rural Poor*, pp. 154–6.

[20] Michael Roberts, 'Gender, work and socialization in Wales *c*.1450–*c*.1850', in Sandra Betts (ed.), *Our Daughters' Land* (Cardiff, 1996), pp. 19–20. For a wider discussion of 'churching' see W. Coster, 'Purity, Profanity and Puritanism: the churching of women 1500–1700', in W. Sheils and D. Woods (eds), *Studies in Church History, 27: women in the church* (Oxford, 1990), pp. 377–87.

[21] Hugh Owen, *The Life and Works of Lewis Morris 1701–1765* (Anglesey, 1951), p. 143; Catrin Stevens, *Welsh Courting Customs* (Llandysul, 1977), p. 20.

[22] Stevens, *Welsh Courting Customs*, p. 22.

conducted to celebrate the event, but much of the day was devoted to feasting, drinking, dancing and sport. The secular nature of these holidays and lack of religious observance caused some concern to more serious-minded clerics such as the redoubtable Thomas Ellis of Holyhead, who took pride in eradicating wakes from his locality.[23] The traditional football matches between neighbouring parishes, which accompanied wakes, articulated a keen sense of parish loyalty. Richard Suggett and David Howell suggest that such displays of parish unity, if anything, increased during the eighteenth century as a result of poor law provision.[24] The parish had been the unit responsible for the care and supervision of the poor since the passing of the Elizabethan Poor Law in 1601, and this was affirmed in the 1662 Settlement Act. Disputes with neighbouring parishes over responsibility for individual paupers may well have turned some supposedly friendly inter-parish football contests into grudge matches. One of the most hotly contended was the match known as Y Bêl Ddu (The Black Ball) between Llandysul and Llanwenog in Cardiganshire which was replaced in 1833 by a scriptural contest between their respective Sunday schools.[25] The added dimension to the competition may well have led to a greater sense of identification with the local parish, if only in opposition to neighbouring communities who had given offence. There is evidence, therefore, that the parish church continued to occupy a central role in Welsh communities, despite the fact that the majority of parishioners rarely, if ever, attended divine service. Many of these ceremonies and customs actually involved more secular celebration than religious observance, yet the Church provided a familiar background to these rituals in community life. As David Cressy states, 'whether raising a glass or raising a prayer, God was never far from hand'.[26]

Among the most useful sources for clarifying popular attitudes to the eighteenth-century Church are its own records, particularly those gener-

---

[23] G. Nesta Evans, *Religion and Politics in Mid-Eighteenth Century Anglesey* (Cardiff, 1953), pp. 59–60, 63–4.

[24] Richard Suggett, 'Festivals and Social Structure in Early Modern Wales', *Past and Present*, 152 (1996), 103–5; Howell, *Rural Poor*, pp. 140–1. For a discussion of parish unity see Keith Wrightson and David Levine, *Poverty and Piety in an English Village: Terling, 1525–1700* (Oxford, 1979).

[25] Prys Morgan, 'From a Death to a View: the Hunt for the Welsh Past in the Romantic Period', in Eric Hobsbawn and Terence Ranger (eds), *The Invention of Tradition* (Cambridge, 1983), p. 54; Suggett, 'Festivals and Social Structure', 88; Emma Lile, 'Chwaraeon tymhorol yng Nghymru cyn y Chwyldro Diwydiannol', in Geraint H. Jenkins (ed.), *Cof Cenedl*, XVIII (Llandysul, 2003), p. 79.

[26] Cressy, *Birth, Marriage and Death*, p. 477.

ated by its courts. There were no archdeacon's courts within the Welsh
diocese so it was the Bishop's consistory court that dealt with matters of
moral discipline, according to the contemporary phrase, 'for the
reformation of morals and the soul's health'.[27] Any cases of non-
attendance, misconduct in church, blasphemy or moral turpitude fell to the
jurisdiction of the consistory courts, but as they could not impose physical
or financial penalties they were probably less intimidating than secular
courts. The most severe punishment at their disposal was excommunication,
which would exclude the offender from the Christian community.[28] Since
this was quite frequently imposed on a temporary basis until the offender
had shown proper contrition and served penance, excommunication was
perhaps not as terrifying a prospect as might be thought. By the eighteenth
century the tradition of doing public penance clad in white at the church
porch had fallen out of favour. Instead the offender usually read a
declaration of penitence before the parish clergyman, and possibly the
churchwardens and others involved in the case. The penance gradually
became a private rather than a public affair and the sensibilities of the
offender were more carefully protected than in previous centuries when
church courts had been more powerful and effective.

Considering how few cases were brought compared with the number
who failed to attend divine service, even at Easter, it would appear that
only the most inveterate and offensive absentees from church were
presented to the courts. John Gronow of St Bride's Major, Glamorgan,
was one of the few. He was accused in 1737 of absenting himself from
church services for the previous three years and, 'seduced by the
instigation of the Devil', of spending most Sundays playing bowls or other
ball games.[29] No similar cases appear in the surviving documents for

---

[27] For example, NLW, Church in Wales Records, LL/CC/G/905, SD/CCCm(G)/
287a. See also Walter Morgan, 'The Consistory Courts in the Diocese of St
David's, 1660–1858', *Journal of the Historical Society of the Church in Wales*, 7,
11 (1957), 6; P. E. H. Hair (ed.), *Before the Bawdy Court* (London, 1972), pp. 15–
28; Bruce Lenman, 'The Limits of Godly Discipline in the Early Modern Period
with Particular Reference to England and Scotland', in Kasper von Greyerz (ed.),
Religion and Society in Early Modern Europe (London, 1984), pp. 124–45; Martin
Ingram, 'Reformation of Manners in Early Modern England', in Paul Griffiths,
Adam Fox and Steve Hindle (eds), *The Experience of Authority in Early Modern
England* (London, 1996), pp. 47–88.
[28] See Morgan, 'The Consistory Courts in the Diocese of St David's', 12; Martin
Ingram, *Church Courts, Sex and Marriage in England, 1570–1640* (Cambridge,
1987), pp. 52–3, 340–63; J. A. Sharpe, *Judicial Punishment in England* (London,
1990), pp. 22–3.
[29] NLW, Church in Wales Records, LL/CC/G/825.

Llandaff or St David's, despite the fact that a number of accusations of violating the Sabbath do appear in the records of Bangor diocese. This may either suggest a greater enthusiasm for dealing with such offenders in Bangor or it could reflect the stronger position of the Anglican Church in the north of the country.[30] Judging by the figures in the parish visitation returns, absenteeism by parishioners in the southern dioceses may well have been on too great a scale to make the persecution of offenders a practical proposition for the authorities. In the parish of Usk, Monmouthshire, in 1763, for instance, it was noted that of the three hundred inhabitants, sixty to seventy could be considered communicants in the church and of those only around fifteen received communion on a monthly basis.[31] Similarly in 1763, in Margam, Glamorgan, of the four hundred communicants listed in the parish, 160 generally received communion.[32] This pattern was by no means uncommon in the larger parishes in the southern dioceses. In Llandeilo Fawr in Carmarthenshire in 1755 around a hundred communicants were recorded at Easter out of a population of eight hundred who might attend.[33]

The court records also contain frequent cases of assault, brawling and scolding within the church and churchyard during this period which might, at first glance, be taken to suggest a lack of appropriate reverence. The articles of the Llandaff courts indeed describe the accused in these cases as 'not having the fear of God before your eyes'.[34] However, closer examination of the actual cases suggests that such quarrels arose on church ground simply because it was a place of assembly at the heart of the parish community. Some of those who gathered for divine service had existing grievances which, on occasion, led to the exchange of harsh words and even blows. It is significant that in the majority of these cases at least one of the parties involved is described as a gentleman, or as a parish official of some sort. Many of these quarrels arose out of existing tensions and competition between prominent members of the congregation who were vying for pre-eminence in the parish hierarchy. This was the case in 1740 when accusations of scolding in the churchyard of Saint Bride's Major, Glamorgan, were brought against two brothers, Robert and Evan Rees, by Lewis Saunders, gentleman. There were four witness statements in each case in addition to the initial Articles outlining the charges. The accounts

---

[30] NLW, Church in Wales Records, B/CC/C(G)/9, 14, 28, 34 (1750–2).

[31] NLW, Church in Wales Records, LL/QA/2.

[32] NLW, Church in Wales Records, LL/QA/1.

[33] NLW, Church in Wales Records, SD/QA/61.

[34] For example, NLW, Church in Wales Records, LL/CC/G/630, 651, 770, 825, 904, 1159a, 1160.

concur that Lewis Saunders had 'a Considerable Estate' in the parish, that he and the Rees brothers talked loudly in the churchyard after morning service, but agree on very little else. Robert and Evan Rees were both accused of calling Saunders a fool or a blockhead, and complaining that 'such a fellow as he . . . was not worth a groat to take upon him to govern the parish', along with 'other vilifying Expressions'.[35]

In the charge against Evan Rees it was stated that he made his statements in Welsh, and while there is no mention of the language used by Robert, it might reasonably be assumed that his testimony would also be offered in his mother tongue. Two of the witnesses, David Nicholl, a cordwainer, and Griffith Hopkin, a tailor, both aged thirty-eight, were at some pains to explain that they were too far away to hear what was said or even if it could be classified as scolding, although they confirmed that the parties talked 'somewhat loudly at each other'.[36] Miles Edward, the parish clerk and sexton, was putting away the church utensils and locking up at the time. He testified to hearing some persons talking 'in a high and loud manner' outside the chancel but could not hear what was said. Seeing Robert Rees sitting on a gravestone near the church porch he asked him about the dispute and was told 'twas only ye Great Belly had occasioned it'. Miles Edward stated he had no idea who might be meant by the expression 'Great Belly'. All accounts agreed that Edward Walters and Thomas Turbervill, the recently deceased vicar of the parish, were close enough to hear what was said. Walters, described as a twenty-six year old gentleman, stated that Evan and Robert Rees had accused Saunders of being unfit to govern a parish and having nothing to show 'for all he had but a great Belly'. He further explained that the dispute arose over accounts submitted to the parish by Evan Rees as surveyor of highways for St Bride's Major. For his part, Saunders had maintained that these accounts should not be accepted. The judgement in both cases was that the accusations had not been proven and that Saunders was liable to pay the Rees brothers' costs totalling £10. 5s. This was obviously a quarrel between parish gentry and officials in which the local craftsmen had no desire to become involved. The initial accusations were made in September 1740, witness depositions were collected between April and June 1741, and the sentences were issued in January 1742. Even fairly minor cases could prove relatively costly and lengthy ordeals, nor was the outcome likely to dispel the resentment and tension in St Bride's Major. It

---

[35] NLW, Church in Wales Records, LL/CC/G/904–5.
[36] NLW, Church in Wales Records, LL/CC/G/9041–b; 905a–b.

took some considerable resolve and wherewithal to choose to pursue cases through the ecclesiastical courts.

This was by no means the only case where the underlying cause was an accusation of financial mismanagement by a parish official as the following examples show: in 1738 the former churchwardens of Llangadog, Carmarthenshire, were excommunicated after being presented to the court by the current churchwardens for failing to make good a sum of money missing from the church accounts during their period in office;[37] in 1754 Richard Jenkin was said to have accused William Deere, the overseer of the poor of Llyswyrny, Glamorgan, of defrauding the parish of 20s. Since this accusation was shouted aloud in a vestry meeting conducted in the church porch, 'without any Respect to the place you then stood upon', it resulted in a case before the consistory court, the outcome of which is unknown;[38] and finally, in 1756 financial matters were also at the heart of the brawl which occurred at a vestry meeting in the church porch of Coedcernyw, Monmouthshire.[39] Joseph Thomas, who was busily engaged as churchwarden, overseer of the poor, surveyor of highways and constable of the parish, along with John Barkley, the parish clerk, were so incensed at what they deemed to be the unwarranted interference of the curate, James Evans, that they jostled, squeezed and pinched him. A number of witnesses attested to the fact that the curate had lost a button from his coat in the fracas and his assailants were duly found guilty of the assault and punished by a sentence of excommunication. Their contention was that the curate had no business involving himself in the parish accounts as he resided in his other parish of Marshfield and owned no land nor paid any taxes in Coedcernyw. Any resentment did not seem to stem from his office as a clergyman, therefore, but from his insistence on checking on the integrity of the parish officials.

Clearly, the church was a place where members of the community of varying social standing congregated. In a society where rank and degree still played an important part, it is not surprising that social divisions were visibly manifested in church. The social order was, after all, traditionally perceived as being ordained by God and this was reflected in the allocation of seating in places of worship. It was probably the defence of social status which lay behind many of the quarrels and assaults which took place on ecclesiastical ground, rather than disrespect for the Church itself. Inevitably, the question of seating in the church was a major cause of

---

[37] NLW, Church in Wales Records, SD/CCCm(G)/280.
[38] NLW, Church in Wales Records, LL/CC/G/1111.
[39] NLW, Church in Wales Records, LL/CC/G/1159–61.

dispute.[40] The best places were reserved for the more affluent who paid the most towards the upkeep of the parish church, and they were most likely to defend any challenge to their position by bringing cases before the consistory courts. There was also a territorial dimension to such disputes as various farms and holdings within the parish were traditionally allocated specific seats in the church. In 1738, for example, a complaint was brought against Griffith Roberts, a gentleman of Kidwelly.[41] According to the complaint, when the church in Kidwelly had been restored some fifty years previously it had been necessary to ascertain who 'owned' which seat. At that time, one seat had been allocated exclusively for the use of the clergyman's wife and the wife of the Mayor of Kidwelly. Griffith Roberts, however insisted on sitting there regardless, arguing that the seat had been built on the site of a pew attached to a dilapidated house called Henblase in the town of Kidwelly. Since the house was his property he therefore prevented the clergyman's wife from sitting there because technically the seat belonged to him.

One man who appeared to have been particularly aggrieved by the question of seating in the church was Thomas Lewis of Llanishen, Glamorgan. The Lewis family of Llanishen were a cadet branch of the Lewises of Y Fan, a prominent family among the Glamorgan gentry.[42] Lewis, as owner of Llanishen House and the most substantial holding in the parish, brought a case against Thomas Morgan, also described as a parish gentleman. The Lewis family, as the chief family in the parish, had for generations enjoyed the occupancy of a prominent church pew placed at the arch dividing the chancel from the the body of the church, near the communion table. With blatant disregard for the social status of the family of Llanishen House, Thomas Morgan had constructed a new seat in 1752 which was then located between the Lewis pew and the rails surrounding the communion table. Morgan's seat adjoined the existing pew but was built nine inches higher so that it obscured the view of the communion table and altar. From the quite detailed description there is no doubt that the new seat was a tight fit, squeezed between the original seat and the communion table in order to claim precedence over the Lewis family. This was tantamount to a challenge to the existing order of supremacy in the

---

[40] See Evans, *Religion and Politics*, 16–17; Water T. Morgan, 'Disputes concerning Seats in Church before the Consistory Courts of St David's', *Journal of the Historical Society of the Church in Wales*, 11 (1961), 65–89.
[41] NLW, Church in Wales Records, SD/CCCm(G)/277.
[42] Penry Williams, 'The Political and Administrative History of Glamorgan', in Glanmor Williams (ed.), *Glamorgan County History. IV: Early Modern Glamorgan* (Cardiff, 1974), p. 168.

parish, and it was no surprise that Thomas Lewis rose to the challenge through the medium of the consistory court.[43]

Many of these cases are suggestive of an atmosphere of almost Trollopean plotting, competition and intrigue at a parish level; Obadiah Slope might well have felt at home in such circles! Yet they also underpin the idea that the Church retained a central place in the community. Even if bickering arose mainly between the more prominent members of the congregation, the humbler parishioners were frequently drawn in to give evidence and would have been made aware that certain behaviour was unacceptable within the confines of the church and its grounds. There is little or no evidence in the records of the ecclesiastical courts to suggest any real disrespect towards or dissatisfaction with the church at a parish level. Specific instances of neglect on behalf of the clergy caused anger and grief, but there is no suggestion that these emotions were translated into resentment towards the Church as an institution rather than rage towards some of its representatives. There are numerous cases of failure to pay tithes or church rates, but nothing to suggest that this was anything more than a simple disinclination to pay taxes.[44] Despite the perceived shortcomings of the Church in south Wales, therefore, there is little evidence from the mid-eighteenth century to suggest that it had lost its place in the affections of the population as a whole. Nonconformity would provide an effective challenge by the end of the eighteenth century, but at the time when the Methodist Revival was beginning to gain ground in Wales, the position of the Church still seemed unassailable. The parish church had, after all, played its part in generations of family history, baptising, marrying and burying local people since time immemorial. If there were signs of irreverence, they arose from the familiarity engendered by a church and churchyard at the heart of a community, fulfilling various functions associated with worship, tradition, respect for the memory of the departed and recreation for the living.

---

[43] NLW, Church in Wales Records, LL/CC/G/1089.

[44] See Walter T. Morgan, 'Cases of Subtraction of Church-Rate before the Consistory Courts of St David's', *Journal of the Historical Society of the Church in Wales*, 9 (1959), 70–91.

CHAPTER FOUR

'AN ALARM SOUNDED TO THE SINNERS IN SION': JOHN KELSALL, QUAKERS AND POPULAR CULTURE IN EIGHTEENTH-CENTURY WALES

RICHARD C. ALLEN

In their study of cultural shifts from the eighteenth century onwards, John Golby and Bill Purdue explained that changes in popular culture were 'largely made by the people, their appetites, demands and aspirations' in response to the development of a consumer society based upon 'greater spending power, urbanisation and new forms of communication'. This culture was 'both spirited and robust'.[1] Their chapter, 'The "old" popular culture' acknowledged that many festivities remained attached to traditional feast days in the agricultural and religious calendar, but they still questioned the representation of pre-industrial society as 'commercially unsophisticated'. While eighteenth-century society was principally based on rural communities and their economies, there were competing forces which challenged existing patterns of behaviour. They contend that the pre-industrial economy and society of England was unique in Europe, suggesting that 'the long tradition of economic individualism, the acceleration of social mobility and the conflict engendered by Puritanism had all stamped themselves on the culture of the people'.[2] Similar views of cultural consumption have been aired by Neil McKendrick, John Brewer and J. H. Plumb who traced the development of a consumer society and its impact, especially on the middling sorts.[3] Yet,

---

[1] J. M. Golby and A. W. Purdue, *The Civilisation of the Crowd: popular culture in England 1750–1900* (revised pbk edn. Stroud, 1999), p. 7.
[2] Ibid., p. 18.
[3] Neil McKendrick, John Brewer and J. H. Plumb, *The Birth of Consumer Society: the commercialisation of eighteenth-century England* (London, 1982).

as Jeremy Black observed, there is a danger 'in seeing society as consumer-led, with culture as just a response to market forces'.[4] Golby and Purdue are inclined to agree and emphasised the way that 'the enduring context of a rural and decentralised society' necessarily restricted significant alterations to popular culture, and thereby centuries-old traditions continued to exist.[5]

There were undoubtedly challenges which eroded this common culture. In his work on traditional customs in early modern Europe, Peter Burke observed that the upper orders increasingly withdrew from participation in popular culture in the seventeenth and eighteenth centuries, while the spread of literacy, communication links and the 'commercial revolution' also had an impact.[6] Moral reform campaigns against such behaviour and attempts to 'proselytise, cajole or discipline the populace into the acceptance of a remodelled way of life, marked by more suitable, more moral and more abstinent habits' further ate away at traditional customs.[7] In 1682 the London Quaker, John Kelsall Snr (1650–84) was contemptuous of the world in which he lived and its vain customs. In this year he wrote *A Testimony against Gaming, Musick, Dancing, Singing, Swearing and People calling upon God to Damn them. As also against drinking to excess, Whoring, Lying and Cheating* . . .[8] His reaction to the perceived depravity of early modern society was mirrored by co-religionists in Britain and in Europe. In 1706 another Quaker minister, Christopher Meidel, produced a widely-circulated broadside entitled *A Time to Dance?* which called on people to avoid 'Fiddling, Dancing, Singing, Playing, Masquing, Gaming, Bowling, Ringing, Fencing, Bull- and Bear-Baiting, Cock-Fighting, Ranting and Revelling', and above all the taverns and ale-houses which encouraged excessive drinking.[9] Among these influential social reformers was John Kelsall Jnr (1683–1743) who

---

[4] Jeremy Black, *Eighteenth Century Britain* (London, 2001), p. 161.
[5] Golby and Purdue, *Civilisation of the Crowd*, p. 20.
[6] Peter Burke, *Popular Culture in Early Modern Europe* (pbk edn. Oxford, 1994), pp. 16, 29, 244–86.
[7] Golby and Purdue, *Civilisation of the Crowd*, p. 10.
[8] John Kelsall, *A Testimony against Gaming, Musick, Dancing, Singing, Swearing and People calling upon God to Damn them. As also against drinking to excess, Whoring, Lying and Cheating* . . . (London, 1682).
[9] Library of the Society of Friends, London (LSF), Broadsides 'A', 146. 'To my neighbours and others, in and about Stratford, near Bow, in Essex, Assembled to Dance on the 1st of the 3[r]d month, called May-Day, 1706.' See also Richard C. Allen, '"Turning hearts to break off the yoke of oppression." The travels and sufferings of Christopher Meidel *c*.1659–*c*.1715', *Quaker Studies*, 12, 1 (2007), 54–72.

followed in his father's footsteps and became a powerful advocate of his views in Wales. Although born in England, he would later spend the majority of his life in north Wales. This voice against self-indulgent behaviour was echoed by William Powell who publicly condemned swearing and drunkenness as 'the Bane of Society, and Destruction to Body and Soul'.[10] For these men at least, the world was contaminated by sinfulness. They were 'profoundly suspicious of worldly pleasures', and determined to encourage 'the habits of moral and social discipline, efficiency and restraint, decorum of bearing and propriety of speech, sobriety, caution and thrift'.[11]

It was while the younger Kelsall was clerk of the Dolobran Meeting, near Welshpool in Montgomeryshire, that Friends decided to translate his father's work into the vernacular in order to strengthen their resolve against such diversions.[12] Abhorrence of ungodly behaviour in places of public diversion led commentators, such as the young Kelsall, to challenge traditional patterns of community life.[13] Consequently, by refusing to join in time-honoured pastimes, these moral reformers distanced themselves from their neighbours and this led to a clash between popular culture and reformed behaviour. As illustrated above, at the forefront of opposition to unreformed behaviour stood The Religious Society of Friends (Quakers).[14] The intention here is to focus on some of the activities frowned upon by the Friends, as expressed by Kelsall Jnr, and to explore the divergence between popular culture and religious ideologies in Wales in the

---

[10] William Powell, *Swearing and Drunkenness, the Bane of Society, and Destruction to Body and Soul* (London, 1727).

[11] G. H. Jenkins, *Literature, Religion and Society in Wales 1660–1730* (Cardiff, 1978), p. 85.

[12] For further details of the code of behaviour sponsored by the Welsh Quaker communities, see Richard C. Allen, *Quaker Communities in Early Modern Wales: from resistance to respectability* (Cardiff, 2007), ch. 5.

[13] Examples of social diversions in the early modern period are provided in P. Burke, *Popular Culture in Early Modern Europe* (revised edn. Cambridge, 1994); J. Barry and C. Brooks (eds), *The Middling Sort: culture, society and politics in England 1550–1800* (Basingstoke, 1994); Tim Harris (ed.), *Popular Culture in England c.1500–1850* (Basingstoke, 1995); John Brewer, *The Pleasures of the Imagination: English culture in the eighteenth century* (London, 1997); B. Reay, *Popular Cultures in England 1550–1750* (London, 1998); Michael Roberts, 'More prone to be idle and riotous than the English? Attitudes to male behaviour in early modern Wales', in M. Roberts and S. Clark (eds), *Women and Gender in Early Modern Wales* (Cardiff, 2000), pp. 259–90.

[14] The terms 'Quaker(s)' and 'Friend(s)' will be used interchangeably in this chapter.

eighteenth century. This study will question whether Welsh social mores and popular activities were as debauched as the Quakers and other religious commentators claimed to be the case elsewhere in Britain.[15]

The Quakers first appeared in Britain during the aftermath of the British Civil Wars in the mid-seventeenth century, and continued to practice their beliefs in opposition to the later Restoration government and the Established Church.[16] George Fox and his followers disseminated the Quaker belief in 'the inner light', liberty of conscience and egalitarianism throughout Britain.[17] In 1653 John ap John, a former Congregationalist at Wrexham, introduced the new religion into Wales and he was assisted by the evangelising visits of a number of Quaker missionaries.[18] Not surprisingly their radical message marked them out as dangerous subversives and they were heavily persecuted in the years before the Act of Toleration (1689) enabled Friends to worship freely in their meeting houses.[19] It is during this later period that John Kelsall Jnr was born (c.1683) into a respectable Quaker family. Before he was three years old his parents died, and in May 1687 Kelsall and his brother went to live with their grandmother in Lancashire. Both boys were educated locally before

---

[15] For details of the reform campaigns waged against the behaviour of early modern society see M. Ingram, 'Ridings, Rough Music and 'the reform of popular culture', *Past and Present*, 105 (1984), 79–113; R. B. Shoemaker, 'Reforming the City: the reformation of manners campaign in London, 1690–1738', in L. Davison, T. Hitchcock, T. Kearn and R. B. Shoemaker (eds), *Stilling the Grumbling Hive: the response to social and economic problems in England, 1689–1750* (Stroud, 1992), pp. 99–120; R. Hutton, *The Rise and Fall of Merry England* (pbk edn. Oxford, 1994), ch. 4; M. Ingram, 'Reformation of Manners in Early Modern England', in P. Griffiths, A. Fox and S. Hindle (eds), *The Experience of Authority in Early Modern England* (Basingstoke, 1996), pp. 47–88.

[16] For the Welsh historical context see G. H. Jenkins, *Protestant Dissenters in Wales, 1639–1689* (Cardiff, 1992).

[17] This is discussed in Fox's *Journal*. See John L. Nickalls (ed.), *The Journal of George Fox* (Cambridge, 1952), passim. For a modern analysis of the origins of Quakerism, Fox and his supporters, see H. L. Ingle, *First Among Equals. George Fox and the creation of Quakerism* (Oxford, 1994).

[18] For details, see W. G. Norris and N. Penney, 'John ap John and early records of Friends in Wales', *JFHS* Supplement 6 (1907); Richard C. Allen, 'Taking up her Daily Cross': Women and the early Quaker movement in Wales, c.1653–1689', in Roberts and Clarke (eds), *Women and Gender in Early Modern Wales*, pp. 104–28; C. Trevett, *Quaker Women Prophets in England and Wales, 1650–1700* (Lewiston, New York and Lampeter, 2000); Allen, *Quaker Communities*, ch. 1.

[19] Allen, *Quaker Communities*, ch. 4.

attending the non-Quaker Abbeystead School.[20] John rebelled in his youth, becoming an 'ungovernable boy' who took pleasure in 'foolish talking, vain jesting and idle communications', and it was said that he had an 'uneasie fretful Spirit' which made him 'very disobedient to those yt sought my welfare'.[21] Later in life he warned parents of the need to consider educational provision carefully for in their formative years children were particularly vulnerable to worldly influences.[22]

In spite of his regular attendance at Quaker meetings he adopted many 'worldly' customs, most notably doffing his hat to social superiors and using 'heathen' days and months in everyday speech. This, Kelsall acknowledged later, caused 'harm yt accrues from an habitual, evil custom'.[23] The death of his grandmother in August 1699, however, affected him greatly as he became aware of 'how undutifull I was to her'.[24] Following a brief period teaching at a Quaker school at Yelland and his removal to Lancaster there was a marked change in his lifestyle. On 22 July 1700 he wrote to his uncle: 'Oh! yt I had a place seperate from all mankind so yt I might avoid the vanity yt is seen in idle discourse and too much babling with vain laughter &c. wch things I can truly say I have much striven against.'[25] It was shortly after this (c.1701) that he took up a teaching position at the Friends' school at Dolobran.[26] He was an exemplary student-teacher, educating his students as well as advancing his own intellectual capacity by becoming proficient in Greek, Latin, mathematics, geometry and trigonometry, and having a 'great inclination to poetry'.[27] It is from this period that his opposition to popular activities can be clearly detected.

Kelsall's diaries and correspondence, which cover the first half of the eighteenth century, illuminate the ascetic lifestyle and hardships expected of eighteenth century Welsh Quakers, as well as the changing popular culture of England and Wales. By the beginning of the eighteenth century

---

[20] LSF, Ms. 194/1 ('A Journal of the historical account of the chief passages, concerns and exercises of my [John Kesall Jnr] life . . .'), pp. 2–5.
[21] Ibid., pp. 9, 11.
[22] Ibid., p. 12.
[23] Ibid., pp. 18–19.
[24] Ibid., pp. 23–4.
[25] LSF, Ms. 194/2 (A book of letters sent by John Kelsall c.1700–1728), pp. 1–2 (letter to Timothy Cragg, 12.6.1700); H. G. Jones, 'John Kelsall: A study in religious and economic history', unpublished University of Wales, Bangor, MA thesis, 1938, p. 14.
[26] LSF, Ms. 194/1, pp. 57, 61–2; LSF, Ms. 194/2, pp. 9–10 (letter to T. Cragg, 2.5.1701).
[27] LSF, Ms. 194/1, pp. 49, 93–4.

most Friends were far removed from their radical mid-seventeenth century roots.[28] As a religious community they maintained amiable relationships with their neighbours and were distinguished by their belief in equality and pacifism. But their abhorrence of the excessive consumption of alcohol led them to oppose some traditional social activities. Arguably, the wider study of Welsh Quakerism and its response to the rise of consumerism and the prevailing modes of behaviour offers a fresh perspective upon the existence and workings of a counter culture.[29] The culture of Quakers and other nonconformists stood in direct opposition to the 'frivolity and self-indulgence of drama, painting, sculpture, music and dance, or even less serious forms of popular leisure'.[30] Moreover, for Friends it was imperative that members should strive to 'overcome the world' by rejecting popular culture and worldly possessions. The divergence between popular culture and reformed behaviour, and calls for plainness and a simple, godly life, led many Quakers to challenge the prevailing norms of society. Yet, at the same time, this austerity led to an inexorable decline in their membership as many found themselves unable to meet such harsh strictures. Their code of conduct was developed partly as a response to the amorphous nature of the Society in the early decades of their history, but also as a means of controlling wayward behaviour. For example, in the late-1650s, and particularly in the post-Restoration years, there was a genuine desire among leading members to distance themselves from anyone who displayed 'ranterish' characteristics. The activities of James Nayler in Bristol in 1656, and the infamous re-enactment of Christ's entry into Jerusalem, occasioned widespread outrage. This forced Friends to insist upon sanctions, and naturally, as time passed, the code they developed became a highly inflexible set of rules.[31]

---

[28] David Scott, *Quakerism in York, 1650–1720*, Borthwick Paper, 80 (York, 1991); Nicholas Morgan, *Lancashire Quakers and the Establishment 1660–1730* (Halifax, 1993); Adrian Davies, *The Quakers in English Society 1655–1725* (Oxford, 2000); Rosemary Moore, *The Light in their Consciences: early Quakers in Britain* (Philadelphia, 2000); Kate Peters, *Print Culture and the Early Quakers* (Cambridge, 2005).

[29] See Allen, *Quaker Communities*, ch. 5–6.

[30] Reay, *Quakers and the English Revolution*, p. 118.

[31] For details see W. G. Bittle, *James Nayler, 1618–1660: the Quaker indicted by Parliament* (York, 1986); Leopold Damrosch, *The Sorrows of the Quaker Jesus: James Nayler and the Puritan crackdown on the free spirit* (Cambridge, Mass.; London, 1996). The code is comprehensively discussed in D. J. Hall, 'The Discipline of the Society of Friends', unpublished University of Durham, MA thesis, 1972.

With the imposition of self-censorship, Friends sought to ensure that no member brought the Society into disrepute by acting inappropriately both in meetings for worship and in public. Even Kelsall frequently felt drowsy in meetings and would have to stab himself with pins to keep himself awake.[32] In June 1705 and May 1708 members were warned that they should avoid sleeping in meetings. Much later in May 1731, Kelsall complained that Friends were increasingly 'unwilling to give . . . offence' and were reluctant to testify against the 'lifeless superstitious ministry of the Priests'.[33] As Geraint Jenkins has observed, this ambivalence was a clear sign that Friends were increasingly becoming accepted in the wider community as well as the fact that 'Welsh Quakerism was becoming increasingly innocuous'.[34] It is possible that Kelsall may have anticipated the rise of Methodism; it was, he wrote, 'my belief God will raise in due time a people out of Friends or others who will be commissioned to strike at the root and branch of Antichrist, without regard to the frowns or favours of high or low clergy or others'.[35] A Friends' refusal to acknowledge his/her inappropriate behaviour would lead to disownment. Thus, at the time Kelsall first arrived at Dolobran in 1701, the Shropshire and Montgomeryshire Monthly Meeting censured Oliver Thomas for his 'disorderly walking' and 'ill behaviour', and were prepared to testify publicly against him. The meeting reported that he was still keeping 'ill company' and he was eventually censured for drunkenness and 'all other vain practisis and misbehaviour'.[36]

The Quaker meeting placed great importance on educating their children, while also restricting outside influences.[37] The monthly meetings

---

[32] LSF, Ms. 194/1, p. 21. cf. Richard C. Allen, 'Establishing an Alternative Community in the North-East: Quakers, morals and popular culture in the long-eighteenth century', in Helen Berry and Jeremy Gregory (eds), *Creating and Consuming Culture in North-East England, 1660–1832* (Aldershot, 2004), pp. 101–2.

[33] Glamorgan Archive Service (hereafter GAS), D/DSF/379, Shropshire and Montgomeryshire Monthly Meeting minutes, 1693–1714 (26.4.1705, 26.3.1708); LSF, Ms. S.190, pp. 249–50 (31.3.1731).

[34] Jenkins, *Literature, Religion and Society in Wales*, p. 183.

[35] LSF, Ms. 194/1, p. 239 (c.1731).

[36] GAS, D/DSF/379 (24.12.1701, 31.1.1702, 29.10.1702, 26.11.1702, 25.12.1702).

[37] For Quaker attitudes towards education see also Allen, 'Establishing an alternative community', pp. 103–6, and for details of Quaker education see L. J. Stroud, 'The History of Quaker Education in England, 1647–1903', unpublished University of Leeds, M.Ed. thesis, 1944; G. Mason, 'Quaker Women and Education 1642–1840', unpublished University of Lancaster, MA thesis, 1987; David L. Wykes, 'Quaker schoolmasters, toleration and the law, 1689–1714',

were encouraged to support the instruction of fellow members and to increase their levels of literacy. As already noted, from 1701 to 1714 Kelsall was the schoolmaster at the Dolobran Monthly Meeting. During his many years teaching children, he was anxious to ensure that his pupils avoided the temptations of the world. He later wrote that the 'function of a school-master' was 'no light exercise, but a serious and weighty employment' that required 'a more qualified temper, and a greater stock of patience'. He found the responsibility of disciplining his charges arduous, and was acutely aware of the 'diverse tempers, capacities and inclinations of children' as well as the expectations and 'indulgences' of parents. He further observed that 'idleness & negligence is very odious & offensive, yet stubbornness & disobedience is far more hurtfull and of greater exercise to a teacher'.[38] In conjunction with a sound education, the Society sought to ensure that young Friends secured suitable employment. They thereby provided apprenticeships for the younger members of their community and ensured that those in their charge did not indulge in popular pastimes.[39]

Although such attitudes followed the standard practices adopted in many early modern apprenticeships,[40] Kelsall wrote that Quaker parents, elders and employers had a duty to avoid the 'harm' caused by allowing younger members 'to associate with the children of the world'.[41] This probably reflected his own experiences at a non-Quaker school in north-west England. Moreover, when he gave up his teaching post at Dolobran

---

Journal of Religious History, 21 (1997), 178–92; Camilla Leach, 'Advice for parents and books for children: Quaker women and educational texts for the home, 1798–1850', *History of Education Society Bulletin*, 69 (2002), 49–58; Geoffrey N. Cantor, *Quakers, Jews, and Science: religious responses to modernity and the sciences in Britain, 1650–1900* (Oxford, 2005); Camilla Leach, 'Religion and Rationality: Quaker women and science education 1790–1850', *History of Education*, 35, 1 (2006), 69–90.

[38] LSF, Ms. 194/1, pp. 61–2.

[39] Allen, 'Establishing an alternative community', pp. 106–8; R. C. Allen, '"Remember me to my good friend Captain Walker". James Cook and the North Yorkshire Quakers', in Glyndwr Williams (ed.), *Captain Cook: explorations and reassessments* (Woodbridge, 2004), pp. 24–6. Kelsall's two sons Amos and John were apprenticed to a Quaker clockmaker/shopkeeper at Frodsham in Cheshire and to a brassfounder at Birmingham, while Elizabeth, his daughter, was sent to live with Kelsall's in-laws John and Mary Gilbert. See Jones, 'John Kelsall', p. 24.

[40] See Joan Lane, *Apprenticeship in England, 1600–1914* (London, 1996); C. Brooks, 'Apprenticeship, Social Mobility and the Middling Sort, 1550–1800', in Barry and Brooks (eds), *Middling Sort of People*, p. 73ff.

[41] LSF, Ms. 194/1, p. 17.

in 1714 to work as a clerk for the Darby family at their Dolgellau ironworks, he re-emphasised the intrusive and corrupting influences of the world which reflects the insularity of the Quaker community and his commitment to the Society of Friends.[42] Yet, the demands of his employment, particularly the rapacious nature of the industry he was associated with, gave him little comfort and few opportunities to contemplate spiritual matters.[43] This can be illustrated by extracts from his diaries and letters. Upon taking up this position he sought to 'give no just offence to any, to wrong none, and to keep my word with all' as well as influencing people 'by love [rather] than austerity and oppression'.[44] By 1716, however, he was forced to concede that in his business dealings with various people he would sometimes be 'loaden with their wickedness and hypocrisy'. He bitterly complained about the great injustices perpetrated and 'such covetousness and self-interest . . . that even in small matters they would be unjust and deceitful, minding only things of this present world'.[45] Between 1717 and 1719, after the death of Abraham Darby I (1678–1717), Kelsall was temporarily employed by Samuel Milner of Bewdley, Worcestershire. Judging the Quaker to be insufficiently hard-nosed in his business transactions Milner removed Kelsall from his post. It can be suggested here that Kelsall was clearly out-of-step with his employers who were already wedded to capitalist activity. Indeed, he wrote in his journal that he was dismissed for being 'too easie and mild & not close & severe enough'.[46]

Other aspects of the lives of Friends, including marriages, were also increasingly controlled by the Society.[47] Above all couples were counselled to appreciate the essential ingredients of a successful relationship: sobriety, compatibility and financial security. In all cases of courtship and proposals of marriage the reputation of the Society had to be upheld and any ill-conceived alliance was referred to the local meeting for

---

[42] Ibid., pp. 14–34, 150–6 (7.12.1713–14; 3.3.1714).

[43] For details of the economic changes, including those in north Wales, see Jones, 'John Kelsall', ch. 3; A. H. Dodd, *The Industrial Revolution in North Wales* (Cardiff, 1933); H. Lloyd, *The Quaker Lloyds in the Industrial Revolution* (London, 1975); R. Floud and D. McCloskey (eds), *The Economic History of Britain since 1700* (2nd edn. London, 1994).

[44] LSF, Ms. 194/1, p. 151.

[45] Ibid., pp. 173–4 (9.6.1716).

[46] Ibid., pp. 193–4 (10mo[nth].1719).

[47] In 1653 George Fox established the guidelines that would govern Quaker marriages. For these and later developments see Thomas Lawrence and George Fox, *Concerning Marriage* (London, 1663); W. C. Braithwaite, *The Beginnings of Quakerism* (2nd edn. Cambridge, 1955), p. 146.

their consideration. By the eighteenth century the rules on marriage, particularly to outsiders, were rigorously applied and this reflected a widespread concern that mixed marriages, or marrying outside the meeting, would undermine the unity of the Society. In 1708, Kelsall was much exercised by his bachelor status, but was determined that 'it might be of the Lord's drawing, and not of man's or of my own contrivance'. In a poem, entitled 'On a wife', he wrote that:

> Let not my heart, let not my roving mind
> Be from thy will unto it if inclin'd
> But let thy power and thy constraining love
> Cause it to follow, and thy choice approve.[48]

Despite his uncertainties Kelsall responded to the exhortations of his friends and proposed to Dorothy Vaughan. As it turned out the relationship foundered and while he does not elaborate on the end of his engagement it did cause him considerable soul-searching.[49] When another marriage opportunity presented itself he waited, sought the approval of his future bride's parents, and in May 1711 he wed Susannah Davies at Dolobran.[50] Kelsall's concern to secure the *prior* approval of fellow Quakers was unusual to say the least and may have reflected instances of impropriety in his own family and among members of the Quaker community in north Wales.[51]

In June 1721 Kelsall wrote that his sister, Betty, who was living in Ireland, had married a non-member despite counselling from Friends. He bluntly informed her in a letter that this was a great mistake and it was 'her own fault' as she had indulged herself with 'vain & loose company' and

---

[48] LSF, Ms. 194/1, pp. 103, 105.

[49] Ibid., pp. 106–7. See also GAS, D/DSF/379 (27.1.1711, 24.2.1711).

[50] LSF, Ms. 194/1, pp. 129–38.

[51] For insights into courtship and marriage in the early modern period see Anthony J. Fletcher, 'The Protestant idea of marriage in early modern England', in Anthony J. Fletcher and Peter Roberts (eds), *Religion, Culture and Society in Early Modern Britain: essays in honour of Patrick Collinson* (Cambridge, 1994), pp. 161–81; Elizabeth A. Foyster, *Manhood in Early Modern England: honour, sex and marriage* (London, 1999); David M. Turner, '"Secret and immodest curiosities?": sex, marriage and conscience in early modern England', in Harald E. Braun and Edward Vallance (eds), *Contexts of Conscience in Early Modern Europe, 1500–1700* (Basingstoke, 2004), pp. 132–50; Catherine Frances, 'Making marriages in early modern England: rethinking the role of family and friends', in Maria Ågren and Amy Louise Erickson (eds), *The Marital Economy in Scandinavia and Britain, 1400–1900* (Aldershot, 2005), pp. 39–56.

had 'turn'd her back on Friends'.[52] On another occasion in 1722 Kelsall recorded the cost of the ill-advised marriage of Richard Griffiths to Katherine Edwards. Griffiths had his employment among the Quakers terminated, while his wife, a maid at Dolobran, was also dismissed.[53] The difficulty young Friends had in keeping to the rules on marriage can also be further illustrated when in March 1736 Kelsall's own son, John, informed his father that he had married a disowned Friend. Although the entry does not state where his son had married, presumably it was in an Anglican Church.[54] Like the earlier marriage of his sister, this greatly embarrassed Kelsall as such actions undermined the Society's beliefs and injured his own reputation among Friends.[55] The frequent disownment of members for 'walking disorderly', or entering into a 'marriage before a priest', however, led to an exodus of Friends from the Society in the eighteenth and nineteenth centuries.

The development of Friends as a dissenting community, which dispensed with the rituals of orthodox religious worship, was epitomised by simplicity and plainness in attire, household décor and behaviour. These characteristics are again evidenced by Kelsall's life and in his many observations. In his youth, he had been cautioned by his aunt Dorothy that 'the Times and People went worse & worse'. Clearly, this had made a marked impression on him as he later wrote, 'I gave diligent ear to her reading and words, and pondered them in my mind, thinking how they had fine times at ye meetings . . . and it comforted me when I thought of it.'[56] Although Friends constituted an alternative community, they nevertheless had to live in harmony with their neighbours. There were obvious pressures to conform to the prevailing social mores, and for some members who were wealthy the lure of eighteenth-century fashionable society proved irresistible. Kelsall wrote in his diary in May 1721 of his concern that Friends ought to be more careful about how they spent their leisure time and not 'in careing, talking & contriving abt yt wch is unprofitable &c so yt we may not have occasion to say on a dying bed, oh! yt I had spent my time better wn I had opportunity in conversation & society'.[57] But even steadfast Friends had trouble resisting the consumerist

---

[52] LSF, Ms. 193/1 (Diary, 1716–22), pp. 36–7 (20.4.1721).
[53] Ibid., p. 131 (9.8.1722).
[54] LSF, Ms. 193/2 (Diary, 1734–7), p. 36 (9.1.1736); Jones, 'John Kelsall', pp. 32–3.
[55] There are cases when Quaker parents were called to account by the local meeting after their children married outside the society. For example, see GAS, D/DSF/351, Monmouthshire Monthly Meeting minutes 1703–19 (2.12.1708–9).
[56] LSF, Ms. 194/1, p. 7.
[57] LSF, Ms. 193/1, pp. 29–30 (6–7.3.1721).

paraphernalia of polite society. In 1722 Kelsall condemned the 'general decay of zeal', the 'days of ease' and 'running into the world and the vanities thereof'. He bitterly regretted the fact that members were not as zealous as they had been in the years of persecution,[58] and was very conscious of the reprehensible behaviour of his Quaker employers, the Lloyds of Dolobran. In August 1727 Charles Lloyd II (1662–1747) and his son, Charles Lloyd III (1697–1767), faced financial ruin as their business collapsed. Despite the shame of Charles Lloyd II's £16,000 debt Kelsall still pleaded on his behalf at the Yearly Meeting at Marlborough in Wiltshire, but without success. Prior to Kelsall's return to Dolobran, both Lloyd and his son, who owed a further £6,000, had absconded 'whereby a great uneasiness and vexation followed in the country'.[59] Charles Lloyd II was officially declared bankrupt on 17 November 1727. Two years later he was testified against by the Society and was called upon to make restitution to his creditors. In 1742 he was nevertheless reconciled with Friends. His son was also declared bankrupt in January 1728 but was assisted by his wife's aunt who provided £1,717 to pay off his creditors. In October 1728 Charles Lloyd III attempted to make the forge profitable, but the business again failed and by summer 1729 he gave up the Mathrafal (Dolobran) forge and Bersham furnace.[60]

The unwillingness of many Friends to partake in the indulgent pleasures of community life, forced them to remain separate. In Kelsall's diaries and correspondence there are criticisms of such vanities and foolish pastimes. In a letter to Richard Lewis of Germantown in Pennsylvania in 1715, Kelsall advocated, along with like-minded Friends, that members of the Society should avoid cross-pockets, button-holes, powdering their wigs 'so as to bee seen', and cutting their hair without the consent of their local meeting. He argued that, 'unless people come to a true sense of ye root & ground of pride and vanity in themselves, I fear we shall have but little reformation amongst us'.[61]

---

[58] LSF, Ms. 193/1, pp. 140–1 (9.10.1722).

[59] Charles Lloyd II had gone to London, while his son had initially taken refuge in Boulogne.

[60] For details see LSF, Ms. 194/1, pp. 233–4 (30.6.1727, 7.7.1727, 15.7.1727, 8 mo[nth] 1727, 9mo.1718, 5mo.1729); LSF, Ms. S.189, pp. 21–2, 32–3, 85–6 (17.9.1727, 6.11.1727–8, 23.8.1728); GAS, D/DSF/2, pp. 620–1 (1–2.2.1730); Jones, 'John Kelsall', 122, 276–81, 283–4, 291–2; E. R. Morris, 'The Dolobran Family in Religion and Industry in Montgomeryshire', *Montgomeryshire Collections. The Journal of the Powysland Club,* 56 (1959–60), 142–4.

[61] LSF, Ms. 194/2, pp. 105–6 (letter dated 1.4.1715).

Throughout his adult life Kelsall acted as the regular representative of
North Wales Friends to the London Yearly Meeting, but he was not
impressed by London society, particularly the 'many spacious works and
curious contrivances of men . . . pride and vanity are very regent and the
glory of this world hath blinded the eyes of many'.[62] He sought, like many
other Friends, to make members aware of the need for plainness in their
lives, and to promote simplicity in apparel while gently reprimanding
those who dressed immoderately. Rules on plainness applied to both sexes
and this clearly distinguished Friends from the rest of society. Kelsall even
went as far as to suggest that young children ought to be responsible for
their behaviour, remarking that God 'strives with ye young in small things
yt are but vanity, as wth the more aged in their greater folly and sins,
leaving all both young & old without excuse'.[63] The code of plainness also
applied to household furnishings. Friends' houses contained little
embellishment and there was a marked absence of pictures or portraits. In
a poem dedicated to his future wife, he wrote 'Reject the world, and
foolish vanities / On heav'nly objects place thy carefull eyes.'[64] Some
Welsh members could not, however, resist acquiring luxury goods.
Clocks, watches, gold and jewellery were all listed as part of their estate as
well as valuable items of clothing.[65]

Friends' insistence on plainness was clearly part of a deliberate
strategy to persuade members to reject eighteenth-century consumerism.
Moreover, in his journal, Kelsall pointed out that such self-indulgence
exacerbated the miserable condition of the poor as they were induced to
spend money on fripperies. He wrote 'I saw them methought as wallowing
in their own blood, sensual, worldly, and brutish, encompassed with
clouds of darkness and in yt very region & shadow of death.'[66] Even when
the adoption of sober clothing by Friends became increasingly
anachronistic in the post-Toleration years, some Welsh meetings endorsed

---

[62] LSF, Ms. 194/1, pp. 79–80. For details of early eighteenth-century London life
and economics see Peter Earle, *The Making of the English Middle Class: business,
society and family life in London 1660–1730* (London, 1989); Roy Porter, *London:
a social history* (London, 1994); Paul Griffiths and Mark S. R. Jenner (eds),
Londinopolis: essays in the cultural and social history of early modern London
(Manchester, 2000); Jeremy Boulton, 'London 1540–1700', in Peter Clark (ed.),
The Cambridge Urban History of Britain, vol. 2: 1540–1840 (Cambridge, 2000),
pp. 315–46.
[63] LSF, Ms. 194/1, p. 11.
[64] LSF, 193/5 (A volume of poetry), p. 90 ('To S.D.').
[65] Allen, *Quaker Communities*, p. 137.
[66] LSF, Ms. 194/1, p. 161 (2.5.1714).

the sentiments of the London Yearly Meeting and called upon their members to abjure 'the fashions & customs of the World . . . in speech, apparell, furniture of houses & all superfluities, so that we may all show forth the vertue of our holy profession in our vertious lives'.[67] Despite such warnings the failure to adhere to the Society's code was evidence of a growing disaffection by members and a rejection of the rules of a religious community that had become clannish and a parody of itself.

While it is clear that some sections of Welsh society respected the Quakers and were persuaded by Kelsall's views, such puritanical values, coupled with his serious demeanour have made him appear a rather morose and introspective figure in Welsh history. While living at Chester he noted that there was 'nothing desireable or pleasant to me in this world . . . even Life itself seem'd but as a burthen, my earnest desires being that I might be truly prepared for the enjoymt of a future happy State'.[68] The constraints of Quaker beliefs were certainly imposed upon younger Friends who were denied access to prose, plays, poetry and community events. Kelsall refers to a cockfighting arena at Dolgellau in 1730 and his avoidance of the horse-race at Chester in 1737 – both occasions that would have been popular with local people but the Quakers opposed them on moral grounds and denounced the gambling associated with them.[69]

Friends made good use of the printing press to educate their members, and this propaganda continued throughout the eighteenth and nineteenth centuries. Tracts published in newspapers and journals, and the copious literature of Friends helped to disseminate their message among the wider community, and challenge anti-Quakerism.[70] For example, in 1720 the London Yearly meeting epistle advised members that they should not 'suffer romances, play-books, or other vain and idle pamphlets, in their houses or families, which tend to corrupt the minds of youth, but . . . that

---

[67] GAS, D/DSF/324, Quarterly Meeting of Cardiganshire, Carmarthenshire, Pembrokeshire and Glamorgan minutes, 1692–1710 (14.6.1705, 7.9.1705).

[68] LSF, Ms. 193/3 (Diary 1737–43), p. 114 (18.9.1742).

[69] LSF, Ms. S.190, p. 226 (1.11.1730); LSF, Ms. 193/2, p. 61 (25.2.1737). For a contemporary attack upon cockfighting by Welsh Friends see Evan Bevan, 'The Evils of Cockfighting', *Gloster Journal*, 13 April 1731, p. 2.

[70] For examples see Anon, *Work for a Cooper* (London, 1679); G. H. Jenkins, 'Quaker and anti-Quaker literature in Welsh from the Restoration to Methodism', *Welsh History Review*, 7 (1975), 403–26, and also in Jenkins, *Literature, Religion and Society in Wales*, pp. 180–2; cf. R. C. Allen '"Mocked, scoffed, persecuted, and made a gazeing stock": The resistance of the Religious Society of Friends (Quakers) to the religious and civil authorities in post-toleration south-east Wales c.1689–1836', in Gilbert Bonifas (ed.), *Cycnos. Publications de la Faculté des Lettres de Nice: Resistances* (Nice, 2003), 23–47.

they excite them to the reading of the Holy Scriptures and religious books'.[71] In 1726 Kelsall produced a broadside entitled, *The Faithful Monitor – or – an earnest exhortation to sobriety and holiness; inviting all people to a timely repentance, and forsaking of sin, before their day be over,*[72] while ten years later he wrote, *An Alarm sounded to the Sinners in Sion.* Unfortunately, this paper has not survived but, like his other writings, it probably would have reflected the attitudes of Welsh Friends to decadent, immoral, frivolous or indolent activities.

Alcohol abuse in the eighteenth century was considered to be a serious problem and Friends, along with other nonconformists, were well aware of the dangers of excessive drinking.[73] In July 1729 Kelsall recorded that some workmen at the Dolobran forge were committed to the stocks 'for being drunk and abusive'.[74] The Dolobran Monthly Meeting and the Quarterly Meeting for North Wales counselled members throughout the eighteenth century to be more temperate and avoid frequenting ale-houses. The aforementioned example of Oliver Thomas' behaviour was matched by that of Humphrey Wynn, and both men were testified against for their drunkenness.[75] These sanctions had both a moral and social impact, and were calculated to ensure that the immoderate behaviour of members did not bring the Society into disrepute with their neighbours, or disrupt the fabric of family life and business probity.

Welsh Friends appealed to members, as well as their non-Quaker neighbours, to refrain from cursing and other excesses. In December 1694, Hugh David was admonished for 'walking disorderly'. He was warned to keep away from Llanfyllin, while the people in the town were advised not to trust him as 'we cannot own him as one of us'.[76] It was not the only

---

[71] *Epistles [from the Yearly Meeting of Friends . . . from 1681 to 1857]* (2 vols. London, 1858), I, pp. 157–8; D. Hall, 'Plainness of Speech, Behaviour and Apparel in Eighteenth-Century English Quakerism', in W. J. Sheils (ed.), *Studies in Church History, 22: monks, hermits and the ascetic tradition* (Oxford, 1985), p. 314.

[72] LSF, Ms. S.188 (Diary 1725–27), p. 176 (14.10.1726). This was published in London in the same year and a Latin copy (*Monitor Fidelis*) is provided in LSF, Ms. 193/3, pp. 139–51.

[73] For details of alcohol abuse in the early modern period see Peter Clark, 'The alehouse and the alternative society', in D. H. Pennington and Keith V. Thomas (eds), *Puritans and Revolutionaries: essays in seventeenth-century history presented to Christopher Hill* (Oxford, 1978), pp. 47–72, and his *The English Alehouse: a social history, 1200–1830* (London, 1983).

[74] LSF, Ms. S.189 (Diary 1727–30), p. 143 (22.5.1729).

[75] GAS, D/DSF/379, (29.10.1702, 26.11.1702, 25.12.1702).

[76] Ibid., (25.10.1694).

time that Llanfyllin was portrayed as a veritable Sodom and Gomorrah for, according to Kelsall's journal entries, there was a great need to reform the manners of the people. In 1722 he was disturbed by 'rude company all night long' and complained that such 'wickedness and profaneness abounds daily scarce can we go to any place but people seem as they had loos'd full reins to do all sort of vanity without any consideration of God or a future being'.[77] Equally, at Oswestry in 1722 and in 1725 Kelsall denounced the 'wickedness of people who were drinking, swearing &c. all night long', and 'the vanity & forgetfulness of God that appeared among people'.[78] In one of his poems, Kelsall also criticised the celebrations which accompanied the Christmas holidays. He wrote:

And oh! Alas, how hath my mournfall heart
In secret griev'd and often wept apart
To hear and see, such as unto the name
Of Christ and Christian usually lay claim
Fiercely contend and argue and dispute
How yt this Day should be in high repute
Observ'd and kept unto the memory
Of our Dear Saviour's blessed nativity

Yet at this time upon this very day
Delight in sports in vanity and play
Indulge themselves as daily unto excess
In gaming and all wickedness
No day nor season the whole year around
With more profane and idle sports abound
Than at this time, methinks I ever see
The people loose full reins to vanity
With singing, dancing, jollity and mirth
The heavens ring and shakes ye hollow earth
The noise of oaths and roaring drunkards pierce
Th' astonish'd skies, and vex the universe
Oh! Horrible! Such wickedness to act
Under pretence of a religious fact.[79]

As a religious body whose moral code penalised inappropriate dress, non-attendance at meetings, and intemperance, Friends were bound to condemn sexual misconduct. Therefore, on 23 June 1721, during a visit to

---

[77] LSF, Ms. 193/1 (Diary 1716–22), p. 117 (9.6.1722).
[78] Ibid., p. 114 (18.5.1722); LSF, Ms. S.187 (Diary 1722–25), p. 293 (30.4.1725).
[79] LSF, Ms. 193/5, pp. 155–8: 'Concerning observation of Christmas (so-called) c.1717'.

Llanantfraed, Kelsall complained about the use of maypoles, suggesting that this simple pastime had a hidden sexual meaning that could corrupt innocent youths.

> W[he]n I came up to them, I ask'd them if they knew w[ha]t they were doing & whether yt work was to God's honour . . . some of them answered they did not well know why they did it, then I told them of the rise of it as may be found in History that Maia a strumpet in Rome . . . [who] placed a pole at her door to entice her lovers to her house &c., and I wish'd them to consider whether they were not making & fitting up yt wch would draw young people to be vain & idle together, they seem'd to be surpriz'd at my words and some of them were very civil.

It was, he stated, 'a great pity so few testimonies are borne in publick agst sin & iniquity wch so openly reign amongst us'.[80] Kelsall nevertheless observed in the following year that his words had had some effect as another maypole had been removed and the ground dug up 'so it appear'd to me like a thing blasted'.[81] Records of Friends in Wales, however, show how susceptible Quakers were to sexual impropriety. There are various references to 'lewd practices', 'scandalous behaviour', and the disownments which accompanied such behaviour and, of course, this was often attributable to excessive drinking.[82]

Those members who were expelled from the Society found themselves isolated and traumatised. Separated from their religious affiliations, which had provided them with security and a sense of belonging, they were now exposed to a community whose social mores they did not understand. One disowned Friend wrote that this was unbearable: 'to be abandoned by ones Friends and put in a state of separation from them . . . is so shocking to a human mind as not to be express'd in any words . . . Life at that time seemed of no further use nor value.'[83] For many their only hope was to be readmitted after they had publicly acknowledged their faults and satisfied the local meeting of their contrition. In 1703 Kelsall stated that he could

---

[80] LSF, Ms. 193/1, pp. 37–40 (23.4.1721); LSF, Ms. 194/1, pp. 208–9. In Greek mythology, Maia was one of the Pleiades who bore Zeus a son, Hermes. Later, in Roman mythology, Maia Maiesta (Fauna) was the goddess of fertility, and also identified as Bona Dea. Although also critical of the Welsh and their superstitious practices neither Kelsall nor his family were immune from these beliefs. See Jones, 'John Kelsall', pp. 160–2.

[81] LSF, MS. 193/1, p. 102 (4.4.1722).

[82] Allen, *Quaker Communities*, pp. 147–51.

[83] Tyne and Wear Archives, Ms. 3744/4, and cited in Allen, 'Establishing an Alternative Community', p. 118.

not find 'peace or satisfaction or fellowship with any' except Friends and this was certainly the case with many members who shunned a closer association with the wider community. Later in 1714, after being in the company of non-Quakers, Kelsall felt that he needed to cleanse his body:

> I had need of washing when I came from amongst them, though lawful occasion sometimes led me there, my very heart would [be] as it were sick with the smell and fume of vanity, irreligion and prophaneness that abounded among them, and the same would pretend to religion and talk thereof but they were ever like heathens never retaining any right notion or ideas of true religion.[84]

Yet what was the relationship of Friends, particularly Kelsall, to the Welsh civil and ecclesiastical authorities? Undoubtedly Kelsall's close relationship with the Lloyd family of Dolobran,[85] his command of the Welsh language,[86] and his undoubted intellectual ability led him to forge good relationships with the 'world's people', notably members of the north Wales clergy and gentry at Corsygedol, Hengwrt, Nannau and Pentrebychan.[87] He referred to them as 'particular acquaintances',[88] and he was often made welcome at their homes where they debated various topics.[89] In 1723, Kelsall recorded that he had 'pretty much discourse' with Parson Jones of Llwynynn and found Parson Humphreys of Ystyncolwyn 'very civil and loving'.[90] Three years later, Kelsall was invited by John Mellor, Master of the Chancery (1665–1733), to visit his home at Erddig, near Wrexham, where he received 'very kind & civil entertainment' and thought his host's views on religion 'very fair, civil & candid'.[91] On at least one occasion while visiting Pentrebychan,[92] Kelsall found that members of the party, believing that another guest's views were unacceptable, supported his forthright condemnation of eighteenth-century social mores. He wrote later in his diary that Humphrey Parry, a local

---

[84] Davies, *Quakers in English Society*, pp. 35, 37, and citing LSF, S.194/1, pp. 72, 161–2.
[85] For an example, see Ms. 194/2, pp. 152–4 (letter to Charles Lloyd Jnr, 29.4.1723) wherein Kelsall acknowledge their long-standing friendship.
[86] In 1713 he wrote that he had 'gain'd a tolerable understanding in that language'. See LSF, Ms. 194/1, pp. 143–4.
[87] See Jones, 'John Kelsall', 29, 53–4, 67–8.
[88] LSF, Ms. S.190, p. 346 (9.8.1732).
[89] LSF, Ms. S.187, p. 141 (15.9.1724); Jones, 'John Kelsall', pp. 29–30.
[90] LSF, Ms. S.187, pp. 17 (24.2.1723), 51 (26.8.1723).
[91] LSF, Ms. S.188, pp. 125–6 (18.5.1726); Jones, 'John Kelsall', p. 53.
[92] The home of Thomas Meredith.

dignitary, was 'very uncharitable & censorious', while the others were 'very civil and courteous to me'. Nevertheless, he felt that they were 'light' and 'airy'.[93] It is possible, as Harri Gwynn Jones pointed out, that Kelsall and his views were tolerated simply because his host and the other guests found his seriousness an amusing distraction which they may have played up to.[94]

Kelsall's diary suggests that, apart from his encounter with Humphrey Parry, he was respected by members of north Wales society. This is fascinating given his criticism of ecclesiastical rites and 'the fruitless works & ministry' of the clergy in the latter pages of his journal. He complained of the 'false divining' and the 'deplorable influence' they had upon 'the unsteady and ignorant multitude . . . their own poor misled flock'. He condemned the pomp and ceremony of the Bishops: 'how vastly unlike they appeared to ye poor, innocent, lowly lambs, followers, Disciples & Apostles . . . there was methought no manner of comparison between them, they having not so much as the very show of Godliness nor form of true religion'.[95] As this incident shows, Kelsall was a complex and, at times, contradictory character. He certainly attacked vanity but also succumbed to it. Yet, despite his private and public attacks against the Established Church,[96] he was still treated civilly by most clergymen in north Wales.[97]

In June 1716 John Williams, the curate of Dolgyn, appealed to Friends for Easter tithes. Kelsall explained the Society's position and the curate made no further requests. Indeed, two months later Kelsall was invited to Dolgyn and entertained by Williams there along with the rector of the parish, George Lewis, and Robert Vaughan and his son. On another occasion the dinner party at Dolgyn included Esquire Nanney of Maes y

---

[93] LSF, Ms. S.188, p. 181 (2.11.1726).

[94] Jones, 'John Kelsall', p. 53.

[95] LSF, Ms. 194/1, pp. 157–62, and cited in Jones, 'John Kelsall', pp. 86–7.

[96] LSF, Ms. 194/2, pp. 68–70 (letter to Richard Derwas, vicar of Meifod, 1706 opposing the 1696 publication of the anti-Quaker pamphlet 'The Snake in the Grass'); Jones, 'John Kelsall', p. 87. See also the letter from his cousin in 1710 which noted the hostility towards Nonconformists in the wake of Dr Henry Sacheverell's attack on the Revolution Settlement and his consequent impeachment by the Whig ministry, as well as the ignorance of the Welsh people concerning religious matters. See LSF, 194/3, pp. 96–7 (letter from John Merrick, Cuddington, Cheshire, 1.3.1710).

[97] He nevertheless recorded in November 1722 that on one occasion at Newtown one clergyman had 'some sharp words ab[ou]t Frds' and was 'very hot and peevish'. See LSF, Ms. 193/1, p. 136 (14.9.1722).

Pandy, members of the Vaughan family and the curate.[98] In April 1722 he recorded an evening spent with 'my much respected friend' George Lewis. On this occasion, Lewis had invited Kelsall to discuss a tax imposed on the townspeople to pay for the building of a new parish church. Kelsall noted that Lewis spoke with 'tears in his eyes yt some way might be found yt our frds might not be persecuted on yt account'.[99] Later, he wrote quite firmly to Lewis that Dolgellau Quakers were unable to comply with this demand as it went against the ethos of their Society [100] and that this was an unjust demand. As he observed in the letter

> I must then say that our friends cannot directly or indirectly pay or contribute towards the maintenance or upholding any method of worship and service they have not unity withal otherwise they wou'd manifest themselves to be meer hypocrites – and I am well assured yt thou and many more art sensible . . . yt this is not the result of obstinacy or covetousness, by reason wou'd they conform therein, it wou'd be both more easie and less chargeable unto them, – I am not ignorant of thy concern to avoid the odious name of a persecutor for religion . . . and therefore I wou'd in love desire thee to acquit thyself of this matter and wtever the parish vestry or B[isho]ps court may order, have thou nothing to do therewith, but rather declare thy dislike thereunto . . . I have great love in my heart towards thee, believing there is that principle of truth & sincerity in thee . . . and sorry I should be thy name should ever be recorded in the black list of persecutors for religion.[101]

As good as his word, Kelsall stood firm against this church tax, and in July 1729 was distrained of a large quantity of hops for church repairs and an additional charge of 2s. 3d. which he considered 'very reasonable'.[102]

Kelsall cultivated the good friendship of the Vicar of Meifod who in December 1726 asked him whether a sermon he had written was worth publishing.[103] For Kelsall this was an acknowledgement of his reputation as a scholar, and more significantly his fair-mindedness. It also meant that Friends, post-1689, had achieved a position of respectability in Welsh

---

[98] LSF, Ms. 193/1, pp. 1, 2 (20.4.1716, 23.6.1716, 8.10.1716).

[99] Ibid., p. 119 (14.6.1722). For details of the rebuilding of the Dolgellau parish church (the 'Steeple House') at this time, see *Byegones* (1899–1900), 79.

[100] From their earliest years Friends refused to support the maintenance of a paid ministry. For details see Allen, *Quaker Communities*, pp. 26, 96–8, 119–20; Barry Reay, 'Quaker Opposition to Tithes 1652–1660', *Past and Present*, 86 (1980), 98–120.

[101] LSF, Ms.194/2, pp. 145–7 (letter dated 14.7.1722).

[102] LSF, Ms. S.189, p. 145 (30.5.1729).

[103] LSF, Ms. S.188, p. 178 (28.10.1726).

communities, even if not completely tolerated for their unorthodox views. In 1729 he wrote that he was grateful to God that he had 'so preserved me in my behaviour &c. amongst men that I was now very kindly received again into the country',[104] while in April 1731 Kelsall reflected upon the respectability of eighteenth-century Friends: 'the Government and better sort of people are very kind and civil to Friends, and they have respect & interest with them, yea the very priests in diverse places are, seemingly at least, loving to Friends'.[105] At the local level, particularly in the 1730s when Kelsall was reduced to seeking financial help from the Welsh Yearly Meeting, the gentry continued to treat him with respect. In 1731 his request for a meeting place for Friends to gather at Dolgellau was granted by Robert Vaughan who offered the town hall, and in 1733 a similar arrangement was made to hold a meeting in Beaumaris, Anglesey. In this case Baron Richard Bulkeley agreed to provide premises for the purpose of holding meetings.[106]

The life of John Kelsall and his relationship with the Friends of north Wales and the wider community illustrates the extent to which the Welsh Quakers distanced themelves from the vast majority of Welsh society in the late-seventeenth and early-eighteenth centuries. As shown, they were scornful of contemporary fashions and advocated an alternative culture to the growth of the consumer-led society of the eighteenth century. The rise of consumerism in Britain, along with a rapidly changing political and industrialising landscape, however, pushed Friends towards introspection and clannish behaviour. Kelsall wrote to John Merrick Jnr that Friends were being 'crucified between two thieves: liberty and carnal security',[107] and in response the Society rigidly enforced its strict code of conduct. As Harri Gwynn Jones argued, 'in spite of the somewhat militant expression which some of its members, by their prophecies of judgment, gave to it, Quakerism, as it went on, was becoming less of a militant creed and more of a narrow society'.[108] He also suggested that Friends acquiesced in what had become a traditional and formalised mode of behaviour – 'the dangers of respectability', whereby they established 'ecclesiastical authority' and gradually accepted Robert Barclay's *Apology* as their own 'articles of

[104] LSF, Ms. S.189, p. 149 (13.6.1729).
[105] LSF, Ms. 194/1, p. 238 (*c*.20.2.1731).
[106] LSF, Ms. S.190, pp. 244, 393–4 (6.3.1731, 13.6.1733).
[107] LSF, Ms. 194/2, pp. 97–102 (p. 99: letter dated 27.7.1712).
[108] Jones, 'John Kelsall', p. 81.

faith'.[109] It is thereby argued that Friends had little in common with eighteenth-century community life, and were isolated: 'spiritually as a deliberate Nonconformist body; culturally, as a non-Welsh body; socially, as people who condemned the popular pleasures; economically, as being above the general economic level'.[110] Moreover, by providing moral oversight Quaker communities acted as 'large and censorious families . . . [safeguarding] . . . otherwise rootless and unsupervised individuals . . . from some of the typical features of early modern urban life: alcoholism, bankruptcy, prostitution and crime'.[111] This is now disputed as Adrian Davies has claimed that Friends were not segregated from the wider world, and clearly in his work as a clerk Kelsall had to effectively interact with his neighbours and work colleagues. Moreover, Friends readily welcomed the 'world's people' to their public meetings, particularly if there was a Welsh-speaking minister or eminent Friend from Pennsylvania.[112] In his need for cultured conversation Kelsall also spent considerable time in the company of the affluent and the well-known in Wales and elsewhere. Did this mean that he acted differently from many members of the Society?

Kelsall feared that 'a spirit of ease has got in amongst many professors of Truth spreading like an hidden leprosie' and had begun to undermine the steadfastness of the Society.[113] The desire for respectability and the organizational shift from a sect to a denomination certainly afforded Friends greater acceptance in their local communities but conversely this weakened their missionary spirit.[114] In Kelsall's case there was a determination to uphold the principles on which the Society was based. This is illustrated in his journal entry for 1714 when he wrote that his employment at the Dolgyn ironworks would not compromise the values of

---

[109] Ibid., pp. 92, 96. See also Robert Barclay, *An Apology for the True Christian Divinity, as the same is held forth . . . by the people, called . . . Quakers . . .* (London, 1678).

[110] Jones, 'John Kelsall', pp. 106–7. See also his comments on the failure of Friends to use the Welsh language in meetings. See Ibid., pp. 131–2.

[111] M. Mullett, *Radical Religious Movements in Early Modern Europe* (London, 1980), p. 67.

[112] LSF, Ms. S.190, pp. 234, 244, 416–17 (21.1.1731: 'there was a large meeting'; 6.3.1731: 'there was many people the hall being near full which were civil . . . and many spoke well of what they heard'; 16.10.1733: 'at our meeting Rowland Roberts from Pensylvania (born near Bala), Jno. Goodwin & Ed. Jones from Radnorshire . . . Some of my family was there being pretty many people'). See also Jones, 'John Kelsall', pp. 116–20, 125.

[113] LSF, Ms. 194/2, p. 16; Jenkins, *Literature, Religion and Society*, p. 179.

[114] This argument is discussed more fully in Allen, *Quaker Communities*, ch. 7.

his religious community.[115] In this example he was following the well-worn path of many other Friends who were able to reconcile their role in the world of work with their religious beliefs.[116] Although he was never able to rely on regular employment throughout his life he placed his trust in Divine providence – a sentiment many of his more affluent co-religionists would have endorsed. For many Friends, however, the austere mode of behaviour was becoming outdated. As entrepreneurs during a period of great technological change, members of the Society increasingly found themselves unable to resist the consumerism of the age. As Kelsall forewarned, they would thereafter be unable to retreat into their earlier introspection and would have to cooperate with the world's people. Despite his own reservations this, in part, was the same concession that Kelsall had made in his response to Welsh society.

---

[115] LSF, 194/1, pp. 151–4.

[116] For details of Quakers in business see J. Walvin, *The Quakers: money and morals* (London, 1997); A. Prior and M. W. Kirby, 'The Society of Friends and Business Culture, 1700–1830', in D. J. Jeremy (ed.), *Religion, Business and Wealth in Modern Britain* (London, 1998).

CHAPTER FIVE

EXPLORING THE EVANGELICAL REVIVAL: THE YORKSHIRE EXAMPLE

EDWARD ROYLE

Historians, however tempted, should not resort to providential explanations in history. They are concerned only with second order explanations and so the response to the question, 'Why did the evangelical revival happen?' must be more, or less, than 'God only knows.'[1] W. R. Ward has also reminded us that explanations should not be parochial, although it should be stated that this chapter will operate on a microcosmic level. The revival of the second and third quarters of the eighteenth century swept Europe and beyond, from Moravia to Massachusetts, and any local explanations have to be fitted into this wider context.[2] Following Ward it must be recognised that the international revival had its roots in the shifting refugee populations of central Europe, as Hapsburg persecution of Protestants forced populations to seek refuge in the less hostile territories of the Electors of Saxony and Brandenburg Prussia. In 1722 members of the reconstituted Church of the United Brethren, the Moravians, founded their refugee camp and religious community of Herrnhut in Saxony on the Berthelsdorf estate of the Pietist, Count Ludwig von Zinzendorf. Thence the diaspora of Moravians spread religious revival across Protestant Europe and beyond, to the rest of Germany, Denmark, Britain, and the British north American colonies. Soon they were operating, quite literally,

---

[1] H. Butterfield, *Christianity and History* (London, 1949), pp. 19–20. The temptation is recognised and rejected by H. D. Rack, *Reasonable Enthusiast. John Wesley and the rise of Methodism* (London, 1989), p. 171.

[2] W. R. Ward, *The Protestant Evangelical Awakening* (Cambridge, 1992); D. Hempton, *Methodism. Empire of the spirit* (Newhaven and London, 2005).

from Greenland's icy mountain to India's coral strand.[3]

These missionary endeavours were successful partly because they were ploughing soil already fertilised by Pietism. Anxiety about the increasing formalism of religion was a concern of members of Protestant churches across Europe. In the Lutheran Church, Philip Jakob Spener and Augustus Hermann Franke had fostered Pietism in the new university of Halle, founded in 1694 shortly after Magdeburg had become Prussian. But the movement and its equivalents were far more widespread than this. In Scotland, the so-called Praying Societies continued a tradition of spiritual seeking and emphasis on the Holy Spirit from the earlier seventeenth century, a reminder that the 'world turned upside down' was not entirely set right again during the misnamed Age of Reason. Walter Ker, who was brought to his religious state of mind by survivors of the Shotts revival of 1630, emigrated to the colonies and was active in the Great Awakening in New England in 1734. The latter has been explained, partly at least, as the product of a crisis within the Calvinist elect arising from their anxiety that the next generation was exhibiting a moral and spiritual laxity that called into doubt their status as a people born of the grace of God and sustained by that grace within the elect. The following year, 1735, John and Charles Wesley, together with a fellow Oxford Methodist, Benjamin Ingham, set out for the new colony of Georgia on the same ship as a group of Moravians, and when the Wesleys returned to London in 1738 they again encountered the Moravian missionaries and their influence. The principal transatlantic revivalist, though, was another of the Oxford Methodists, George Whitefield. He was caught up in the Massachusetts Great Awakening in the late 1730s and was also present in 1742 when the same widespread sense of spiritual hunger resulted in a great outpouring of revival at Cambuslang, just south of Glasgow.[4]

John Wesley's background was High Church, even Nonjuring. This

---

[3] Though Reginald Heber may not have been aware of this when he wrote his famous hymn in 1819.

[4] Ward, *Protestant Evangelical Awakening*, provides the best account; see also Rack, *Reasonable Enthusiast*, pp. 158–80 for a stimulating and wide-ranging overview, and, for Whitefield see M. R. Watts, *The Dissenters. From the Reformation to the French Revolution* (Oxford, 1978), pp. 397–401. The Scottish dimension is set out in A. L. Drummond and J. Bulloch, *The Scottish Church, 1688–1843* (Edinburgh, 1973), pp. 45–56, and T. C. Smout, 'Born again at Cambuslang: new evidence on popular religion and literacy in eighteenth-century Scotland', *Past and Present*, 97 (1982), 114–27.

section of the Church of England, drawing on a spiritual tradition that went back to Nicholas Ferrar of Little Gidding and George Herbert, aspired to reinvigorate the spiritual life of the Church beyond the formal moralism of the day. Wesley found particular inspiration in the writings of the Nonjuror, William Law, whose *Serious Call to a Devout and Holy Life* was published in 1729. In Oxford, as a fellow of Lincoln College in the early 1730s, Wesley had gathered with similarly-minded young men, including his younger brother, Charles, George Whitefield, Benjamin Ingham from Osset in Yorkshire, and Christopher Atkinson, later of Thorp Arch near Wetherby, to practise good works and spiritual exercises. This was according to the 'New Method' developed by reforming Calvinists or 'Arminians' in the Netherlands in the 1670s, whereby good works were encouraged not as a means of earning God's grace but of *proving* it. The group that Wesley joined or assisted in forming at Oxford, and which became known as Methodist, was one of several to develop within the Church of England along similar lines at this time, in London and elsewhere. The Moravian, Peter Boehler, formed one such society on 1 May 1738, at the home of James Hutton, a London bookseller, while Charles Wesley lay ill at his house and brother John was visiting. It was at a meeting of this society in Aldersgate Street on 24 May 1738 that John Wesley was famously 'converted'.[5]

All this is far, but not too far, from Yorkshire, for a number of the personalities mentioned had or acquired Yorkshire links. So why did Yorkshire provide a favourable location for the Evangelical Revival, and what can the history of revival in Yorkshire tells us about the origins and nature of the revival in England more generally? Clearly no simple explanation will suffice. The ground has been well surveyed by both John Walsh and Henry Rack.[6] As they have shown, in addition to international factors, including the Moravian impact on England and Whitefield's experience in America, a whole range of domestic factors should be considered. These include the institutional weakness of the Established Church away from the south-eastern quadrant of the country; a possible

---

[5] F. W. B. Bullock, *Voluntary Religious Societies, 1520–1799* (St Leonards on Sea, 1963), pp. 162–75; R. P. Heitzenrater, *Wesley and the People Called Methodists* (Nashville, 1995), pp. 1–95; C. Podmore, *The Moravian Church in England, 1728–1760* (Oxford, 1998), pp. 29–44.

[6] John Walsh, 'Origins of the Evangelical Revival', in G. V. Bennet and J. Walsh (eds), *Essays in Modern English Church History* (Oxford, 1966), pp. 132–62; Rack, *Reasonable Enthusiast*, pp. 171–80.

reaction against Latitudinarianism; existing traditions of spiritual vitality and 'serious' religion, both High Church and Puritan, within the Church of England; and reaction to the political and economic tensions of the 1730s. It is the conjunction of a multiplicity of different causes with accidents of personality and opportunity that produces the unique event in history, so perhaps what historians should be looking for are simultaneous and parallel reasons for religious change which reacted upon and reinforced one another, cumulatively and collectively providing an answer to the question of the origins of the revival: not so much a straight line of cause and effect, as a spider's web of reinforcing connections.

The purpose of a regional study is not to test a generalisation offered for a whole country or continent but, rather, to contribute an interpretation rooted in a specific and limited geographical context, which can then form a part of the mosaic that makes up the national picture. The regional picture of revival in England can then contribute to an understanding of the wider British revival and thence beyond to Europe and North America. In some respects such a regional study will suggest features that will find their correspondences in other places – it would be surprising if they did not – but the uniqueness of each local experience will also be a part of the story. In a more extended study than can be offered here, a comparison and contrast should ideally then be made with other regions, within Britain and abroad, to underline similarities and isolate differences, the purpose being not to test or formulate a general explanatory hypothesis but to refine in more detail the overall picture.

The case for taking Yorkshire as a regional study is that, alongside Cornwall and Wales, it proved to be one of the strongest centres of the revival and, though many of the factors promoting revival were not peculiar to Yorkshire, they do seem to have been present to an unusual degree.[7] These include prominent upper-class support, such as was given by Lord Dartmouth of Woodsome Hall in Almondbury parish, near Huddersfield, and the Hastings family of Ledston Hall in Ledsham parish, near Castleford. Then there were prominent evangelical clergymen who already lived and worked in the area, including Benjamin Grimshaw of Haworth who was born just over the Lancashire border in Blackburn, Benjamin Ingham from Osset near Wakefield and, indeed, John Wesley

---

[7] This has been graphically illustrated in a detailed study of the findings of the 1851 Census of Religious Worship: see K. D. M. Snell and P. S. Ell, *Rival Jerusalems. The geography of Victorian religion* (Cambridge, 2000), distribution maps on pp. 72, 168.

himself, who came from Epworth near Doncaster, part of Lincolnshire but on the Yorkshire side of the Trent. Yorkshire also offered several potentially important circumstances out of which revival might arise, including large parishes with many communities remote from a church, and rapid economic change. It would be a mistake, though, to think of Yorkshire as a single entity. By far the largest county in England, it contained many varieties of local experience. A study of these can further illuminate the richness of the revival. Indeed, it is possible to suggest that the revival that began in the eighteenth century and spilled over into the first half of the nineteenth should be understood, even in a regional context, not so much as a single event as a convergence of several different factors with accidents of personality, leading to revival.

One final introductory point concerns the nature of what is being examined. The revival being studied here, as both John Kent and Henry Rack have pointed out,[8] was not a short-term, organised outburst such as was perfected in nineteenth-century America and still forms the image of religious 'revival' today. Though such events were present within the Evangelical revival, this study will focus upon the broader movement of transformation within the churches. It is an institutional story, though individuals and their experiences, of course, made the institutions what they were. In calling for personal holiness among their followers, the revivalists were seeking to breathe a new spirit, the Holy Spirit, into the Church (and churches) and into national life. Though the emphasis on personal commitment in the nineteenth century was to lead in some quarters to an excessive emphasis on the individual, the revival that began in the eighteenth century was primarily social. The Methodist *societies* formed by the followers of John Wesley were simply the most obvious expression of this essential feature of that religious movement which transformed the institutional expression of religion in England between the mid-eighteenth and mid-nineteenth centuries.

---

[8] John Kent, *Holding the Fort. Studies in Victorian Revivalism* (London, 1978), pp. 9–37; Rack, *Reasonable Enthusiast*, pp. 158–61. Kent has more recently challenged the whole notion of revival, preferring the idea that people were seeking new outlets for that primary religious instinct which is ever-present: John Kent, *Wesley and the Wesleyans. Religion in eighteenth-century Britain* (Cambridge, 2002).

The Church of England

Any study of religion in England must begin with the Church of England. John Walsh set out an important proposition in his doctoral thesis of 1956 on 'The Yorkshire Evangelicals in the Eighteenth Century'. Despite his sub-title, 'with especial reference to Methodism', his argument was that Evangelicalism (signified with a capital E) should be considered distinct from Methodism, not only in the mid-eighteenth century, but also later, laying the foundations for the separate development in the nineteenth century of Evangelicalism as a party within the Church of England. The revival, in other words, should not be equated with Methodism and expropriated by the followers of Wesley. This interpretation is now widely accepted, even by the leading biographer of Wesley.[9]

Yorkshire became one of the strongest centres of Evangelicalism within the eighteenth-century Church of England. According to Walsh, by 1800 'it was the only county in which the Evangelical clergy had in influence, if not in numbers, a dominating position'.[10] The Elland Clerical Society, originally founded by Henry Venn in Huddersfield in 1767, was one of the most successful of such societies formed in the second half of the eighteenth century. Its membership comprised a small elite of Evangelical clergy meeting 'for religious and pastoral discussion'.[11] In 1777 they set up a fund for the education of like-minded young men at Cambridge or Oxford with a view to supplying the next generation of Evangelical ordinands. Other clerical societies elsewhere in the country followed this lead. A second clerical society was set up in Yorkshire to serve the east and south, based on James Stillingfleet's rectory at Hotham, south of Market Weighton in the East Riding.[12]

Though such societies cannot be considered a cause of the revival, their presence helps explain how the Yorkshire Evangelicals sustained revival within the Church and converted tentative beginnings into a mutually-reinforcing fellowship of like-minded clergymen. Strong

---

[9] J. D. Walsh, 'The Yorkshire Evangelicals in the Eighteenth Century, with especial reference to Methodism', unpublished University of Cambridge, Ph.D. thesis, 1956; Rack, *Reasonable Enthusiast*, p. 161.

[10] Walsh, 'Yorkshire Evangelicals', 86–7.

[11] Quoted by Walsh. See Ibid., 252.

[12] Bullock, *Voluntary Religious Societies,* pp. 238–42; Walsh, 'Yorkshire Evangelicals', 233–73. Some of the records of the Elland Clerical Society are held at the West Yorkshire Archive Service, Wakefield, C/84/1.

personalities were undoubtedly important, but what brought these people to Yorkshire in the first place? Some already had links with the region but others were drawn from outside. An important part was played here by lay patronage. The second Earl of Dartmouth, who succeeded to the earldom in 1750 and died in 1801, was a man of strong Evangelical views. He was a near neighbour of Sir John Ramsden who was the patron of Huddersfield where the Dartmouth estates included the manor of Slaithwaite. The appointment of Venn as vicar of Huddersfield (1759–1770) can be attributed to his influence, as can the choice of Stillingfleet for Hotham, a living in the gift of the Crown. Lady Betty Hastings of Ledston Hall, sister-in-law of the Countess of Huntingdon, purchased the advowson of Thorp Arch before her death in 1739. Her heir appointed Christopher Atkinson vicar there in 1749; and the Countess of Huntingdon secured Ledsham for Walter Sellon in 1770. Atkinson's son, Miles, was curate at Leeds parish church and vicar of Kippax; then, from 1793, perpetual curate of his own proprietary chapel of St Paul's, Leeds. Kippax, which adjoins Ledsham parish, was another Crown living and had a succession of evangelical curates and vicars. The school at Thorp Arch was one of several in Yorkshire endowed by Lady Betty Hastings. A pupil there with Miles Atkinson was Joseph Milner, later influential headmaster of Hull Grammar School, whom William Wilberforce was to present to a lectureship at Holy Trinity, Hull in 1768 and a curacy at North Ferriby where he became vicar in 1786. Wilberforce's brother-in-law, Thomas Clarke, was appointed vicar of Hull under the patronage of the Corporation in 1783. Wilberforce also brought John Overton to St Crux in York in 1802. Meanwhile, John Thornton of Clapham bought up the advowson of St Mary's, Hull, in the Evangelical interest.[13]

The opportunity to appoint to curacies in Yorkshire owed a great deal to the structure of the parishes, many of which served large geographical areas divided into several chapelries. The parish clergyman would expect to influence who the curate might be even when he did not have the right of appointment himself. These chapelries, often covering several upland townships, presented both a spiritual and physical challenge as well as being poorly paid, but they also created opportunities for young men who

---

[13] Details of clergy, patronage and appointments are taken from Walsh, 'Yorkshire Evangelicals', 233–317; C. Annesley and P. Hoskin (eds), *Archbishop Drummond's Visitation Returns, 1764* (3 vols. York, 1997–2001); and G. Lawton, *Collections Relative to Churches and Chapels within the Diocese of York* (2nd edn. London, 1842).

took their religion seriously and felt a vocation to spread the word. One who carved out for himself an evangelical pastorate in a remote chapelry was William Grimshaw, curate of Haworth in the parish of Bradford between 1742 and his death in 1763. There were similar opportunities to the south of Bradford in the parishes of Halifax and Huddersfield. Venn appointed George Burnett as his curate at Huddersfield in 1759 and then moved him to his chapelry of Slaithwaite, where Dartmouth was Lord of the Manor. Burnett's next move was to the nearby Elland chapelry in Halifax parish on the nomination of Dr George Leigh, vicar of Halifax 'who, though no Evangelical, turned a genial eye on the Gospel cause'. Dartmouth continued to support a succession of curates at Slaithwaite.[14]

In this way the Evangelicals spread their connections and, having established themselves with the help of sympathetic patrons, were able, through these patrons and their own control over subordinate curacies, to bring in other clergy of like minds to themselves to create what is now referred to as 'a critical mass'. As in the contemporary political system, where representation in many parliamentary constituencies was a matter of the patrons' preference, the Church of England for good and ill was also shaped by the power to nominate. The concern of the patrons of Evangelicalism was revival not reform, as they exploited the old system, including pluralism, for all it was worth. When the Earl of Dartmouth secured from the Crown the vicarage of Dewsbury for Matthew Powley in 1777, he nevertheless nominally kept him on at Slaithwaite where he had been perpetual curate since 1767, putting Thomas Wilson in as a resident substitute. This situation continued until 1785 and was justified by the fact that after Venn's departure from Huddersfield in 1770 the right of presentation to Slaithwaite was no longer in Evangelical hands so Dartmouth did not want to create a vacancy. Powley did not resign until 1785 when John Lowe, an Evangelical, became vicar of Huddersfield and

---

[14] See note 13; also C. A. Hulbert, *Annals of the Church in Slaithwaite . . . from 1693 to 1864* (London and Huddersfield, 1864), pp. 68–103. The description of Leigh is from Walsh, 'Yorkshire Evangelicals', 237. In the parish of Whalley, just over the border into Lancashire, patronage worked very differently. Here the provisions of the Bounty Act of 1714 were exploited by local Tories to take control of the patronage of perpetual curacies within the parish for political rather than religious ends; Evangelicalism made a late start in Whalley. See M. F. Snape, *The Church of England in Industrialising Society. The Lancashire Parish of Whalley in the eighteenth century* (Woodbridge, 2003), pp. 94–5, 150–62.

could be trusted to arrange a proper Evangelical succession.[15]

The early revivalists

Grimshaw had been converted following his ineptitude in handling an infant death experienced by two of his parishioners in Todmorden in 1734. Marriage and two children of his own were then followed by the death of his wife in 1739. Out of this personal torment emerged a man committed not to the easy moralism of set sermons, but a passionate wrestling with human nature and sin, and a commitment to gospel preaching from the heart. The role of such preaching should not be underestimated as an important contributory factor to the Evangelical revival. Not only did Grimshaw preach twice each Sunday, but also began monthly visitations to twelve places in his and other parishes where he preached to gatherings of families in remote places. By 1750 there were 51 places on his round and he was preaching twenty or thirty times a week in all weathers.[16] In this work he was probably influenced by 'Scotch Will' (William Darney) a travelling pedlar active in Lancashire and West Yorkshire in 1743 where he set up a number of little religious societies for prayer and fellowship. Here we can see the cross-fertilisation of influences from the Scottish praying societies and outbursts of revival north of the border.[17]

In his analysis of Wesley's itinerant preachers, John Lenton has shown how the West Riding produced more of these preachers than any other county – seventy (15.6 per cent) compared with thirty-two in the next highest county, Cornwall. To some extent this was through the contagion of numbers producing a density of activity which fed on itself. In upper Airedale, Calderdale and Ribblesdale, Darney and Grimshaw affected, almost infected, others with their energy and enthusiasm, and not simply within the Church of England. Baptist congregations expanded from the chapel at Rossendale into Yorkshire where Grimshaw's converts supplied several leaders in the Hebden Bridge area of the upper Calder Valley.[18]

---

[15] Walsh, 'Yorkshire Evangelicals', 245–7.
[16] J. W. Laycock, *Methodist Heroes in the Great Haworth Round, 1734–1784* (Keighley, 1909); F. Baker, *William Grimshaw, 1708–1763* (London, 1963). For a brief summary, see A. Longworth, *William Grimshaw* (Peterborough, 1996).
[17] Rack, *Reasonable Enthusiast*, pp. 218–19.
[18] J. H. Lenton, *My Sons in the Gospel. An analysis of Wesley's itinerant preachers*. Wesley Historical Society Lecture, 2000 (Oxford, 2000), p. 14; W. E.

Further south, in the lower Calder Valley, Benjamin Ingham was active. After his time in Georgia with John Wesley, he returned to Ossett where he held nightly religious meetings in his mother's house and began keeping a school to teach poor children to read and write. Preaching one Sunday at a church near Ledsham, he found his congregation included the four younger Hastings ladies – Anne, Frances, Catherine and Margaret – who lived with their older half-sister, Lady Betty, at nearby Ledston Hall. They invited him to Ledsham church where they were deeply affected by his preaching, especially the youngest, Margaret. She in turn influenced her sister-in law, Selina, Countess of Huntingdon, who was undergoing her own religious crisis and conversion to Evangelical views in 1739. The Countess became a powerful supporter of the revival, especially after the death of her husband in 1746. She soon parted company with Ingham, though, and her work was to be mainly in conjunction with another of the original Oxford Methodists, George Whitefield, whose university studies had partly been funded by Lady Betty Hastings. Ingham remained closest to Lady Margaret, whom he married in 1741 when she was already in her early forties and he only twenty-nine.[19]

The Moravians were a major influence on Ingham. Like Wesley, he had first met them on the ship to Georgia and then subsequently in London. By June 1739 he had formed some forty religious societies when he was prohibited by the archbishop from preaching in any church in the diocese of York and so took to the fields and barns. He sought help from the Moravians and in November was visited by John Toeltschig whom he had met in Georgia and with whom he had visited Herrnhut in 1738. Toeltschig returned the following year and in 1742 the Moravians formally agreed to begin a mission in Yorkshire and to take on the oversight of Ingham's societies. Beginning with two farms near Halifax, they soon spread out and by 1743 they had turned six preaching and thirteen other regular meeting places into eleven preaching and forty-seven other regular meeting places. In January 1744 Ingham used Lady

---

Blomfield, 'The Baptist Churches of Yorkshire in the 17th and 18th centuries', in C. E. Shipley (ed.), *The Baptists of Yorkshire* (Bradford and London, 1912), pp. 98–111.

[19] B. S. Schlenther, *Queen of the Methodists. The Countess of Huntingdon and the eighteenth-century crisis of faith and society* (Durham, 1997), pp. 14–37; L. Tyerman, *The Oxford Methodists* (London, 1873), pp. 57–154; H. M. Pickles, *Benjamin Ingham. Preacher amongst the Dales, Forests and Fells* (Coventry, 1995), pp. 11–32.

Margaret's money to buy the Moravians an estate near Pudsey to be known as Fulneck.[20]

Ingham and the Moravians were not the only preachers active in this part of Yorkshire at that time. One of the most energetic was John Nelson, a stonemason from Birstall, about seven miles north-west of Ossett. Nelson was converted by hearing John Wesley preach in Moorfields while working in London and he returned to Yorkshire to preach the message. Like Grimshaw, Darnley, and Ingham at the same time, he began to form little religious societies out of those whom he had brought to a new height of spiritual awareness through his preaching. So laymen and clergymen together brought about the great spiritual awakening in Yorkshire. For example, William Shent, a Leeds barber and peruke maker, was taken by his wife, Mary, to hear Nelson preach in Birstall and in late 1742 they invited Nelson to preach at Shent's shop in Briggate, Leeds, thus bringing Methodism to Leeds. Sammy Hick, an apprenticed blacksmith, heard John Nelson preaching in the open air at Aberford, near Ledsham, and thereafter became a powerful lay influence in the area, centred on his blacksmith's shop in Micklefield. Pressed for the militia in 1744, Nelson travelled with his regiment to York where he lost no time in bearing witness to the gospel in the most difficult of circumstances, attending church but also preaching by popular demand in the fields around York. Soon afterwards his regiment was posted to Sunderland but, on being released from the militia when the Countess of Huntingdon purchased a substitute, in the Autumn of 1744 he returned to York. It was probably through this visit that a small group of Methodists began meeting at a house in Acomb, a village just outside the city and the first recorded place of Methodist meeting in the area.[21]

So far this study has played down the term 'Methodism'. This has been deliberate, for it was applied by contemporaries quite indiscriminately to all manner of unofficial preaching which stressed the immediacy of the

---

[20] G. Stead, *The Moravian Settlement at Fulneck, 1742–1790* (Leeds, 1999), pp. 6–10, 22–4; Podmore, *Moravian Church*, p. 50.

[21] 'An Extract of John Nelson's Journal' (1767), in T. Jackson (ed.), *The Lives of Early Methodist Preachers* (4th edn. London, 1871), reprinted in 4 volumes (Stoke-on-Trent, 1998), I, pp. 31–137; J. C. Hartley, *John Nelson and the Evangelical Revival in West Yorkshire* (London, 1988); D. C. Dews, *Ranters, Revivalists, Radicals, Reformers and Revolutionaries. A celebration of Methodist local preaching in West Yorkshire* (Leeds, 1996), pp. 3–7, 59–65; J. Lyth, *Glimpses of Early Methodism in York* (York and London, 1885), pp. 39–45, 48, 282.

Holy Spirit, with its implied challenge to clerical order and threat to
emotional stability and rationality. In fact those people called 'Methodists'
had many differences as well as much in common. Wesley differed from
Whitefield over the nature of the elect, Wesley taking an Arminian
position and Whitefield a Calvinistic one. Wesley disagreed with Ingham
over the latter's closeness to the Moravians for he disapproved of their
quietism. Ingham then broke with the Moravians over their desire to
evangelise members of the Church of England, while he and his wife were
at odds with Selina, Countess of Huntingdon over the Hastings' family
inheritance. The revival in Yorkshire has deliberately been presented as
something independent of Wesley, although associated with men who
were close to him. Wesley in fact began to visit the area only in 1742,
after the revival had started, and his first base was Nelson's societies
which the latter handed over to his control in that year. John Wesley's
contribution was that of organiser, putting these scattered flowerings of
revival into an enduring organisation, but the prominence he later
achieved should conceal neither the varieties of early Methodism nor the
fact that he was only one influence among several, and by no means the
first, in the Yorkshire revival of the 1740s.[22]

The appeal of the revivalist preachers

Those who were attracted to these preachers and their meetings probably
attended for many reasons, including curiosity and entertainment. Only a
minority stayed to join the societies but this fact alone is evidence of a
failure by the church to meet their spiritual wants. The excitement,
spontaneity and directness of this preaching have to be contrasted with the
formalism of conventional church services at this time. Accident, whether
providential or not, has its part to play in history, but accidents become
opportunities for men and women to exploit. So, while accident of
personality is an important half of the story, the other half concerns their
ability to shape those circumstances which then aided the spread of the
movement.

Walsh suggested two reasons for the appeal of the preachers. The first
is that, outside of the towns, the people were savage and simple,
susceptible to revivalist preaching. The second, perhaps related to this, is
that, as the leaders of old dissent leant towards rationalism and
Socinianism, their followers became open to the preaching of the old

[22] Walsh, 'Origins of the Evangelical Revival', pp. 134–8.

puritan gospel from other quarters.[23] There may be something in both of these suggestions. Certainly, the success of the Baptists can be traced back to 1680 with the conversion of William Mitchell of Heptonstall in the upper Calder Valley, across the moor from Haworth. Travelling with his cousin, David Crossley, he was preaching in Yorkshire and Lancashire just as the Toleration Act of 1689 was making possible the establishment of dissenting conventicles. A church, though not yet Baptist, was founded in Rossendale by 1696 and other churches, definitely Baptist, quickly followed including Rodhill End and Stoneslack (1717). From these early beginnings came two important daughter churches: Salendine Nook (1743), the first of many Baptist churches in the parish of Huddersfield; and Rawdon (1715) from which came churches in Bradford (1753), Halifax (1755) and Leeds (1779), among others. Soon the moorlands in the parishes of Huddersfield, Halifax and Bradford were covered with Baptist chapels.[24] In the lowlands to the east, following the establishment by James Scott at Heckmondwike in 1756 of an Academy devoted to Trinitarian theology and evangelical doctrine, there was a similar revival among the more urban Independents.[25] The same rejection of rational theology and an openness to the new preaching with its emphasis on saving grace was also apparent within the Church of England, not only with Grimshaw, Ingham and Wesley, but also with Henry Venn and those fellow incumbents who gathered in his vicarage for fellowship in what became the Elland Society.[26]

Walsh's invocation of the savage simplicity of the people echoes Wesley's now-famous journal entry as he approached Huddersfield for the first time as late as 1757: 'A wilder people I never saw in England. The men, women, and children filled the street as we rode along, and appeared just ready to devour us.'[27] In this context it is relevant to note the social and economic structure of upland Pennine parishes in the West Riding, where communities of independent weaver farmers lived close to the wildness and majesty of nature, where the smallness and powerlessness of

---

[23] Walsh, 'Yorkshire Evangelicals', 87–8; see also his 'Origins of the Evangelical Revival', pp. 158–60.

[24] Shipley, *Baptists of Yorkshire*, pp. 73–98.

[25] J. G. Miall, *Congregationalism in Yorkshire* (London, 1868), pp. 146–52; R. T. Jones, *Congregationalism in England, 1662–1962* (London, 1962), pp. 152–4.

[26] Walsh, 'Origins of the Evangelical Revival', 136–8.

[27] *The Journal of the Rev. John Wesley* (4 vols. London, 1903), II, p. 386, entry for 9 May 1757.

mankind was obvious, and preachers in homely language spoke directly from the heart to answer the psychological needs of at least some of their hearers. The same explanation has been offered for the appeal of the revival to people who daily confronted their own mortality in pit or fishing village.[28] Again, this does not entirely explain the revival for, although the appeal of the evangelical preachers might also hold good for other parts of the country such as Cornwall, not all such places were equally strong centres of the revival. Furthermore, some of these explanations are absent from other parts of Yorkshire where the revival was equally strong, such as the city of York.

A further step is therefore needed to go beyond the people and their beliefs to look at some of the explanations that focus upon the relationship between the lie of the land and the structure of the Established Church. In 1935, Frank Tillyard pointed out how Methodism appeared to complement Dissent in that it put down its strongest roots in those parts where Baptists, Independents or Presbyterians were weakest, and Brian Greaves in 1961 stressed the size of parishes and the relative weakness of the Church of England on the ground. The implication of these views is that the revival, especially in its Methodist form, was strongest where there was room for it to develop left by the weakness of rival forms of religious organisation. In another context Alan Everitt has noted the importance of remote parish boundaries and large open parishes with no dominant landlord, for the development of rural Dissent.[29]

The environment of revival

These studies would appear to offer promising grounds for understanding why the revivalist preachers were to make such headway among the people of Yorkshire, or, at least, the people of the Pennine uplands of West Yorkshire. In the remainder of this study, these theses will be tested

---

[28] A. D. Gilbert, *Religion and Society in Industrial England. Church, chapel and social change, 1740–1914* (London, 1976), pp. 60, 66–7.

[29] F. Tillyard, 'The Distribution of the Free Churches in England', *Sociological Review*, 27, 1 (1935), 1–18; B. Greaves, 'An Analysis of the Spread of Methodism in Yorkshire during the Eighteenth and early Nineteenth Centuries (1740–1831), with special reference to the environment of this movement', unpublished University of Leeds, MA thesis, 1961; A. Everitt, *The Pattern of Rural Dissent: the nineteenth century* (Leicester, 1972), pp. 22–6. These issues are discussed further in Snell and Ell, *Rival Jerusalems*, pp. 185–98.

to see how far, when taken in conjunction with the other factors mentioned above, they can help explain the Evangelical revival in Yorkshire. In order to demonstrate the limitations of this approach, comparative material will be drawn from two contrasting areas of Yorkshire: the upland Pennine parishes of Huddersfield and Almondbury in the west of the county, and the city of York and its neighbouring lowland rural parishes in the vale of York to the east.[30]

Of nearly ten thousand parochial livings in England in the mid-eighteenth century, about 650 were in Yorkshire. They came in all shapes and sizes, though on average parishes in the north of England were larger than those in the south. In Yorkshire the average size of a parish was a little over 6,000 acres compared with just under 2,500 acres in the south-east.[31] But even within Yorkshire there were extremes: Halifax parish was the largest, extending over 75,740 acres and including in 1801 a population of 63,434. Almondbury was smaller, but with over 34,000 acres it was the seventh largest parish in the county, with a population of 17,431 in 1801. Huddersfield was nearly 13,000 acres with a population of 14,400. By contrast, the average size of the thirteen parishes falling wholly within York's city walls was around ten acres; the smallest being only four acres with a population of 691.[32] Many of the social explanations for revival have been fashioned with parishes like Almondbury and Huddersfield in mind. And yet York was also an early centre of revival and a stronghold of Methodism, so much so that at the 1851 Religious Census both Huddersfield and York shared similar figures for both the proportion of attendances at worship to population, and the shares of those attendances held by both the Church of England and the Methodists.[33] So what, if anything, did these two places have in common? A few examples might give some insight into the revival and the way it could take hold in different environments.

First, the vicar of Almondbury was an old, nearly blind High

---

[30] For the methodology used here, see E. Royle, *Need Local History be Parochial History?* Cambridge Institute of Continuing Education, Occasional Paper no. 4 (Cambridge, 2002).

[31] Gilbert, *Religion in Industrial Society*, p. 100.

[32] G. S. Minchin, 'Table of Population' in William Page (ed.), *The Victoria History of the County of York* (3 vols. London, 1907–1913), II (1912), pp. 485–548, especially pp. 500–1, 525 and 533–4.

[33] E. Royle, 'The Church of England and Methodism in Yorkshire, *c.*1750–1850: from monopoly to free market', *Northern History*, XXXIII (1997), 137–61.

Churchman called Edward Rishton. In his Visitation Return to Archbishop
Drummond in 1764, he complained of 'Methodists [who] are pretty
numerous in the remoter parts of this parish'. He was referring to two
townships about five miles as the crow flies and across three valleys from
the parish church. Here we would appear to have classic evidence for
Methodist revivalism in a remote part of an over-large parish. But in this
instance all is not what it seemed, for these townships adjoined the parish
of Huddersfield along the river Colne, and the valley-bottom village of
Slaithwaite extended into both parishes. As we have already seen,
Slaithwaite was an evangelical stronghold and in 1764 Venn's curate was
Samuel Furly, an Evangelical in the Arminian mould of Wesley rather
than the Calvinism of his vicar. His chapel stood on the river bank, a few
yards from Almondbury parish, and it served the townships on both sides
of the river. Rishton's complaint was actually levelled against Furly who
'holds what he calls lectures, but I call conventicles', so here the mischief
on the parish boundary resulted not from unlettered Methodist preachers
but from the Evangelical movement within the Church of England.[34]

While vicar of Huddersfield, Venn was an enormously popular
preacher and when he left he helped his former congregation establish
Highfield Chapel in the parish because his successor as vicar was not an
Evangelical. Though this chapel was intended to be an Anglican
proprietary chapel in the Evangelical tradition, it soon became the centre
of Calvinistic Independency in the town. As one contemporary recalled,
'After Mr. Venn left, the people were all squandered away from the
church'.[35] Both Methodism and Nonconformity fed off the squandered
successes of the Established Church. One of the leaders of the first
Wesleyan chapel of 1775 was a grocer, Thomas Goldthorpe, who had
been converted at the parish church in Venn's day. Another prominent
Methodist, John Dyson, had been converted by Thomas Wilson at
Slaithwaite, and then joined the Methodists when he moved to
Huddersfield and was unable to obtain a pew in the parish church.[36]

---

[34] Annesley and Hoskin, *Archbishop Drummond's Visitation Returns, 1764*, I, pp.
15–17; J. Jago and E. Royle, *The Eighteenth-Century Church in Yorkshire.
Archbishop Drummond's primary visitation of 1764*, Borthwick Paper No. 95
(York, 1999), p. 30.

[35] 'Memoir by the Rev. John Venn', in Henry Venn (ed.), *The Life and a Selection
from the Letters of the late Rev. Henry Venn* (London, 1836), pp. 44–5. A footnote
explains defensively that 'squandered' means 'dispersed'.

[36] John Rylands Library, University of Manchester [JRL], Methodist Archives,

Though several of the township parochial chapels were rebuilt during these years, church extension in Huddersfield itself did not get underway until after 1815 and the parish church was not rebuilt with extended accommodation until 1836.[37] The example of Huddersfield, therefore, suggests that the revival was powered as much from within the Established Church as from without and that the institutional weaknesses of the church – over-large parishes and too few places of worship – were matched by a spiritual vitality, which spilled over into Dissent. This created a hunger for spiritual nourishment, which the revivalist preachers with their outdoor preaching and unorthodox methods sought to satisfy.

This picture is confirmed in the unlikely setting of the cathedral city and county town of York. Here many of the usual generalisations are inapplicable: the parishes were small; there were apparently adequate numbers of clergymen and if the revivalists succeeded only where they found gaps, York would appear to have offered them little scope. Once again all was not as it seemed. The problem in the city and rural parishes in the vale of York was the poverty of the livings, especially in the smaller parishes, leading to extensive pluralism. Thus within the city, most churches offered either 'morning' or 'afternoon' services only and, although any parishioner who wanted two services on a Sunday could easily find them within a few yards of his parish, this did not build up parochial loyalty. The displaced parishioner could just as easily wander off to a meeting room or chapel to hear a sermon and sing hymns in a less formal and restrained style.[38] Outside of the city, some of the village parishes each encompassed several villages and here there was a problem similar to that in the large Pennine parishes. It was easy for a village without a church to offer a ready home to Dissenters. In 1764, at Kirby Wharfe, south of Tadcaster, of ninety-two families in the parish one was Catholic and fifty were Methodist. But this rural parish contained two villages: the parish church was in Kirby Wharfe itself and here the church

---

MAW LHB.29.4, manuscript by P. Ahier, 'Methodism in Huddersfield', Lecture, 25; Hulbert, *Annals of the Church in Slaithwaite*, p. 111.

[37] Honley (1756), Meltham (1785), Slaithwaite (1787), Scammonden (1812); E. Royle, 'Religion in Huddersfield since the mid-eighteenth century', in E. A. H. Haigh (ed.), *Huddersfield. A most handsome town* (Huddersfield, 1992), pp. 104, 117.

[38] Annesley and Hoskin, *Archbishop Drummond's Visitation Returns, 1764*, vol. 3, pp. 144–69; Borthwick Institute of Historical Research, York, RD/AIN/1, manuscript Report on the State of the Rural Deanery of the City and Ainsty of York, December 1845, 167.

was supreme; the Methodists were in the other village of Ulleskelf, a mile
away, where there was no church and a local farmer led the Wesleyans
while a labourer led a group of Benjamin Ingham's followers.[39]

There is also a parallel with Huddersfield in the support given to the
revival from within the Established Church. Methodism obtained an early
foothold in the city. Wesley did not visit York until 1752 but in 1747 he
had visited the nearby village of Acomb where John Nelson had
established a Methodist class three years earlier. After this 1747 visit the
Acomb Methodists started a class in the city, which met in various
locations close to the Minster in buildings on non-parochial land. In a city
with so many clergy there always were going to be some who opposed the
revivalist preachers and some who supported them; Methodism thrived
between the two. In 1759 a purpose-built chapel was opened, one of the
earliest in Yorkshire. So successful was the York society that in 1775 they
had to put galleries into the chapel to accommodate the crowds.[40]

Further impetus was given to York evangelicalism in 1771 when
William Richardson began his fifty-year incumbency at St Michael-le-
Belfrey church. Richardson joined the Hotham clerical society and, like
many Anglican Evangelicals, was often accused of Methodism by the
opponents of 'vital religion'. It was a charge he heartily repudiated. Yet it
remains true that, like Grimshaw and Venn before him, many of his
converts did become Methodists, one of whom was Robert Spence, a
pillar of the Methodist society in York until his death in 1824. As in
Huddersfield, the revival in the pulpits of the Established Church was
spilling over into the wider community of Dissent.[41]

The best way to understand the mechanisms of the revival is to study
the licences granted by the Archbishop for dissenting meetings under the
Toleration Act.[42] From the 1760s there is a proliferation of such licences,
often in the names of the same people or combinations of the same with
other names, indicating a number of restless searchers after the truth. In
areas such as Huddersfield this indicates the extent and distribution of

[39] Annesley and Hoskin, *Archbishop Drummond's Visitation Returns, 1764*, II, pp. 97–8.
[40] Lyth, *Glimpses of Early Methodism*, pp. 76, 82–6, 89–94, 120.
[41] *A Brief Memoir of the late Rev. Wm. Richardson, sub-chanter of York Cathedral* (2nd edn. York, 1822); R. Burdekin, *Memoirs of the Life and Character of Mr. Robert Spence* (York, 1840), p. 16.
[42] Borthwick Institute, Faculty Books, 1737–1816 (Fac.Bk. I–III); Dissenters' Meeting House Certificates, 1712–1852 (DMH), 4 boxes, *passim*.

house meetings before the formal establishment of a society with a chapel. In York it indicates the lively sectarianism of spiritually independent and self-confident individuals among the lower ranks of urban society. One such group can be traced through their spiritual autobiography, written by their leader in 1799. They began their journey as young people, attending various churches, seeking one that satisfied their spiritual needs. They were at first attracted by the Methodists, but conviction of the power of the grace of God led them to Calvinism and they attended the Countess of Huntingdon's preachers. Further conviction of the power of the new birth led some of them to reject infant baptism and form a congregation of Baptists. By 1806 they had become Unitarian Baptists, led by a shoemaker.[43] Such a group as this will be familiar not only to historians of the evangelical revival but also of religious movements in England during the mid-seventeenth century, or of Germany during the Reformation. It is salutary to be reminded of this constant feature in religious revivals, which takes us back to the origins of the Evangelical revival among the refugee peoples of central Europe at the end of the seventeenth century.

Within the scope of this study it has not been possible to give a definitive explanation for the Evangelical revival, even in one county, but an attempt has been made to contribute something towards a better understanding of its complexity. In offering a few suggestions for how, if not why, revival occurred in Yorkshire, some factors have been identified which, if treated comparatively, might be generalised to throw light on the wider picture. Many influences were experienced in the county that were of wider significance: the importance of the Moravians; the role of energetic preachers, both ordained and lay; and the existence of a widespread dissatisfaction with existing religious services and teaching in both the Established Church and Dissent. But if this analysis has confirmed the usual generalisations about the structural inadequacy of the Established Church in large upland parishes with scattered populations experiencing the early consequences of industrialisation, it can be argued that this weakness was also true, for different reasons, of parishes in the agricultural vale of York, and even of the tiny parishes in the cathedral city itself. Further, while pointing to the weaknesses of the Church of England, this study has also sought to confirm that revisionism about the eighteenth-century Church of England which suggests structural inadequacy should not be equated with spiritual inadequacy in the way

---

[43] D. Eaton, *A Narrative of the Proceedings of the Society of Baptists in York* (2nd edn. London, 1809), pp. 1–28.

that some Victorian reformers implied. In considering old-fashioned High Churchmen like Edward Rishton, and energetic new evangelicals like Henry Venn or William Richardson, it has been shown that the revival did not descend from Heaven upon a religious desert, but rather received much support from within the Established Church. Following John Walsh's thesis that the process of revival began within the Church of England, it has been suggested that the spread of revival to Nonconformity and the new Methodist movement resulted from the tensions set up between the strength of revival in some parishes and the inadequacy of the structures of the Church to satisfy it. In Yorkshire the revival within the Church was unusually strong and its institutional structures were unusually weak. Taken together these two facts go a long way towards explaining why the Methodist movement established such a strong and independent presence in the county.

CHAPTER SIX

'TRANSCRIPTS OF MY HEART':
WELSH METHODISTS, POPULAR PIETY
AND THE INTERNATIONAL EVANGELICAL
REVIVAL, 1738–1750

DAVID CERI JONES

Whether one adopts the official *versus* unofficial, elite *versus* popular or learned *versus* unlearned dualism, drawing a stark distinction between the religion practiced by clergy and that taken up by the laity, a far too dramatic polarisation between the spirituality of the leaders of religious movements and those of their followers is introduced. Much of the methodological framework underpinning the debate on popular religion has been developed by historians preoccupied by the extent to which Protestantism took root in England during the sixteenth and seventeenth centuries.[1] Other historians have argued that such an approach can be inappropriate when examining religious belief in later periods. It was to escape the oppositional implications of the popular religion model that David D. Hall suggested that the concept of 'lived religion' might better capture the overlapping and highly complex layers of meaning attached to any expression of religious commitment.[2] Echoing these misgivings, David Hempton has argued that the concept of popular religion during the eighteenth century is potentially misleading, as by this time Christianity throughout the British Isles consisted of a diverse mix of beliefs and practices that defies simple categorisation.[3]

---

[1] For example, see the discussion in Christopher Marsh, *Popular Religion in Sixteenth Century England* (London, 1998), pp. 6–12.
[2] David D. Hall (ed.), *Lived Religion in America: towards a history of practice* (Princeton, 1997).
[3] David Hempton, *The Religion of the People: Methodism and popular religion c.1750–1900* (London, 1996), pp. 70–1.

At the most fundamental level, Methodism, in its earliest decades at least, displayed a remarkable degree of homogeneity. There tended to be little distinction between the spirituality of the revivalist and those who were revived. It is all too easy to lose sight of the fact that Methodism was, initially, a movement of people who were drawn together by a range of shared religious experiences. The universal availability of experiences, such as the new birth, appealed to those independently-minded middling sorts who formed the backbone of the Methodist movement and who were eager to better themselves by taking full advantage of the opportunities for influence and power that the gradual modernisation of the country brought their way. Despite what may be regarded as a difference in intensity there tended not to be a dramatic difference between the religious lives and experiences of Howel Harris, Daniel Rowland and William Williams, Pantycelyn, and many of their followers, at least during the first thirty years of the revival.[4] Methodism, as Nathan Hatch has shown, was an integral part of a much more extensive trend towards the democratisation of Christianity,[5] the emergence of autonomous religious movements in which individuals were urged to take responsibility for their own religious lives.[6] As a result of this development, Methodism, which was the first Protestant movement to elicit anything approaching a positive response in Wales,[7] presents the historian with a particularly clear view of the spirituality of many of its rank-and-file members.

Popular spirituality can be approached from a number of perspectives, and a range of sources can be used to shed light on its different layers. Historians of Methodism are particularly fortunate because of the numerous and extensive collections of primary source material that are available to them, including personal papers in the form of journals, diaries and letters, as well as the more mundane official documentation of the movement. Literary sources are also plentiful, and range from both printed and unprinted sermons, hymns and books and, perhaps most useful of all, one of the earliest religious periodicals. This chapter, takes one of these sources, the Calvinistic Methodist periodical, best known in its second incarnation as *The Weekly History*, and attempts to uncover some

---

[4] John Kent, *Wesley and the Wesleyans: religion in eighteenth-century Britain* (Cambridge, 2002), p. 6.

[5] Nathan O. Hatch, *The Democratization of American Christianity* (New Haven, 1989).

[6] This is a theme in most of the essays in Deryck W. Lovegrove (ed.), *The Rise of the Laity in Evangelical Protestantism* (London, 2002).

[7] Glanmor Williams, 'Wales and the Reformation', in G. Williams, *Welsh Reformation Essays* (Cardiff, 1967), p. 30.

aspects of Welsh Methodist spirituality by analysing the contributions that
were made to it by a select band of the Welsh revival's most committed
rank-and-file members.

In many ways *The Weekly History* became the public face of
Calvinistic Methodism after the division had taken place between George
Whitefield and John Wesley in the early 1740s. The strategic importance
of the magazine is increased still further if, following recent historiographical
trends, the Evangelical Revival is approached from an international
perspective.[8] Despite there being many apparently separate Methodist and
evangelical awakenings during the first decade of the revival they all were
regarded as contributors to a single 'pan Protestant phenomenon'[9] that was
both trans-national and trans-Atlantic in its scope. According to W. R.
Ward these religious awakenings have to be traced back to a single source:
the dramatic crisis of confidence pervading the Protestant enterprise at the
hands of rejuvenated Catholic powers who were determined, in the wake
of the Treaty of Westphalia (1648), to recoup some of the losses of
territory that it had enshrined.[10] The dispersal of Protestant minorities from
parts of Germany, particularly the Salzbergers and Moravians, precipitated
the spread of many of their pietistic ideas and also led many to adopt their
highly individualistic and experimental piety in a bid to halt the progress
of Protestant decline. Despite wide geographical and cultural separation,
therefore, these religious awakenings can all be traced back to the fears
and concerns of the Protestant establishments in each country.

The one common factor in many of these awakenings was the
influence of the itinerant revivalist, George Whitefield. Harry Stout has
called him the first evangelical celebrity.[11] Whitefield took full advantage
of improvements in the speed of travel, and communications, particularly

---

[8] For works which attempt to interpret the Evangelical Revival within an
international context see Frank Lambert, '*Pedlar in Divinity': George Whitefield
and the transatlantic revivals* (Princeton, 1994); David Ceri Jones, '*A Glorious
Work in the World': Welsh Methodism and the international evangelical revival,
1735–1750* (Cardiff, 2004); David Hempton, *Methodism: empire of the spirit* (New
Haven, 2005).

[9] John Walsh, '"Methodism" and the Origins of English-Speaking Evangelicalism', in Mark A. Noll, David W. Bebbington and George A. Rawlyk (eds),
*Evangelicalism: comparative studies of popular Protestantism in North America,
the British Isles, and beyond 1700–1990* (New York, 1994), p. 20.

[10] W. R. Ward, *The Protestant Evangelical Awakening* (Cambridge, 1992), pp. 19–
21.

[11] Harry S. Stout, *The Divine Dramatist: George Whitefield and the Rise of
Modern Evangelicalism* (Grand Rapids, Mich., 1991), p. xiv.

the more efficient mail service and also the growth of the marketplace, which brought a greater range of commodities within the reach of a larger number of people.[12] His international profile made him an obvious figurehead of the revival, a position from which he was able to draw the disparate awakenings into a more unified evangelical renewal movement. Whitefield had been the first evangelical to make an impact outside of his own community, and had begun to draw large crowds to listen to his dramatic sermons in London as early as 1736. Upon hearing of evangelicals in other countries, he immediately set about establishing links with them, creating a network of correspondence that kept the leaders of the various infant awakenings in close contact with one another. As the revivals developed and became more complex, these *ad hoc* personal contacts became insufficient, and so with the help of some well-placed financial backers, Whitefield sought to establish more permanent methods of communication, including a more sophisticated letter distribution network, a weekly religious periodical and an energetic programme of evangelical publishing. These mechanisms served to draw otherwise scattered evangelicals into what Susan O'Brien has called a 'trans-Atlantic community of saints'.[13]

The rank-and-file Welsh Methodists could not, however, have participated in the international revival without the commitment of Howel Harris and George Whitefield. The two revivalists met for the first time during March 1739, when Whitefield and Harris teamed-up in Cardiff, a meeting that set in motion the close alignment of the Welsh revival and what was to become English Calvinistic Methodism. Whitefield's brief visit to Wales had followed a brief exchange of letters, and having 'agreed on such measures as seemed most conducive to promote the common interest of our Lord'[14] they established regular contact. Whitefield became a regular visitor to Wales and began to advise Welsh Methodists on matters relating to the successful propagation of the revival. By way of exchange, Harris began to visit London, and soon came to play an invaluable role in the development of Calvinistic Methodism, particularly after serious divisions arose between the Moravians, the Wesleyans and

---

[12] Neil McKendrick, John Brewer and J. H. Plumb (eds), *The Birth of a Consumer Society: the commercialization of eighteenth-century England* (Bloomington, 1982); Lambert, *'Pedlar in Divinity'*, pp. 25–36; W. R. Ward, 'John Wesley, Traveller', in W. R. Ward, *Faith and Faction* (London, 1993), pp. 249–63.

[13] Susan O'Brien, '"A Trans-Atlantic Community of Saints": The Great Awakening and the First Evangelical Network', *American Historical Review*, 91 (1986), 811.

[14] Iain H. Murray (ed.), *George Whitefield's Journals* (London, 1960), p. 230.

the Calvinists. He eventually became the outright leader of English Calvinistic Methodism in 1748. Far from being a backward looking and strictly indigenous outpouring of primitive religious enthusiasm, the Welsh revival was at the forefront of an international campaign which, according to David Bebbington, was to give rise to a brand new Evangelical movement.[15]

Having relied on meetings and private correspondence during the later 1730s, Whitefield and his fellow Calvinistic revivalists realised, particularly following his extended visit to the American colonies during 1739 and 1740, that their revival could not be sustained in such a haphazard fashion any longer. Conscious of the threat posed to his revival following the split with the Wesley brothers, Whitefield secured an interest in the struggling periodical, *The Christian's Amusement*. This journal had been printed and edited by the London-Welsh printer, John Lewis, from September 1740 until March 1741. Whitefield struck a deal with Lewis by which he took over as chief editor and provided a regular supply of material for inclusion in the magazine's pages, while Lewis continued to do much of the practical editorial work. In April 1741 the magazine was re-launched with a new title, *The Weekly History*, and was printed cheaply on four folio pages. It rapidly established itself as the mouthpiece of the Calvinistic Methodist movement as its pages were filled with accounts of Whitefield's activities, news about the revival, conversion narratives and letters from many of the rank-and-file converts as they struggled with some of the problems that their involvement in the movement invariably entailed.[16] The London-based magazine also spawned two other sister publications: in Scotland, James Robe and William McCulloch edited *The Glasgow Weekly History* between December 1741 and December 1742;[17] and in the American colonies, Thomas Prince began to publish *The Christian History* in March 1743.[18] Both magazines relied heavily on material from the London edition, but the three versions each contributed to the sense of solidarity that existed

---

[15] David W. Bebbington, *Evangelicalism in Modern Britain: a history from the 1730s to the 1780s* (London, 1989), pp. 1–19.

[16] For the change in the editorial policy of the magazine see Susan Durden, 'A study of the first Evangelical Magazines, 1740–1788', *Journal of Ecclesiastical History*, 27, 3 (July 1976), 260–2; Jones, 'A Glorious Work in the World', p. 83.

[17] Its contents have been discussed in some detail in T. C. Smout, 'Born Again at Cambuslang: new evidence on popular religion and literacy in eighteenth-century Scotland', *Past and Present*, 97 (1982), 114–27.

[18] J. E. van Wetering, 'The Christian History of the Great Awakening', *Journal of Presbyterian History*, 44 (1966), 122–9.

amongst Calvinistically-inclined evangelicals throughout the British Isles and the American colonies. The London version of the magazine enjoyed the longest life and circulated with some interruptions for almost eight years, despite having to change its format and title on four separate occasions.[19] It eventually ceased publication in 1748, a few years after a dejected and bankrupt John Lewis had defected to the Moravians.[20]

Like the correspondence from which they emerged, the magazines had a clear didactic purpose. They quickly established themselves as the first port of call for rank-and-file Methodists who wished to learn about what was happening in some of the more distant corners of the evangelical world. The accounts which they read and, in some instances, those that some of them actually wrote, bore ample testimony to the fact that 'in many nations the Gospel is spreading its healing wings',[21] and that there was a 'glorious work . . . going on in the world'.[22] Their realisation that the revival was making remarkable progress in 'Scotland, Yorkshire, Lincolnshire, Warwickshire, Wiltshire, Germany, Prussia, New England, Pennsylvania and many other provinces'[23] was not mere hyperbole, but the result of their familiarity with the events and personalities involved in the awakenings in many of those places.

Many other Methodists were not content simply to read accounts of revivals in other parts of the world and occasionally adopt internationalist terminology. A few were intent on requesting news about the latest progress of the revival from those, like Harris and Whitefield, who were best placed to advise, and by writing accounts of their localised experience. The anonymous correspondent who wrote to Whitefield in April 1742 and whose letter was printed in *The Weekly History* was typical:

---

[19] During the Autumn of 1742 the title was changed to *An Account of the Most Remarkable Particular of the Present Progress of the Gospel in England, Wales, Scotland and America, as far as the Rev. Mr. Whitefield, His Fellow Labourers and Assistants are concerned* (London, 1742–3), while in the Autumn of 1743 it became *The Christian History or General Account of the Progress of the Gospel in England, Wales, Scotland and America, as far as the Rev. Mr. Whitefield, His Fellow Labourers and Assistants are concerned* (London, 1743–8).

[20] National Library of Wales, Calvinist Methodist Archive, The Trevecka Letters (hereafter NLW, Trevecka) 1330, John Lewis to Howel Harris (15 June 1745).

[21] 'Extract of a Letter from a Minister in the Country to his Friend in London (3 February 1742)', in John Lewis (ed.), *The Weekly History or, An Account of the Most Remarkable Particulars Relating to the Present Progress of the Gospel*, 46 (Saturday, 20 February 1742).

[22] NLW, Trevecka 708, Howel Harris to Marmaduke Gwynne (22 October 1742).

[23] NLW, Trevecka 2803, Howel Harris to Bro. Jenkins (22 November 1742).

How much do I long for the pleasure of a line from you: I have written to
you twice since I had any from you – But your time is much better
employed. Glory be to God for the continued success of the Gospel by
your ministry.[24]

The revivalists, delighted that their vision of an international community
of saints was being met with enthusiasm, were invariably true to their
word and their responses offered full and comprehensive accounts of the
latest progress of the revival. Such letters were intended to be read by the
immediate recipient first, but they were clearly also designed to be read, or
at least read aloud, by the recipient's local Methodist community. Howel
Harris, for example, in response to a letter from the Breconshire
landowner, Marmaduke Gwynne,[25] wrote a letter that was genuinely
international in its scope noting that 'there are above 100 ministers
everywhere up and down the world now employ'd in the Great Work'.[26]

There are also several examples which show that some Welsh
evangelicals wrote their own accounts of the awakenings. For example,
after a visit to Llangeitho in August 1743, Brother Williams, in a letter to
an anonymous friend, wrote-up his impressions of Daniel Rowland's
sermons. The letter is a particularly vivid account of the effects of
Rowland's preaching and was subsequently reprinted in the Calvinistic
Methodist magazine for the wider evangelical readership. He wrote:

> I am newly returned from hearing that famous man of God, the Reverend
> Mr [Daniel] Rowland . . . There was a dozen of the Members of our
> Society, and exceeding sweet was the Lord to our Souls, both in our going,
> while there, and coming home. Wonderful was the Power Mr. Rowland
> had on the Sabbath.[27]

Few Methodists from Wales matched George Whitefield's wife for the
frequency with which she wrote or the strategic role which her letters
played. Elizabeth James, a widow from Abergavenny in Monmouthshire,

---

[24] 'From Mr. A. T. to the Rev. Mr. Whitefield (Edinburgh, 1 April 1742)', in
Lewis (ed.), *Weekly History*, 55 (Saturday, 24 April 1742).

[25] J. E. Lloyd and R. T. Jenkins (eds.), *Dictionary of Welsh Biography* (London,
1959), pp. 331–2; John A. Vickers (ed.), *Dictionary of Methodism in Britain and
Ireland* (London, 2000), p. 145; A. H. Williams, 'The Gwynne's of Garth *c*.1712–
1809', *Brycheiniog*, XIV (1970), 76–96.

[26] NLW, Trevecka 708, Howel Harris to Marmaduke Gwynne (22 October 1742).

[27] 'From Brother E__n W__ms, to Brother L__t (29 August 1743)', in Lewis (ed.),
*An Account of the Most Remarkable Particulars Relating to the Present Progress
of the Gospel*, IV, I, pp. 76–9.

had married Whitefield in November 1741, following a brief courtship
with Howel Harris.[28] Marriage saw her full integration into the life of
Whitefield's Tabernacle at Moorfields in London, but her regular letters to
Harris and some of the other Welsh exhorters with whom she remained
friendly,[29] quickly became one of the richest sources of news for many in
Wales. It was a role she was able to play to maximum effect when she
accompanied Whitefield on his longest and most extensive colonial tour
between 1744 and 1748. Many of her letters home were rushed into print
by John Lewis, enabling Methodists in London and further afield to
closely follow Whitefield's progress.[30] By this stage in the revival many
Methodists, particularly in Wales, were also regularly contributing
significant sums of money in support of Whitefield's Orphan House
project at Bethesda in the recently founded colony of Georgia. Elizabeth
Whitefield's letters assumed added significance as they became a crucial
point of contact between those who gave what they could barely afford to
an evangelical enterprise at one of the more distant corners of the known
world.[31]

The response to many of the published letters from grass-roots
Methodists in Wales was invariably enthusiastic. Anne Thomas of
Longhouse in Pembrokeshire, one of the best informed of all the Welsh
Methodists, was thrilled to receive copies of *The Weekly History* in 1742:

> I receiv[e]d . . . the Weekly Histories which you was so kind as to send me
> . . . I think my soul has received some Benefit in reading them. O how
> sweet is it to hear how the Lord brings in his work.[32]

---

[28] Arnold A. Dallimore, *George Whitefield: the life and times of the great
evangelist of the 18ᵗʰ century revival* (2 vols. Edinburgh, 1980), II, pp. 103–13.
[29] For example, see 'From Mrs Whitefield to Brother Herbert Jenkins (12 April,
1744), in John Lewis (ed.), *Christian History*, V, III, pp. 56–7.
[30] 'From Mrs Whitefield, Dated from Portsmouth in New England (14 November
1744)', in Lewis (ed.), *Christian History*, VI, III, pp. 74–8; 'From Mrs Whitefield
to Howel Harris (27 June 1747)', in Lewis (ed.), *Christian History* (1747), pp.
117–19.
[31] See the circular letter addressed to all the main leaders of English and Welsh
Calvinistic Methodism. NLW, Trevecka 1340, Elizabeth Whitefield to Harris,
Jenkins, Adams and all at the Tabernacle (July 1745).
[32] 'The Copy of a letter from Mrs Anne T__s of Pembrokeshire in Wales to Mr
Howel Harris in London (Longhouse, 3 September 1742)', in Lewis (ed.), *Weekly
History*, 80 (Saturday, 16 October 1742).

Similarly, after receiving the latest issue of *The Weekly History* in March 1742, John Oulton, a dissenting minister from Leominster on the Welsh border, wrote to Howel Harris:

> With pleasure and refreshment I read ye experimental Gospel Letters in the weekly history (and hope they will be continued) Especially as they are a transcript of my own Heart respecting Sin and Grace.[33]

Oulton's letter is a perfect illustration of the way in which Harris and Whitefield intended their propaganda to function. The mere transmission of news played only a small part in their overall purpose. They wrote letters such as these with the intention of provoking a specific response from their readers. That Oulton was 'refreshed' by hearing the latest news was only part of that aim. Perhaps more significant was the way Oulton saw his own experience mirrored in that of other Methodists. Harris intended that his writings would provoke people to pray for similar experiences to those that they read about, which would then spread the revival from place to place. His rationale was, therefore, little different from that which Jonathan Edwards had outlined shortly after the end of the awakening at Northampton in 1735. Both were convinced that news of a revival in 'any place, tends greatly to awaken and engage the minds of persons, in other places'.[34] For the somewhat smaller band of Welsh Methodists who wrote letters, participation in the international communications network became a vital part of their involvement in the revival. It afforded them the opportunity to use their newly discovered literacy skills and to carve out a niche for themselves within the movement. For the majority of other evangelicals, who either received letters from their leaders or followed the course of events in *The Weekly History* and its successors, these letters were exciting and vibrant, containing as they did up-to-the-minute information which reinforced the impression that they were at the heart of a movement which had great significance and to which they were invaluable members.

If imitation lay at the core of the rationale behind such a sophisticated circulation of revival news, perhaps one of the most significant functions of *The Weekly History* was its transmission of the distinctively Methodist re-interpretation of religious experience. Perhaps more than any other group the Methodists contributed to the redefinition of the experience that lay at the heart of the movement – conversion or the new birth. The

---

[33] NLW, Trevecka 504, James Oulton to Howel Harris (3 March 1742).
[34] Durden, 'A Study of the First Evangelical Magazines', 257.

originality of their interpretation lay not so much in any major theological reform, but in their stress on the immediate attainability of the new birth and on the desirability of reaching a position of certain salvation. David Bebbington has somewhat controversially argued that it was their emphasis on assurance that most distinguished the early Methodists from their Puritan forebears.[35] Jonathan Edwards in particular, influenced by Enlightenment epistemology, most conspicuously by John Locke's rejection of innate ideas and preference for the power of sensory experience, argued that individuals could be certain about spiritual matters through 'a new inward perception or sensation'[36] created by the Holy Spirit at the moment of conversion.[37] In practice, this led the Methodists to elevate the importance of the conversion experience, infusing it with dramatic intensity and the certainty that God could be immediately and consciously known. Although not all evangelicals held assurance to be the very essence of faith, they all expected it to be reached fairly shortly after conversion.[38] Edwards argued that such assurance depended on the presence of the Holy Spirit in the life of each convert. He expounded his theory in meticulous detail in *The Distinguishing Marks of the Work of the Spirit of God* (1741), raising them into empirical tests and infallible indicators of genuine Christian experience.[39]

Standardised accounts of evangelical conversion appeared in a variety of places. The published journals of George Whitefield and the diaries of John Wesley are, in effect, extended conversion narratives tracing the Christian life from its initiation to the archetypal holy death. A few evangelicals published modest autobiographical accounts, but those who were minded to record their experiences tended to do so most often in

---

[35] David Bebbington, 'Revival and Enlightenment in Eighteenth-Century England', in Edith L. Blumhofer and Randall Balmer (eds), *Modern Christian Revivals* (Urbana, Illinois, 1993), pp. 21–2. For a helpful critique of Bebbington's thesis see Garry J. Williams, 'Was Evangelicalism created by the Enlightenment?', *Tyndale Bulletin*, 53, 2 (2002), 283–312.

[36] Bebbington, *Evangelicalism in Modern Britain*, p. 48.

[37] See George M. Marsden, *Jonathan Edwards: a life* (New Haven, 2003), 59–64; Norman Fiering, 'The Rationalist Foundations of Jonathan Edwards's Metaphysics', in Nathan O. Hatch and Harry S. Stout (eds), *Jonathan Edwards and the American Experience* (New York, 1988), pp. 73–7.

[38] David W. Bebbington, 'Revival and Enlightenment in Eighteenth-Century England', in Andrew Walker and Kristin Aune (eds), *On Revival: a critical examination* (Carlisle, 2003), p. 73.

[39] Whitefield did the same in his *The Nature and Necessity of New Birth in Christ Jesus, in Order to Salvation* (Bristol, 1737). The sermon was so important that it was published in Welsh in 1739.

letters. Some of the best of these letters found their way into the pages of *The Weekly History*, and thereby became one of the most important sources of information for rank-and-file members on the signs of genuine conversion. Whitefield encouraged John Lewis to supplement the evangelical theology of conversion that his converts heard or read about in his many sermons, by making case studies of model conversions a regular feature in his magazine. Lewis, therefore, solicited readers who felt able to write accounts of their conversions to forward them to him for consideration. In a letter included in an early issue of *The Weekly History*, Lewis spoke through the words of an anonymous correspondent to explain this new approach:

> The best way is for every person simply to write what he once was in a state of nature, how and by what means he came to have the dawnings of light and grace upon his soul, and how it has been with him since this time . . . The distress'd, tempted soul will hereby see that many of his brethren and Sisters in the kingdom and patience of Jesus, have walked in the same road before him. What will heaven be, but searching into and comparing of one anothers experiences, joined with praising God for the same.[40]

Of the many accounts written by both English and Welsh evangelicals, Lewis, undoubtedly with Whitefield and probably Harris's guidance, selected the most striking for inclusion. The accounts invariably followed the well-established conventions of the conversion narrative genre which had been refined by some of the more radical Puritans[41] and their Pietist successors.[42] By the advent of the Methodists these narratives had become sophisticated enough to accommodate a wide variety of evangelical experience. According to Bruce Hindmarsh, Methodist narratives tended to follow the biblical template of creation, fall, redemption and new creation.[43] For example, in April 1742, John Lewis included in *The Weekly History* a letter from an anonymous correspondent which described 'a fresh instance of the quickening, comforting influences of the good

---

[40] Anonymous letter in Lewis (ed.), *Weekly History*, p. 13.
[41] Owen C. Watkins, *The Puritan Experience* (London, 1972), 18–36; Patricia Caldwell, *The Puritan Conversion Narrative: the beginnings of American expression* (Cambridge, 1982).
[42] W. R. Ward and R. P. Heitzenrater, 'Introduction', in W. R. Ward and R. P. Heitzenrater (eds), *The Works of John Wesley, XVIII: journals and diaries, I: 1735–38* (Nashville, TN., 1988), pp. 1–24.
[43] D. Bruce Hindmarsh, '"My chains fell off, my heart was free": early Methodist conversion narrative in England', *Church History*, 68, 4 (December, 1999), 921–2.

spirit'.[44] Its author constructed a dramatic and vivid narrative outlining his experience of the anxieties of the new birth:

> I was alone employ'd in a Branch of my worldly Business in the Twilight of the Evening, and without much Attention, or Design, revolving in my Mind these Lines:
>
> He will present our Souls
> Unblemish'd and compleat
> Before the Glory of his Face
> With joy divinely great.
>
> With sudden almost as a Flash of Lightening my Soul was ravish'd with a joyful Assurance that our Blessed Saviour, my dear Jesus, will one day present my worthless Soul, polluted and vile as it now is, before the Presence of CHRIST at once filled me throughout with transporting pleasure.[45]

This example highlights some of the key motifs of early Methodist religious experience. Despite admitting to an apparently ungodly youth, the writer's sudden, subconscious reprise of a verse from a well-known hymn, suggests at least some measure of latent spiritual knowledge, perhaps the result of a godly upbringing. The imagery employed reinforces the evangelical's stress on the immediacy of the new birth and the reality of the emotions that invariably accompanied it. The writer's attention was arrested like a 'Flash of Lightening', reinforcing both the terror of sin and the reality of the wrath of God. Characteristically, there was no long drawn-out period of conviction of sin, as the writer testified to being quickly assured of acceptance and forgiveness, proven tangibly by an 'overwhelming sense' of the love of God and 'transporting pleasure'. Although they admitted that there could be, and often were, variations in each individual conversion experience, the early evangelicals pared conversion down to the minimum: an awareness of personal sinfulness, forgiveness and an assurance of acceptance by God, demonstrable, in classic enlightened fashion by verifiable signs, almost always located in the feelings and emotions, or what Jonathan Edwards would have preferred to call the 'affections' of the convert.[46]

---

[44] 'The Copy of a Letter from a Friend in the Country (26 April 1742)', in Lewis (ed.), *Weekly History*, 57 (Saturday, 8 May 1742).
[45] Ibid.
[46] Bebbington, 'Revival and Enlightenment in Eighteenth-Century England', in Blumhofer and Balmer (eds), *Modern Christian Revivals*, pp. 22–3.

Such accounts proliferated in both the evangelical letter-writing network and in the pages of *The Weekly History*. Despite the somewhat formulaic style, the narratives offered valuable exemplars whereby many Methodist converts could compare their individual experiences with the grand narrative, stretching from creation all the way through to new creation as outlined by their leaders. The communications network became what Margaret P. Jones has called a 'public space',[47] in which the experience that lay at the heart of Evangelicalism became standardised. Methodists in Wales, Scotland, England and the American colonies were, therefore, able to relate to one another with such apparent ease precisely because they had all passed through the same experience and all spoke one another's language.

Beyond its role as an indispensable guide through the intricacies of the conversion experience, *The Weekly History* was also put to a number of other more sophisticated uses. Many female members of the revival found *The Weekly History* invaluable as they struggled to apply their newly-discovered faith to every facet of their lives. A considerable amount of the pioneer revivalist's time and energy was taken up with shepherding their new converts. While much of this was done on a face-to-face basis, particularly within the context of the Methodist societies, as the movement expanded this became increasingly difficult. Letters, therefore, came to play an important role in the provision of pastoral care, and some of the most helpful of them were deemed worthy of publication in *The Weekly History*.

It would appear at the outset that women used the network as a kind of self-help forum and that they did so far more readily than men. Their letters differ from those written by male correspondents in that they tended to focus far more on matters of the soul and the practice of piety; men tended to be more concerned with issues relating to the prospects and future direction of the revival movement.[48] There is evidence too that Methodists in England and Wales found Howel Harris to be the most sympathetic of all of the revivalists, and more ready to engage in the kind of protracted spiritual counselling that many of them demanded. For his

---

[47] Margaret P. Jones, 'From "The State of My Soul" to "Exalted Piety": women's voices in the *Arminian/Methodist magazine*, 1778–1821', in R. N. Swanson (ed.), *Studies in Church History*, 34: *gender and Christian religion* (Woodbridge, Suffolk, 1998), p. 273.

[48] Compare with Gail Malmgreen, 'Domestic Discords: Women and the Family in East Cheshire Methodism, 1730–1830', in J. Obelkevich, L. Roper and R. Samuel (eds), *Disciplines of Faith: studies on religion, politics and patriarchy* (London, 1987), pp. 55–70.

part, Harris demonstrated an awareness of their difficulties and throughout his career he attached particular importance to being 'instrumental to comfort any of the poor deep precious Lambs that are equally dear to the dear shepherd, with the strongest and bravest soldier'.[49] A large portion of his correspondence consisted of letters from converts struggling with the problems of Methodist membership. By writing to Harris many of the typical concerns of Welsh Methodists were brought to the attention of a far wider audience. The contents of *The Weekly History* diversified as the needs of its contributors altered in line with the changing priorities of the revival movement.

It is probably fair to say that many of the Welsh evangelicals who wrote to Harris initially did so with very little, or even no, expectation of a reply. They wrote for the cathartic effect of unburdening their anxieties. Accordingly, Ann Harry, from St Kennox in Pembrokeshire, wrote simply to 'acquaint [you] of some of my experiences'.[50] In February 1742 Ann Evans, a Welsh member of Whitefield's Tabernacle in London, wrote to Harris after hearing one of his sermons. She was able to trace her deliverance from spiritual depression and doubts about the authenticity of her conversion to a letter that Harris had written to a certain Sister Hart, and which was either read aloud in the Tabernacle society or circulated informally among some of its members. Ann Evans's experience illustrates the way in which Harris's letters often took on a relevance far beyond that which even the astute Harris first envisaged. Her indebtedness to Harris's correspondence led her to call for even more letters as those that she had already had access to had proved to be of 'so great youse to me',[51] and had supplemented the help she had received from the 'means of grace' on offer at the Tabernacle.

For other evangelicals, however, their letters to Harris led to a more established correspondence. To Elizabeth Thomas of Longhouse, one of his closest friends in Wales, Harris wrote an earnest letter encouraging her during a period of particularly intense trial. His letter is typical of the care and attention that Harris gave to many of his converts and indicative of the way he supported them through many of the spiritual peaks and troughs that they experienced. Packed with scriptural references and allusions, Harris employed in the classic manner of the best examples of Puritan

---

[49] 'The Copy of a Letter from Mr. Howel Harris, to Mrs. E. P. in London' (4 February 1742)', in Lewis (ed.), *Weekly History*, 46 (Saturday, 20 February 1742).
[50] NLW, Trevecka 983, Ann Harry to Howel Harris (15 September 1743).
[51] NLW, Trevecka 482, Ann Evans to Howel Harris (13 February 1742).

casuistry,[52] closely reasoned scriptural arguments in order to demonstrate to Elizabeth Thomas the true source of her problems and direct her to the best solution for them. He wrote:

> I love & Praise Him for dealing so tenderly with thee but thou shalt soon find more depths of love & tenderness in His compassionate Heart . . . I doubt not but thy Heaven born soul is more & more weary of that vile abominable & sinning nature that thou hadst from Satan . . . I am well persuaded thy cry is Lord let me be nothing that thou mayest be all in all to me & deliver me from myself.[53]

Similarly, in a letter to another unnamed correspondent, Harris once more utilised carefully selected scriptural principles to point the reader towards the resolution of her problems. His emphasis on the positive didactic purpose of spiritual trials and temptations was just part of the theological rationale that lay behind Harris's approach to his pastoral counselling. If trials were intended to have a sanctifying effect and to spur Methodists on to live better and more wholehearted Christian lives, Harris assumed the role of schoolmaster, whose function it was to interpret the significance of these trials and to encourage individuals to persevere and draw the right lessons from them. To this end he counselled:

> You are taught to wait all your appointed time, till your Charge come. – He will come, and will not tarry: and the lower he humbles us, the higher he raises us up again.[54]

One of the most effective techniques that Harris employed was to place his converts' problems within an eschatological context by focussing on the long-term significance of the international evangelical movement. The early Methodists' belief that they were part of the fast approaching millennial reign of Christ, led them to locate themselves in the vanguard of the cosmic struggle between the kingdom of God and the kingdom of the devil.[55] For example, in a letter to Jane Godwin in March 1743, after

---

[52] For more, see Ian Breward, 'William Perkins and the Origins of Reformed Casuistry', *The Evangelical Quarterly*, XL, I (1968), 3–20; D. Dewey Wallace, *Puritans and Predestination: Grace in English Protestant Thought, 1525–1695* (Chapel Hill, 1982).
[53] NLW, Trevecka 797, Howel Harris to Elizabeth Thomas (10 February 1743).
[54] 'A Letter from Mr. Howel Harris, to a Sister under Trials', in Lewis (ed.), *Weekly History*, 53 (Saturday, 10 April 1742).
[55] For example, see John F. Wilson (ed.), *The Works of Jonathan Edwards, IX: a history of the work of redemption* (New Haven, 1989), p. 353. For the context of

addressing her particular pastoral difficulties, Harris reminded her of the latest events of the international revival and how, despite obvious setbacks both individually and corporately, 'the work goes still on sweeter and sweeter'.[56]

For many, joining the Methodist movement could entail considerable personal sacrifice. Membership often resulted in bitter criticism and, at times, violent and other forms of persecution. For the majority, opposition took the often hidden form of the disapproval of family members, or of alienation between husbands and wives, children and parents, neighbours and old friends. Membership of the revival was, therefore, not something that was usually embarked upon lightly, but demanded remarkable commitment and copious reserves of stamina and resilience. References to this kind of community disapproval are largely absent from the pages of *The Weekly History*, most probably because for many it was an accepted part of their daily lives and, therefore, not regarded as worthy of too much complaint! There can be little doubt, though, that the loss of friends, the gossip of neighbours and members of one's extended family or, more seriously, the possibility of losing one's livelihood, all the more public in the small closely-knit village communities in which most Welsh Methodists tended to live,[57] was more difficult to bear than the extant records indicate, despite the obvious stoicism of the first generation of converts.

However, the threat of more overt violence and intimidation was never very far away, especially during the revival's first decade. The Methodists, of course, lived in unusually tense political times. Fears that their enthusiasm was a reversion to the kind of individualistic religious anarchy of the mid-seventeenth century held particular resonance for the Hanoverians, ever on their guard against the threat of a possible Jacobite rebellion. The Methodists, therefore, became an easy target for mob violence, often inspired by the local clergy and landowners who believed that their authority was under threat. William Seward's death at the hands

---

Edwards's work see John F. Wilson, 'History, Redemption and the Millennium', in Hatch and Stout (eds), *Jonathan Edwards and the American Experience*, pp. 131–41.

[56] NLW, Trevecka 827, Howel Harris to Jane Godwin (25 March 1743).

[57] J. D. Walsh, 'Methodism and the Mob in the Eighteenth Century', in G. J. Cuming and D. Baker (eds), *Studies in Church History, 8: popular belief and practice* (Cambridge, 1972), p. 213.

of a mob at Hay-on-Wye in 1740[58] sent shock waves through the Movement, and the revivalists had to quickly improvise with an explanatory theology of persecution that reinforced traditional Calvinistic ideas of Divine Providence, stressing God's ultimate sovereignty over every aspect of life and death.[59] A letter from Sarah, the wife of Samuel Mason, the printer, and one of Harris's closest London friends, illustrates the extent to which these ideas had been adopted by members of the revival:

> The death of Mr Seward was awfully surprising . . . Why did blessed Seward leave this world so soon, why did so bright a star thus set at noon. But stay what bold enquirer asks to know . . . can we fathom wisdoms deep design. By our undiminished reasons . . . let all agree in silence to adore and by remarking querys sin no more But humbly wait the Glorious Rich display of God's Perfection in the rising way. They'll brightly shine in one eternal Ray Amen Hallelujah.[60]

Although Seward's martyrdom was unique in the history of the revival, *The Weekly History* and its successors published colourful accounts of Methodists who got into close scrapes with angry mobs and skirmishes with ecclesiastical and secular authorities. For many, physical persecution could be fairly superficial resulting in little more than mild embarrassment and inconvenience. For example, two Methodists were ambushed and catapulted into a river by a rope stretched across a bridge as they returned from a meeting in November 1744,[61] and three exhorters were overcharged the toll when they crossed a bridge over the river Wye in Breconshire.[62] Other more prominent figures faced the full censure of the ecclesiastical establishment. James Ingram, Howel Harris's servant and travelling companion, was carted off to Brecon gaol by a press gang. Even after his release, which Harris had secured with the assistance of the Countess of Huntingdon and James Erskine, Lord Grange, Ingram lived

---

[58] Geoffrey L. Fairs, 'Notes on the Death of William Seward at Hay, 1740', *Cylchgrawn Cymdeithas Hanes Methodistiaidd Calfinaidd*, LVIII, 1 (March, 1973), 12–18.

[59] Alexandra Walsham, *Providence in Early Modern England* (Oxford, 1999), pp. 8–32.

[60] NLW, Trevecka 316, Sarah Mason to Howel Harris (28 February 1741).

[61] 'Mr J. W. to Brother J. E. (20 November 1744)', in Lewis (ed.), *Christian History*, VI, IV, pp. 69–72.

[62] 'The Copy of a Letter from Brother J__s to Brother Cennick (26 March 1743)', in Lewis (ed.), *An Account of the Most Remarkable Particulars*, III, II, pp. 3–6.

with the possibility of being dragooned into military service at any time.[63] However, none matched James Beaumont for the relish with which he seemed to attract the hostility of the mob.[64] On two occasions in 1742 he found himself threatened with imprisonment in the stocks after the heckling of mobs had failed to silence him. Whilst the motivation for such harassment arose as much from the belligerence of individuals like Beaumont, there is little doubt that it was also related to the way the Methodists were thought to threaten the traditional way of life of many remote Welsh villages. The Methodists were deeply distrusted in these communities because of their disdain for many aspects of popular culture.[65] Although it is too early to speak of Methodism as an agent of social control in these formative years, for numerically, of course, they were still few in number,[66] there is little doubt that the revival was largely successful in countering the belief in magic and superstition, and weaning local people away from popular entertainments like theatre, dancing, cock-fighting and bull-baiting. Although many historians have been quick to condemn the Methodists for suppressing traditional festivities,[67] they usually fail to recognise that they provided what was for many a far more attractive counter-culture. Emotionally-charged religious revivals, comm-unal gatherings to hear famous preachers like Harris, Whitefield and

---

[63] See 'From Brother James Ingram, a Welch Exhorter, to a Brother in London (19 June 1744)', in Lewis (ed.), *Christian History*, V, IV, pp. 68–9, and Geraint Tudur, *Howell Harris: from conversion to separation, 1735–1750* (Cardiff, 2000), p. 143.

[64] See Geraint Tudur, '"Like a Right Arm and a Pillar": the Story of James Beaumont', in Robert Pope (ed.), *Honouring the Past and Shaping the Future: religious and Biblical studies in Wales. Essays in honour of Gareth Lloyd Jones* (Leominster, 2003), pp. 138–9.

[65] For an indication of the prevalence of popular beliefs and customs in early eighteenth century Wales, see Geraint H. Jenkins, 'Popular Beliefs in Wales from Restoration to Methodism', *Bulletin of the Board of Celtic Studies*, XXVII, 3 (November, 1977), 440–62.

[66] See J. D. Walsh, 'Elie Halévy and the Birth of Methodism', *Transactions of the Royal Historical Society*, 25 (1975), 11–17; W. R. Ward, 'Was there a Methodist Evangelistic Strategy in the Eighteenth Century?', in Nicholas Tyacke (ed.), *England's Long Reformation, 1500–1800* (London, 1998), pp. 285–305; David Hempton, 'Established Churches and the Growth of Religious Pluralism: a case study of Christianisation and secularisation in England since 1700', in Hugh McLeod and Wener Ustorf (eds), *The Decline of Christendom in Western Europe, 1750–2000* (Cambridge, 2003), pp. 81–90.

[67] For example, see David Hempton and John Walsh, 'E. P. Thompson and Methodism', in Mark A. Noll (ed.), *God and Mammon: Protestants, money and the market, 1790–1860* (New York, 2001), pp. 108–10.

Daniel Rowland, and the reassuring fellowship of the society meetings, meant that for many upwardly-mobile middling people, evangelical religion was compellingly attractive.

The political insecurities of the mid-1740s forced the Methodists in England and Wales to repeatedly protest their loyalty to both the Hanoverians and the Established Church of England. Between 1744 and 1745, when political stability was particularly threatened, Howel Harris was among the first to urge his fellow Methodists to set aside special seasons for prayer and fasting to invoke God's help for the deliverance of the nation. To James Beaumont he wrote in February 1744:

> We are like to be called to the Field of Blood soon . . . the French fleet now lay at anchor in one of our Ports being come over with a firm Resolution to dethrone his Majesty & set the Pretenders Son of the Throne of England & consequently not only take away all Toleration & liberty of Protestants but establish Popery again . . . Next Monday we have settled for fasting and prayer for the Kg & Nation we all hold it our Duty to preach loyalty to the King set over us by the Ld & as he is a Protestant & tolerates the true Religion & as he is laid deeply on our hearts too.[68]

It was the guarantee of the continuation of religious toleration that led the Methodists, like all other Protestant groups, to enthusiastically support George II. Methodists in Wales, led by Harris, fasted and interceded for their king and his armies, and avidly followed the course of military campaigns in Europe and further afield. From being suspected of subversion, Jacobitism and even Popery, and at times facing the full brunt of mob violence, the Methodists reinvented themselves as model subjects of the British state. When the Jacobite armies were finally defeated, they enthusiastically celebrated the nation's deliverance and Harris rejoiced that 'our national trials have been . . . instrumental in turning the hearts of many to the King'.[69] In one sense, old tensions with the Church were forgotten during these years as even erstwhile opponents came together to resist their common enemy. Linda Colley has persuasively argued that the prevalence of popular and elite anti-Catholicism during these years, born of repeated conflict with France and Spain, worked to focus attention on the elements that united the peoples of the British Isles rather than upon those things that divided them. The most potent unifying factor of all was

---

[68] NLW, Trevecka 1118, Howel Harris to James Beaumont (18 February 1744).
[69] 'From Mr Howel Harris, at Trevecca, near the Hay, in Breconshire, South Wales to Mr Thomas Adams, at the Tabernacle House, near Moorfields, London', in Lewis (ed.), *Christian History* (1747), pp. 21–3.

Protestantism, and when that appeared to be most at threat, many clung to it tenaciously.[70]

For a few Welsh Methodists participation in the international revival did not operate on a solely spiritual level. The individualism inherent in the evangelical message was ameliorated to some extent by an attempt to create a community based on the principal of mutual responsibility, not only for the spiritual well-being of every member but for their temporal and practical needs too. During his time as sole editor of *The Christian's Amusement*, John Lewis attempted to establish a network of sympathetic contacts to whom converts could turn for practical help, particularly when membership of the revival resulted in financial hardship.[71] The response to his suggestion was initially very positive. He was able to advertise the services of Sister Betty Angus who owned a clothes shop[72] and Brother Jacob Humphreys, who was a watch and clockmaker.[73] We know also that Howel Harris later benefited from the largesse of a number of wealthy Methodists who kept him clothed, fed and even helped him furnish his home after his marriage in 1744.[74] Lewis's attempt at pooling resources in this way undoubtedly harked back to the communitarian spirit that characterised the Apostolic Church and was further evidence of the preoccupation with some of the ideals of primitive Christianity.[75] The experiment did not last very long. While the London Methodists remained within the confines of the Fetter Lane Society it had the potential to work well, but once an element of competition had entered the revival, following the divisions between the Moravians, Arminians and Calvinists, there was less opportunity for sharing practical resources as individuals and groups became more competitive and less cooperative.

---

[70] See Linda Colley, *Britons. Forging the Nation, 1707–1837* (London, 1992), pp. 11–54; Colin Haydon, *Anti-Catholicism in Eighteenth-Century England: a political and social study* (Manchester, 1993), pp. 129–63.

[71] 'Editorial Comments', in John Lewis (ed.), *The Christian's Amusement containing Letters Concerning the Progress of the Gospel both at Home and Abroad etc. Together with an Account of the Waldenses and Albigenses*, no. 13.

[72] Ibid.

[73] Ibid.

[74] NLW, Calvinist Methodist Archive, Howel Harris's Diary (hereafter NLW, Howel Harris's Diary) 41, entries dated 13–15 March 1739; NLW, Trevecka 404, George Whitefield to Howel Harris (28 November 1741); NLW, Trevecka 2811, Howel Harris to Anne Williams (18 February 1744).

[75] J. D. Walsh, 'John Wesley and the Community of Goods', in Keith Robbins (ed.), *Protestant Evangelicalism. Britain, Ireland, Germany and America, c.1750–1950: essays in honour of W. R. Ward* (Oxford, 1990), pp. 25–50.

This is not to say that the communitarian ideal evaporated altogether, but for many this was most commonly expressed through their responses to advertisements for the latest religious literature. It was mainly through adverts in *The Weekly History* that the writings of Whitefield, Jonathan Edwards and the Scottish Presbyterians, Ebenezer and Ralph Erskine,[76] found their way into Welsh homes. Harris was usually the immediate agency by which such religious literature was circulated, but some of his closest associates acted as links in the distribution chain. In March 1743 Thomas Bowen's requests for copies of the works of the Erskine brothers, and some of the hymns of John Cennick, to hand to other Welsh Methodists was characteristic of the way some individuals played a relatively unobtrusive part in the international revival.[77]

A select few discovered that their involvement in the international revival became the means by which they found their marriage partners. In Wales, two individuals in particular stand out. Elizabeth James had married George Whitefield in November 1741 and Sarah Gwynne, daughter of Marmaduke Gwynne of Garth married Charles Wesley in August 1747, a relationship that seems to have developed out of the close friendship between her family and the Wesley brothers. Whilst these two marriages were clearly exceptional, not every Welsh Methodist married one of the revivalists, others married partners that they met in their local societies or at the various local and national Methodist gatherings which they regularly attended. Crucially, many of these marriages did not take place without Howel Harris's recommendation. For example, Elizabeth Thomas's marriage to John Sims in January 1746 only finally went ahead after Harris had assured her father of Sims' good character,[78] and Watkin Watkins felt that he had to seek Harris's advice before he married Hester Parry in 1744.[79] These marriages are indicative of some of the most powerful motives compelling grass-roots Methodists to participate in the international revival, namely fellowship, friendship and the security of a well-structured support network.[80]

Finally, many Welsh Methodists had a vested interest in the progress of the revival overseas. Their support of Whitefield's Orphan house

---

[76] See Nigel M. de S. Cameron (ed.), *Dictionary of Scottish Church History and Theology* (Edinburgh, 1993), pp. 35–6, 298–302.

[77] NLW, Trevecka 826, Thomas Bowen to Howel Harris (25 March 1743).

[78] NLW, Trevecka 1348, Howel Harris to John Thomas (5 August 1745).

[79] NLW, Trevecka 1158, Watkin Watkins to Howel Harris (March 1744).

[80] Eryn Mant White, '"The World, the Flesh and the Devil" and the Early Methodist Societies of South West Wales', *Transactions of the Honourable Society of Cymmrodorion*, 3 (1997), 48, 54.

project at Bethesda, Georgia, came to assume particular importance during
the mid-1740s. Whitefield had intended the Georgia orphanage to be a
place to 'preach chiefly to children's hearts . . . [and] instruct them by the
Church of England's Articles'.[81] Its funding relied on the enthusiasm of
his fellow Methodists in England and Wales, who were encouraged to give
what money they could spare in support of the project.[82] The Welsh
Methodists wholeheartedly responded to Whitefield's appeals for help,
and they followed its progress closely through many of the letters written
by either its superintendent, some of its residents or Whitefield himself,
which were circulated in the letter writing network and printed in *The
Weekly History*. Howel Harris, predictably, became one of the most
enthusiastic fund-raisers for the project. He publicised it wherever he
went, usually appealing for funds at the close of sermons, when his
listeners were emotionally most vulnerable and, therefore, more amenable
to persuasion. Visiting south-west Wales in February 1748, Harris wrote:

> Last night aftr Bro Wms preachd I discoursed a little . . . I opend abt ye
> Orphan House & made a collectn here & gatherd some many aftr openg ye
> Mattr & shewg home how God has placd us in various stations in this Life
> to some poor & some rich &c shewd how I was free to beg for God's poor
> opend . . . [at] ye orphan house.[83]

Two days later at Penywennallt in Carmarthenshire, he collected £1. 11s.
6d.[84] The next day he added together all the money that he had collected
on the tour and recorded a grand total of £41. 12s. ½d. from the members
of just thirty-six societies.[85] By contributing financially to this
philanthropic venture the Welsh Methodists were claiming a stake in the
worldwide propagation of the evangelical faith. Their not inconsiderable
financial sacrifices were repaid by the receipt of regular up-to-date
information about some of the ways in which their money was being
used.[86]

---

[81] Quoted in Lambert, '*Pedlar in Divinity*', p. 156.
[82] For more on the Orphan House see Neil J. O'Connell, 'George Whitefield and
Bethesda Orphan-House', *Georgia Historical Quarterly*, 54 (1970), 41–62; Boyd
S. Schlenther, *Queen of the Methodists: the Countess of Huntingdon and the
eighteenth century crisis of faith and society* (Durham, 1997), pp. 83–95.
[83] NLW, Howel Harris's Diary 129, 5 February 1748.
[84] NLW, Howel Harris's Diary 129, 7 February 1748.
[85] NLW, Howel Harris's Diary 129 (inside front cover).
[86] 'The Copy of a Letter from Mr Periam, Schoolmaster at the Orphanhouse in
Georgia, to Bro S__s in London (May 1 1742), in Lewis (ed.), *An Account of the
Most Remarkable Particulars*, II, III, pp. 19–26; 'From Mr Jonathan Barber

Participation in the international evangelical network in such a wide variety of ways meant that many Welsh Methodists had a much more sophisticated sense of identity than has been often assumed. Despite some recent work that has attempted to show their close affinity with native Welsh culture,[87] there is little doubt that the early Welsh Methodists were capable of maintaining a fairly complex sense of their identity. As Geraint Tudur has amply demonstrated, Howel Harris was deeply conscious of his Welsh identity and remained committed, despite so many additional responsibilities, to Wales and his Welsh converts.[88] But Harris was also able to move in a number of circles at the same time with apparent ease. At various times he confessed to being a Methodist, an Evangelical, a Calvinist, a Protestant and a Christian, all identities that indicate various layers of local, national and international allegiance. He and Whitefield had been the architects of the merging of English and Welsh Calvinistic Methodism in January 1743, a fact that ensured that the fortunes of the two revivals would be inextricably linked.[89] There is also little doubt that many Welsh Methodists were just as conscious of belonging to a trans-national and trans-Atlantic evangelical movement as they were of being part of a distinctively Welsh awakening. But perhaps even more fundamental than this, they saw themselves as small cogs in the great history of redemption. They were, first and foremost, citizens of the worldwide kingdom of God, and fully expected all temporary national and denominational divisions to be subsumed once the millennial age had dawned, an age that many of them firmly believed was imminent. It was this consideration more than any other that led many of them to seek fellowship with those from other countries who were also expecting to be caught up in this same cosmic drama.

(Superintendent as to Spiritual Affairs) of the Orphan house in Georgia, to the Rev. Mr Whitefield (Sept. 3 1743)', in Lewis (ed.), *Christian History*, V, I, pp. 63–6.

[87] E. Wyn James, '"The New Birth of a People": Welsh Language and Identity and the Welsh Methodists, *c.*1740–1820', in Robert Pope (ed.), *Religion and National Identity: Wales and Scotland c.1700–2000* (Cardiff, 2001), pp. 14–42.

[88] Geraint Tudur, '"Thou Bold Champion, Where art Thou": Howell Harris and the issue of Welsh identity', in Pope (ed.), *Religion and National Identity*, pp. 43–60.

[89] The merging of English and Welsh Calvinistic Methodism is discussed in considerable detail in Jones, '*A Glorious Work in the World*', pp. 191–238. Some additional contextual material may also be found in Alan Harding, *The Countess of Huntingdon's Connexion: a sect in action in eighteenth-century England* (Oxford, 2003).

CHAPTER SEVEN

'THE MOST SINGULAR AND ECCENTRIC LITTLE SECT OF THIS GENERATION': THE WHITE QUAKERS OF IRELAND, C.1840–1854

JAMES GREGORY

In early Victorian Britain, radicals were fascinated by the White Quakers of Ireland and examined their simple domestic arrangements, communism in property, opposition to taxation and tithes, hygienic and clothing reform, and alleged abandonment of marriage. Their guiding principles were promoted in print and observed in their meetings and occasional public appearances. Thus far, however, there has been relatively little written about this fascinating community.[1] This study locates the White Quakers in the broader context of the history of the Society of Friends (Quakers) in Ireland, studying their attitudes to Quakerism and religious authority. Although they clung to many of the practices of a 'Peculiar People',[2] their doctrines and way of life were viewed as scandalous by other Quakers and indeed society at large.

Joshua Jacob, the leader of the White Quakers, was born in the southern Irish 'Quaker town' of Clonmel,[3] so-called because of its importance as a centre of Quaker economic activity. His family were wealthy, but when their business collapsed Jacob was obliged to make his

---

[1] This chapter is based upon an earlier study provided in *Quaker Studies*. See James Gregory, 'Some account of the Progress of the Truth as it is in Jesus': The White Quakers of Ireland', *Quaker Studies*, 9, 1 (2004), 68–94.

[2] The term 'peculiar' is discussed in Thomas Clarkson, *A Portraiture of Quakerism* (3 vols. 2nd edn. London, 1908), I, pp. ii–iii. The terms 'Quakers', 'Friends' and the 'Society' will be used interchangeably in this study.

[3] See L. Boylan, 'Joshua Jacob, 1801–1877', *Journal of Co. Kildare Archaeological Society*, 16, 4 (1983/4), 349–54.

own way in the world. After receiving an education in England and Ireland he was apprenticed to a Dublin grocer and candlewick manufacturer, and later established a profitable business selling cheap packets of tea and sugar. His marriage to Sarah Fayle in 1829 produced seven children, and the Quaker community recognised his 'good standing'. They commented that he was 'a regular attender of meetings for worship and discipline, a good neighbour, kind to the poor, and greatly respected'.[4] Like many other conservative Friends, Jacob grew increasingly anxious that the Society was becoming more worldly.[5] In 1835, fearful that the morality of Friends was in jeopardy, he preached intemperately against Quaker worldliness.[6] Inevitably this aroused significant opposition, but his call for a return to the virtuous life found acceptance among 'the more rigid professors, in many of the Monthly Meetings', who shared Jacob's view.[7] Following his disownment in 1838 a 'chosen remnant' joined him to form a breakaway sect and Jacob was selected as their leader. Supporters included Jacob's brothers, Samuel and William, and his sister Mary, while others, as a consequence of Quaker 'endogamy', were his cousins.

The White Quakers, as the new group became known, were distinguished by the plain, undyed clothing they wore in contrast to the more familiar but, according to Jacob and his followers, unregenerate 'Black Quakers'. Jacob felt driven to give up his business interests, dispose of his furniture and household goods, and by 1842 had formulated a new code of conduct towards property and consumption for the White Quakers. Jabob's wife, Sarah, was 'united heart and hand' with his decisions and gave her support for the symbolic public destruction of decorated china and earthenware.[8] She proved to be an effective member of the women's meeting and played an important role in the crucial transitional phase.[9] Unfortunately her commitment to the White Quakers

---

[4] *National Anti-Slavery Standard* (New York), 28 October 1847, pp. 86–7.

[5] On this conservatism see E. H. Milligan, '"The Ancient Way": The Conservative Tradition in Nineteenth Century British Quakerism', *Journal of Friends' Historical Society (JFHS)*, 57, 1 (1994), 74–101; E. Isichei, *Victorian Quakers* (Oxford, 1970), pp. 16–25.

[6] An instance of his intemperancy occurred in 1837 at Samuel Bowley's funeral. He told mourners the deceased had been spiritually blind and unsanctified, though, according to the *Irish Friend*, Bowley was an esteemed Friend. See Mountmellick Friends, *Some account of the Progress as it is in Jesus* (Dublin, 1843–4. Hereafter cited as *Progress*), vol. 12; *Irish Friend* (December, 1837), p. 16.

[7] *Littell's Living Age* (New York), vol. 15, p. 184; 20 November 1847, p. 374; *National Anti-Slavery Standard*, 28 October 1847, p. 87.

[8] S. Greer, *Quakerism; or the story of my life* (Philadelphia, 1852), p. 379.

[9] Ibid., p. 377.

declined and she was subsequently ostracised by other members. In March 1843 Sarah and Jacob were divorced.[10] This was a regular occurrence as membership of the sect divided many families and friends. Members scorned their former friends, 'denouncing and inveighing all sorts of bitter things against . . . [those] who were unprepared to go the wholehog with them'.[11] The White Quakers were mostly from good families, comparatively well-educated, wealthy and of hitherto the 'highest respectability'.[12] About fifty adults joined the sect during the early 1840s, and their children were also raised according to the values of the White Quakers. Jacob set a personal example which ensured that members would 'learn to serve themselves in the creation; to make their own beds, and to clean their rooms every morning'.[13] Yet, despite welcoming 'all' to their meetings, the White Quakers, until the years leading to the Great Famine, had little success in recruiting from outside of the Quaker middle classes.[14] An exception to this was Isaac Dickenson, a painter, whose lower status was the subject of private reflection and public examination by Quaker opponents.[15] By the late-1840s recruits were drawn from humbler, non-Quaker backgrounds and few of the original members remained.

The sect's development from Jacob's disownment until late-1844 was recorded in *Some account of the Progress of the Truth as it is in Jesus*. This journal published in forty parts provides a documentary account of the sect's formation and later development, including a short pedigree of the Jacob family; the correspondence of both supporters and opponents; minutes of their meetings; and material relating to the sect's pre-history, most notably accounts of dreams from 1832 onwards.[16] This source is invaluable in that it provides a unique insight into the establishment of

---

[10] *Progress*, vols. 6, pp. 7, 9, 24; vol. 18, p. 43.

[11] *National Anti-Slavery Standard*, 28 October 1847, p. 87.

[12] Greer, *Quakerism*, p. 382. One Quaker, R. D. Webb, recalled that there were 'many rich people, particularly rich women'. See *Littell's Living Age*, vol. 15, p. 184; 20 November 1847, p. 374.

[13] *Progress*, vol. 7, p. 71.

[14] Ibid., vol. 37, p. 51.

[15] Ibid., vol. 4, p. 35; vol. 6, p. 41; vol. 7, pp. 40–1; vol. 17, p. 25. In vol. 38, p. 46 Dickenson was described as a 'Protestant'.

[16] This was published with a part number which was separately paginated. Though undated the parts (averaging 70 pages) can be dated from material published in each issue. Library of the Society of Friends, London (hereafter LSF) has two copies: the first is an incomplete set of four volumes, the other bound in three volumes. The first volume of the three-volume copy includes a MS index, contained in a notebook with a printed calendar for 1880–1.

several houses and meetings;[17] Jacob's imprisonment in Four Courts Marshalsea for the refusal to return money vested in the community but belonging to his deceased brother's children;[18] the 'putting away' of his wife Sarah and later 'marriage' in March 1843 to Abigail Beale (1797–1849); the enforced auction of goods at the community house at William Street, Dublin (October 1843)[19] and the establishment of a house at Usher's Quay.[20] The *Progress of Truth* ceased publication in late-1844,[21] but other accounts of the White Quaker community on the Newlands estate outside Dublin exist. This was portrayed as a cheerful and self-sufficient vegetarian paradise but in reality it was a failure.[22] By 1850 a significant number of the original group had deserted,[23] some doubtless prompted to leave by Jacob's controversial relationship with Abigail, and several female White Quakers had been 'rescued'.[24] With the early death of some members[25] few of the original community remained.[26] The sect began as an internal protest movement against moral failings, formed itself into a society of self-proclaimed authentic Quakers and later operated as a community with a mere handful of former Friends, albeit with a co-founder, still in charge.

The sect's religious and socio-political ideas were published and made

---

[17] Meetings existed at Dublin, Waterford, Mountmellick, Clonmel. On support elsewhere see *Progress*, vol. 28, pp. 25–7.

[18] Ibid., vol. 15, pp. 10–27.

[19] Ibid., vol. 17, pp. 43–9.

[20] A former hotel converted into a community house by workmen whose praise for the sect appeared in Ibid., vol. 40, pp. 64–5. For a description see Ibid., vol. 39, pp. 64–5 (by George Ruby, a Fourierist), pp. 66–7 (reprinted with other material in *New Moral World*, 28 September 1844, p. 112); *Family Herald* used his account, 27 April 1844, p. 814. For the critical White Quaker response see LSF, vol. D, fol. 224.

[21] *Lloyd's Weekly London Newspaper*, 20 October 1844, p. 5.

[22] Primary accounts of Newlands include: 'Singular Sects. A Day with the White Quakers', *Howitt's Journal*, 38 (18 September 1847), p. 18; summarised in *National Anti-Slavery Standard*, 28 October 1847 (and reprinted there, 4 November 1847, p. 92; and in *Chamber's Journal*; *Littell's Living Age*); *Reasoner*, 21 February 1849, p. 128; *Family Herald*, 1850, p. 154; Joseph Barker's *The People*, vol. 3, 25 (reprinted in *National Anti-Slavery Standard*, 24 October 1850, p. 88); *Newcastle Weekly Chronicle*, 15 January 1876. By 1851 the community was near Rathfarnham, see Boylan, 'Joshua Jacob', 353.

[23] For consequent desertions see *Progress*, vol. 7, pp. 26–8, 51.

[24] Ibid., vol. 6, pp. 36–8; vol. 7, pp. 22–3. For examples of abductees see Ibid., vol. 40, pp. 6–8.

[25] For example, Abigail Jacob died in 1849.

[26] Boylan, 'Joshua Jacob', 351.

manifest: 'We cannot call Christ our Saviour in sincerity without witnessing Him in this way.'[27] As they saw it, their task was:

> simply and entirely the work of God. Different from all other communities, we live by faith; no plans, no commerce, no speculations, no contrivances, no taking thought for the morrow, nor taking thought for any of those things which the nations of this world seek after, because our Father who hath begotten His Son in us, and has given us this faith, knoweth what he have need of, and will supply all our need.[28]

They rejected the world's 'heap of things'[29] and religious duties were privileged over family ties. Their lifestyle was chaste, temperate and healthy.[30] They rejected the services of physicians, lawyers, priests and servants, and assumed a pacifist position.[31] Ostentatious displays of wealth were frowned upon and they banned items, including chronometers, carpets, bells, mirrors, wallpaper, silverware, mahogany furniture, sofas and pictures.[32] For the White Quakers their needs were simple:

> Only a change of raiment, simply made without dye. We cook, bake and wash, scour the floors, make and mend our clothes and shoes; in which, as well as useful learning, the children are instructed, having no thoughts of toys or pastimes in use in the world.[33]

Obedience by children, and 'in all to the Spirit of God', was insisted on as 'unity is held in the bond of peace'.[34]

They regarded themselves as a 'pure body' attempting to reform a once highly favoured church.[35] They claimed a line of continuity with the first generation of Friends which had subscribed to the 'highest and purest standard of Christian religion and worship'.[36] The sect was not alone in seeking to return to that earlier period of asceticism. Tensions within the

---

[27] *Progress*, vol. 6, p. 45.
[28] Ibid., vol. 40, pp. 19–21 (p. 19).
[29] Ibid., p. 20.
[30] Ibid.
[31] Ibid.
[32] On 'plainness' as religious ideal, a symbol of spirituality, and aesthetic judgement see P. Collins, 'Quaker Plaining as Critical Aesthetic', *Quaker Studies*, 5, 2 (2001), 121–39.
[33] *Progress*, vol. 40, p. 20.
[34] Ibid.
[35] Ibid., vol. 4, p. 64. This argued that they were 'endeavouring to stand in the testimonies and practices of our ancient Friends'.
[36] Ibid., vol. 8, p. 23.

Society of Friends led to divisions. Friends such as John Wilbur and Joseph John Gurney sought to change the Society albeit in quite different ways.[37] In the *Progress of Truth,* Jacob reprinted John Barclay's letters (c.1818) against modernising children's religious education,[38] and one of his own letters written to Richard Allen in 1837 revealed his innate conservatism in describing the Moral Reform Society as 'inconsistent with the principles of our religious Society'. He was distressed 'to see those who profess the only guide into all truth, and dependence on it alone, now turning to this human invention as a substitute',[39] and that tracts full of 'modern trash . . . such as Gurney and others being too much resorted to and delighted in'.[40]

In their youth, Jacob, Abigail Beale and Mary Pim, had met and corresponded with John Conran (1739–1827), who had been involved in the late-eighteenth century Irish Quaker schism, and described as 'a champion in his day'.[41] Conran had a profound influence on Jacob following their meeting when he was an apprentice. He heard about sufferings at the hands of 'false brethren' and was charged with continuing Conran's defence of the doctrine of Christ's divinity. Jacob and his close friends were not only hostile towards 'evangelical' modernisers whose beliefs they interpreted as a danger equivalent to deism, but they publicly charged in speeches and publications their relatives, friends and 'weighty' brethren, with worldliness. The response to their assault on backsliding was expulsion. The issues were thoroughly aired, but Jacob's argument was effectively refuted by the large influential majority. Yet he refused to accept the decision of those he described as 'ranters, fanatics, heretics, deep dark spirits, Hicksites, unbelievers, without love, without natural affection, disturbers of the peace, mad, deluded, self-righteous, devils'.[42] Jacob's supporters, including women, were forcibly ejected from meeting houses.[43] Further response was shaped, naturally, by their subsequent

---

[37] For details of early-nineteenth century Irish 'heresies' as well as Hicksites, Beaconites and Gurneyite divisons but not White Quakerism see William Hodgson, *The Society of Friends in the Nineteenth Century: a historical view of the successive convulsions and schisms therein during that period* (2 vols. Philadelphia, 1875–6).

[38] *Progress*, vol. 40, pp. 22–31.

[39] Ibid., vol. 18, p. 12 (letter dated 28 June 1837).

[40] Ibid., vol. 1, p. 16.

[41] Ibid., vol. 6, p. 39. See entry in LSF, MS 'Dictionary of Quaker Biography'. For details of the schism see Hodgson, *Society of Friends in the Nineteenth Century*, I, ch. 2. For a letter from Conran to Abigail Beale see *Progress*, vol. 14, pp. 46–8.

[42] *Progress*, vol. 4, p. 29 (Mary Pim to the English Quaker Sarah Squire).

[43] Ibid., pp. 16–18.

activity as a separate sect. The Society's fears were borne out and this led to a formal declaration of the sect's schismatic status. When *The Times* reported the sect's extraordinary behaviour in Waterford in 1842, London Friends moved swiftly to distance themselves from this by issuing a statement confirming that Jacob was no longer a Quaker.[44]

Behaviour on both sides was intemperate. White Quakers attacked their opponents even though this publicised family quarrels and hostilities, and complicated the schism.[45] The legal proceedings by Joseph Beale against Jacob and his sister-in-law, Anne Jacob, in defence of her children's inheritance, added to the tensions. According to the sect's decision to pool all property, £9,000 had been placed in common funds by Anne Jacob. Beale, acting as the family's 'nearest friend', alleged that Anne was weak-minded and that Jacob had applied unusual pressure to persuade followers, particularly females, to surrender property amounting almost to £20,000.[46] Individual Quakers appealed to the authorities and resorted to disreputable tactics such as sending people to beg charity from the sect in order to bankrupt or embarrass them.[47] Handbills and papers spread misinformation and angry words were exchanged.[48] Following the allegation that White Quakers had embraced the sexual immorality of Owenite free-love under the guise of religion, they received anonymous letters which condemned Abigail and her mother-in-law as harlots.[49] The sect received a large number of hostile letters and, despite the claim to high moral ground, some couched their criticisms in extraordinarily vulgar terms. One correspondent, upbraiding the sect's leader for his illicit

---

[44] *The Times*, 7 January 1842, p. 5.
[45] For example, *Progress*, vol. 3, p. 30. For Joseph Beale's business fraud, and William Beale's 'awful conduct' and excessive drinking see Ibid., vol. 40, pp. 50–1.
[46] Ibid., vol. 15, pp. 10–18. For Jabob's comments on Beale's character see Ibid., pp. 19–27.
[47] Ibid., vol. 3, p. 71.
[48] See the hostile paper reprinted in Ibid., vol. 27, pp. 33–4.
[49] For example, a letter from a Waterford Quaker. See Ibid., vol. 7, pp. 33–5. For likening Elizabeth Beale to Jezebel see Ibid., vol. 6, p. 54, and for the Owenite movement see W. H. G. Armytage, *Heavens below. Utopian experiments in England, 1560–1690* (London, 1961), pp. 202–3; B. Taylor, *Eve and the New Jerusalem. Socialism and feminism in the nineteenth century* (London, 1983), pp. 80–82, 174–5; E. Royle, *Robert Owen and the Commencement of the Millennium: a study of the harmony community* (Manchester, 1998), p. 152; J. E. M. Latham, *Search for a New Eden. James Pierrepont Greaves (1777–1842): the sacred socialist and his followers* (London, 1999), p. 172; G. Malmgreen, 'Ann Knight and the Radical Subculture', *Quaker History*, 71 (1982), 110.

relationship with Abigail Beale, graphically referred to Jacob's 'Tea-Pot as it is technically called Poking its nose into forbidden Ground'.[50] Such coarse language merely confirmed the sect's view that the Society had itself degenerated into immorality.

The White Quaker episode deeply embarrassed, pained and shamed Friends. Their publications exposed family conflicts and the alleged moral failings of prominent southern Irish Quakers. They caused rifts between husbands, wives and children, and appeared to advocate free-love. The Society sought to suppress public knowledge of the schism and avoided discussing the affair in its journals. Only opaque allusions were made in one article in *The Friend*, in response to a publication by a radical English supporter.[51] The conservative *Irish Friend* was also wary though isolated paragraphs and correspondence reveal that the concerns of the White Quakers were shared by others (assuming such letters were not from members of the sect). Between 1837 and 1841, the *Irish Friend* seemed receptive to new ideas. They contemplated serialising a biography of John Conran, printed calls for plain clothing and habitation, and inserted paragraphs which opposed the compromises involved in commercial activities.[52] Initially the journal appeared to align itself with the Society's rejection of the White Quaker position, and in June 1839 printed a passage from Isaac Penington's *Works* which enjoined tenderness in dealing with weaknesses, possibly as an allusion to the Society's new 'fault finders'.[53] Nonetheless, in May 1841 a letter was published from a correspondent in Islington which stressed the commitment of early Friends to the simple life.[54]

Refuge in another denomination was not really an option as Jacob believed that joining another religious group would involve compromising his attitude towards material consumption. He knew little about non-Quaker belief and practice since the Society had discouraged members from visiting other places of worship, and he had helped revive rules making such visits the grounds for discipline or disownment.[55] In

---

[50] *Progress*, vol. 28, p. 7.

[51] 'H', 'Communism not Christianity', *Friend*, 7 January 1849, pp. 8–9.

[52] *Irish Friend*, 1837 on Conran. For plain dress and dwellings, and concerns over trading see Ibid., August 1839, p. 63; September 1841, p. 135.

[53] Ibid., extract from Penington in June 1839, p. 47.

[54] Ibid., letter from 'J.P.', May 1841.

[55] On the misery of disownment and isolation through 'Peculiar Practices' after expulsion, for convinced 'birthright' Quakers if unable to accept the humiliating position of 'attender', see Isichei, *Victorian Quakers*, pp. 67, 134–9. Isichei emphasises the 'constant reminder' to English Quakers of American schisms but

1841 he disrupted the Anglican Christmas service at Waterford Cathedral and condemned Anglicanism as a lifeless 'whore'.[56] Catholicism was also strongly criticised for its Pope and priesthood, yet a handbill addressed *To those calling themselves Roman Catholics*, censured his gaoler's description of Catholics as unlettered and turbulent.[57] He objected to denominational labels, claiming that they were 'only Nicknames which the devil has invented to keep people from the right way of the Lord; there being in reality none but the two, the good and the bad, the sheep and the goats, the wise and the unwise'.[58] Jacob knew little or nothing of other sects, such as Southcottians and Swedenborgians, and was unimpressed by apologists.[59] He was acquainted with Shakerism through his contact with English reformers, but he rejected their commitment to the celibate life.[60] It is then all the more surprising that Jacob should convert to Catholicism after the disintegration of the White Quaker community. No doubt this was related to his subsequent marriage to a Catholic woman.[61]

White Quakers looked first of all to the Bible as a guide to their behaviour and thereafter sought counsel from early Quaker texts. Jacob also admired the writings of James, Bishop of Armagh, and, like many conservative Quakers, the quietist Madame Guyon. A paragraph in the *Progress of Truth* on the medieval Paterine sect, who opposed clerical marriage, represented a model of 'primitive' Christianity,[62] while extracts from the writings of George Fox, Isaac Penington, John Woolman and Robert Barclay were also included. In addition, Jacob privileged old prophetic material and the more recent prophecies of the Quaker, Job Scott. The *Progress of Truth* was not simply recommended reading, but was intended to modify and direct behaviour. Furthermore it offered a justification for some aspects of the White Quaker code, notably opposition to clergymen and church tithes, walking barefooted, and Jacob's deportment in prison, all of which emulated the activities of early Friends.[63]

Although the sect's behaviour and precepts seem exotic, their attitude

---

neglects the Irish warnings.
[56] *Progress*, vol. 8, p. 1 1.
[57] Reprinted in *Waterford Chronicle*, 25 March 1843.
[58] *Progress*, vol. 37, p. 37.
[59] Ibid., vol. 40, pp. 33, 67. Southcottianism is discussed in Ibid., vol. 7, p. 10 (following Barmby on Southcott, pp. 6–7).
[60] *New Moral World*, 15 February 1845, p. 268.
[61] Boylan, 'Joshua Jacob, 1801–1877', 349–54.
[62] On Armagh see *Progress*, vol. 9. On the Paterines see Ibid., vol. 18, p. 10.
[63] Ibid., vol. 7.

to religious authority was consonant with the debate which exercised the Quaker world at that time. This had particularly manifested itself in the American Hicksite schism and Beaconite-Gurneyite evangelicalism.[64] The Bible was a problematic text for the White Quakers on the grounds that the devil was the 'greatest scripturian in the world'.[65] Following a visit by William B. Kirkpatrick, a presbyterian minister, the *Progress of Truth* asserted that evangelicals knew nothing of God beyond 'what was gathered in human wisdom and natural understanding of man'.[66] White Quakers, therefore, maintained the 'Inward Light' tradition as the 'grand fundamental of White Quakerism',[67] but they were often criticised for it,[68] especially in 1851 during the controversy surrounding Sarah Greer's autobiography.[69] Quaker apologists and commentators were perhaps too embarrassed to allude to the sect in their critique of her work, but a non-Quaker, the Rev. Edward Nangle, believed that this was just a doctrinal development.[70] This emphasis on the 'Inward Light' led to charges of antinomianism, especially as the *Progress of Truth* cited the writings of the seventeenth century antinomian, William Dell.[71] Jacob and others repudiated the charge and White Quakers denied that their beliefs were linked with Ranter sectarians and their concept of sin.[72] In 1840 the White Quaker, Rebecca Ridgway, vehemently denied the Ranter connection as they had been 'an immoral loose people who gave out, that what was sinful in others was not sin in themselves, and consequently they were guilty of many gross sins; they used to go into the Meetings of our

---

[64] The Gurneyite journal, *Inquirer*, associated the current crisis in Irish Quakerism with Hicksism when making reference to the silencing of a minister and office-bearers at Waterford. See *Inquirer*, November 1838, p. 350.

[65] *Progress*, vol. 7, p. 58.

[66] Ibid., vol. 28, p. 33.

[67] See LSF, Volume D, fol. 224.

[68] See 'N.B.L.', in *Progress*, vol. 8, p. 57. In a letter the English writer Mary Kelty warned 'against believing every spirit'. See Ibid., vol. 12, p. 25.

[69] Greer, *Quakerism*.

[70] The Rev. E. Nangle, *Letter upon Quakerism, or Truth and Error* (London, 1855), p. 25. Quaker responses to Greer include Anon., *Vindication of Friends; (by one not a member) from slanders contained in a book just published entitled Quakerism, or the story of my life* (Philadelphia, 1852); S. Elly, *Ostentation: or critical remarks on Quakerism, or the story of my life* (Dublin, 1852). In the *British Friend* no allusion to the sect is made, see *British Friend*, February 1853, pp. 47–50; April 1853, p. 103.

[71] *Progress*, vol. 4, pp. 8–9; vol. 19, p. 3; vol. 22, pp. 28–31.

[72] Ibid., vol. 3, pp. 22–33.

early Friends singing and dancing'.[73] Jacob viewed free will and free-thought as 'infidelity'. True earthly joy came through the 'leadings and guidance, prompting and restraints' of the Holy Spirit and not through reason, whose right place was 'subservient to revelation'.[74] Action had to be understood and presented as following God's will.[75] Belief in the 'Inward Light' meant a continued watchfulness for the guidance of the Holy Spirit.[76] White Quakers believed backsliders succumbed to the devil's temptations, and their vehement condemnation of this contrasted sharply with their private acts of charity and philanthropy.[77] The return to purity, symbolised through plain clothing and habitation, simple food and subsistence living expressed a clear division between the damned and those working for their salvation.[78]

Though denying the supremacy of Scripture, White Quakers were steeped in it, especially the Old Testament and the Book of Revelation. Quotations from the Bible constantly appeared in their writings and this was partly at least a conscious decision to demonstrate that they were not heretics, though critics naturally viewed this as hypocrisy. Dreams were taken very seriously as they were thought to be significant, offering warnings or comfort from God. Consequently dreams were carefully recorded so that they could be interpreted by the members. The sect's journal recorded numerous personal tests by Jacob and others aimed at scrutinising obedience and discipline. Jacob required members to demonstrate an absolute obedience, for 'this people must be a separate people, not a mixed people; and to enable them to stand for the honour of God, they must go through the trials, siftings and provings that are appointed for their purification'.[79] Some of these tests were cruel, often they were very exacting. One winter morning, a wealthy and aged White Quaker woman was instructed to eat a bowl of stirabout on the steps of the Bank of Ireland, dressed only in thin white calico and without shoes.[80] This test could be read as Jacob's determination to humiliate her beyond what was reasonable and break her free will. On the other hand, it could be

---

[73] Ibid., vol. 15, p. 52.

[74] Ibid., vol. 8, p. 72.

[75] Ibid., vol. 3, p. 4.

[76] Ibid., vol. 3, pp. 22–3.

[77] Ibid., vol. 32, p. 44.

[78] Ibid., vol. 28, p. 33. For Jacob's views on transgressions 'in likeness of Adam's transgression', and the 'new creation in the soul of man' see Ibid., vol. 32, p. 22.

[79] Ibid., vol. 1, p. 57. This refers to the disownment of Mary Keegan in December 1842.

[80] Greer, *Quakerism*, p. 383.

argued that she accepted the trial willingly and was happy to prove her acceptance of the simple life. But the incident may have arisen from more complex motivation. The Bank had become the target of Jacob's hostility because he believed their officials had incorrectly weighed his gold coins.[81] It may be that in requiring her to humble herself in that particular place, he was as much concerned with publicising the Bank's over-zealous profit-making as he was with her salvation. His early followers were mostly wealthy and, therefore, unaccustomed to hard manual work. It was alleged that a 'delicate young lady' had died from overwork when ordered to wash clothes for the whole community.[82] Both of these examples need to be viewed with caution as they were first reported in Greer's questionable autobiography and may have been fabricated by opponents who sought to bring the White Quakers into disrepute.

According to one critical observer the group was a 'white nunnery' where recruits were required to give up their own freedom and submit to the collective will of the community.[83] James 'Shepherd' Smith, an English radical, thought that Jacob did not exercise real authority and that there was 'no appearance of any regular system of government amongst them'.[84] This was patently inaccurate as the usual Quaker practices were instituted and closely followed, including disciplinary meetings, private admonitions, testimonies and letters of disownment. Jacob's leadership rested upon his perceived status as a prophet and despite his disingenuous claims that he was not 'leader' of a sect his authority was strictly imposed. Any questioning of his authority or acts of disobedience were swiftly followed by disownment.[85] Even though Jacob always spoke confidently about his mission, evidence suggests that he constantly wrestled with his doubts.[86] At times of spiritual crisis Jacob turned to Abigail Beale, and her importance to the establishment and early fortunes of the sect should be fully recognised. An obituary in the *Spirit of the Times*, an English radical publication, described her as 'the master-mind and guiding spirit'.[87] While Jacob was clearly the leader of the White Quakers, Abigail's determination and courage proved crucial to the sect's survival, especially

---

[81] *Progress*, vol. 1, pp. 11–15.

[82] Greer, *Quakerism*, p. 383.

[83] *Progress*, vol. 6, p. 22.

[84] *Family Herald*, 27 April 1844, p. 814.

[85] The tract 'Creed and Character of White Quakerism' alleged Jacob was 'spiritual father, ecclesiastical dictator and temporal treasurer'. *Progress*, vol. 32, p. 39. For Jacob's denials see Ibid., vol. 25, p. 29.

[86] Ibid., vol. 35, p. 9.

[87] *Spirit of the Times* (London), 24 November 1849, p. 119.

when he was incarcerated in Four Courts prison for almost five years for refusing to return the inheritance of his nephews and nieces which he had applied to the community's accounts. By default she assumed the leadership in his absence. Abigail, who came from a prominent southern Irish Quaker family, undoubtedly drew upon her formative experiences as the daughter of a manufacturer.[88] Before her departure from the Society of Friends, she was outspoken in her condemnation of those who displayed vanity and worldliness. Together with two other women overseers of the Waterford monthly meeting, Sarah Warring and Anne Goouch, she was disowned after being charged with disrupting Quaker families. At the time, Abigail alleged that this was defamation of character but nevertheless her attempt to prove her innocence failed. Following the intervention of the men's meeting she was disowned as a delinquent.[89] Abigail's role in the White Quakers, underpinned by her intimate relationship with Jacob, was not always well-received by members of the community. Her overbearing manner caused tensions and the testimony of two men who left the sect, Isaac Dickenson and William Roberts, drew attention to her 'hardness' towards them.[90] Abigail's role should be placed in the context of White Quaker ideas on gender and sexuality, which contributed so much to their notoriety in general and the tense relations with mainstream Quakerism. These ideas, and views about celibacy which they rejected, and nudism which they were falsely accused of, were extremely controversial in a period when respectability depended upon the proven virtues of women and the sanctity of marital relations.[91]

The Society of Friends was deeply concerned by the sect's attitude towards commerce and capitalism. J. Goodwin Barmby, the communist, distributed White Quaker literature and styled the sect 'the Communist Church in Ireland'.[92] The White Quakers believed that their community of

---

[88] *Progress*, vol. 3, p. 33.

[89] Ibid., vol. 13, pp. 29–30.

[90] Ibid., vol. 38, pp. 49–54, 71.

[91] Martin Meeker, 'The Doctrine of the Inner Light. Evangelicalism and women in the Society of Friends', in the web-published *Ex Post Facto, the Journal of the History Students Association, San Francisco State University*, 1994, III (1994). An e-text version (http://userwww.sfsu.edu/~epf/1994/friends.html–accessed January 2009) provides the context for this. See also S. S. Holton and M. Allen, 'Officers and Services: women's pursuit of sexual equality within the Society of Friends, 1873–1907', *Quaker Studies*, 2 (1997), 1–29.

[92] For Barmby see Armytage, *Heavens Below*, pp. 196–208; Armytage, 'The Journalistic Activities of J. Goodwin Barmby between 1841 and 1848', *Notes and Queries*, April 1956, 166–9; Taylor, *Eve and the New Jerusalem*, pp. 172–82. Note that *Lloyd's Weekly London Newspaper* described him as a White Quaker. See

goods represented a return to 'primitive Christianity', and according to the *Progress of Truth* community of goods involved 'enjoying all things in common together' so that there would be no distinction between 'those who brought thousands into the community' and others.[93] To that end, new members were encouraged to auction their possessions. This tested wealthy supporters' commitment to the community as well as facilitating public declarations of faith. It also, of course, secured much needed funds for the White Quakers. For example, in February 1844, Elizabeth Pim auctioned her mahogany furniture and delftware.[94] Not everyone was willing to give up their goods in this way. Anne Isaac Jacob was disowned for her refusal to sell on her luxuries to others even though she argued that such transactions encouraged the acquisitiveness of others. In her view, the goods should have been destroyed.[95] This case highlights the difficulties faced by the White Quakers in their desire to reject nineteenth-century materialism. The problem was that the community could not sustain itself and continue to grow without recourse to funds. This central ambiguity demonstrates that Jacob's ideology was not fully thought out and he was frequently found wanting whenever he was embroiled in financial transactions. The court case and his encounter with the Bank of Ireland both reveal an acquisitive streak in his character that is entirely at odds with the outspoken condemnation of worldliness, which precipitated the establishment of the sect in the first place.

Jacob and the White Quakers rejected the capitalist and commercial life which the Society of Friends had so enthusiastically embraced. A dream set in Dublin Bay, and subsequently published in the *Progress of Truth* in 1843, reflected upon his condemnation of the Friends' business activities; the word 'Grab-all' graphically conveyed his outright rejection of their acquisitive way of life.[96] He kept several tracts which questioned the growth of 'mammonism' in the Society.[97] Some of these anti-capitalist ideas had been formed when he was a young apprentice. Later, when he acquired his own business, Jacob became concerned about the long hours he had to work in order to turn a profit. He could have combined with other shopkeepers to press for shorter hours, but instead he chose to close the shop 'on all occasions and times, when higher duties called, having

---

Lloyd's Weekly London Newspaper, 6 October 1844, p. 4.

[93] *Progress*, vol. 37, pp. 47–8; vol. 32, p. 1.

[94] Ibid., vol. 33, p. 47.

[95] Ibid., vol. 14, pp. 11–12; vol. 33, pp. 46–7.

[96] Ibid., vol. 3, pp. 41–3.

[97] Ibid., vol. 15, pp. 43–5, pamphlets c.1838–1840. For Jacob's query, 'How could a true Quaker die possessed of wealth?', see Ibid., vol. 35, p. 12.

dominion over the love of gain'.[98] Factories and joint-stock companies which began to proliferate in the first half of the nineteenth century were also considered to be a danger to health and morality. Rebecca Ridgway argued that they oppressed the poor and made honest labour redundant.[99] Machinery and steam travel were contrasted with a 'true simplicity of life and manners' when man was restored 'to a pastoral life'.[100] Self-sufficiency required that all members shared in the menial domestic duties of the household, but this was also desirable as it was consistent with 'the simplicity and purity of the gospel of Christ'.[101] For the Society of Friends, whose servants were a badge of the respectability they cherished so much, this was shocking.[102] In contrast, the White Quakers held that such notions of respectability and status belonged to the devil.[103] Thus servants could not be employed, though as converts they lived at the William Street and Pound Street communities. They believed that paying for service pandered to material urges and White Quakers issued a condemnatory circular advising against giving money to servants.[104]

At the outset the White Quakers had not intended to establish a separate Society with a new code of ethics, rather Jacob and others had hoped to persuade the Society of Friends to reform themselves. The rise of consumption in nineteenth-century Britain and Ireland proved to be an irresistible force and it was difficult for the predominantly middle class Irish Quakers to abandon the business interests they had so carefully nurtured. The reforming impulse was resisted, and Jacob's reformers had little choice but to withdraw and live their lives according to the utopian vision that they gradually constructed. The experiment was short-lived, reflecting both the unusual social and economic pressures of the age of industrialism, and the conservative attitude to unorthodox households in the Victorian period. The question here is how to evaluate the White Quaker community.

In the first instance the emergence of a breakaway group throws considerable light on the Society of Friends in Ireland in the first half of the nineteenth century, their code of conduct and their organisational structures. Jacob and his followers believed that the Society had turned

---

[98] Jacob to H. D. Griffiths, *Lloyd's Weekly London Newspaper*, 19 May 1844, p. 6.
[99] *Progress*, vol. 7, pp. 29–32. See also vol. 22, p. 36.
[100] Ibid., vol. 35, pp. 52–3 (responding to a letter from Barmby); see also pp. 60–1.
[101] Ibid., vol. 1, p. 23.
[102] Ibid., vol. 28, p. 54. *Progress* reports Abigail and others preparing peat, and Elizabeth Beale sifting flour on her knees.
[103] Ibid., vol. 28, p. 54.
[104] Ibid., vol. 3, p. 69; vol. 9, p. 42.

their backs on the guiding principles of the founding members, on simplicity and plainness. Greer and others viewed White Quakerism as an attempt, at least originally, to return to early Quakerism. Its conservative and inward-looking attitudes distinguished it from the progressive utopianism of Barmby and others.[105] The seceders were preoccupied with the well-being of 'their own little corner of mount Zion'.[106] Some features of White Quaker life now seem peculiar: the faith in dreams, portents and prophecies, were certainly not intellectual or romantic in inspiration. If anything they seem rather old-fashioned.[107] Moreover, the conservative impulse prevailed. Jacob's nephew, and namesake, defended simplicity against evangelicalism, and had contact with the conservative English 'Fritchley' schismatics. Their theological and physiological tenets were echoed by Charles Allen Fox (1849–1929), an Englishman who was disowned in the late-nineteenth century.[108]

White Quakerism began without notions of returning to an Enlightenment-inspired primitive state of society. Notoriety and the need or desire to find friends and converts transformed the sect's public profile. An important factor in this was the decision to print Barmby's writings in the *Progress of Truth*. When Jacob and Abigail were reviled for their 'marriage', Barmby's support was welcome. He and other English radicals were sympathetic where others were scandalised. Despite their aberrant behaviour, one such visitor later wrote in the Owenite journal, *New Moral World*, that household arrangements such as dietary habits, domestic matters and the members' behaviour towards each other were 'distinguished by great practical good sense'. The writer also claimed that White Quaker clothing was not nearly as curious as descriptions implied.[109] Newlands, a White Quaker community, certainly represented developments of 'physical puritanism' paralleled elsewhere, but these were consonant with beliefs and practices already espoused by the sect. Furthermore, Jacob did not accept all of Barmby's communist ideas. He was cautious about examining and reprinting his writings and appreciated their differences when they met.[110]

---

[105] Taylor, *Eve and the New Jerusalem*, p. 175.

[106] *National Anti-Slavery Standard*, 28 October 1847, p. 87.

[107] Ibid.

[108] Milligan, 'The Ancient Way'; R. C. Allen, 'An Example of Quaker Discipline: the case of Dr Charles Allen Fox and the Cardiff Quakers', *Journal of Welsh Religious History*, New Series, 1 (Winter 2001), 46–73.

[109] *New Moral World*, 28 September 1844, p. 112; *Progress*, vol. 40, pp. 65–7.

[110] Jacob distinguished between his community and that of Barmby and others, see *National Anti-Slavery Standard*, 24 October 1850, p. 88. On his selective reading

Inevitably, the White Quakers have been remembered for their sexual radicalism, as epitomised by the practise of divorcing unsympathetic spouses and exaggerated by false reports of public nudity. Greer condemned Jacob's 'most monstrous indelicacy and licentiousness' which found justification in the doctrine that to the pure all things were pure 'whenever he inclined to honour any of his female followers with a temporary preference'.[111] The press were extremely critical both at the time and subsequently. For example, in 1843 the *Leinster Express* questioned the spirituality of the White Quakers and identified them with Owenite free-love and Protestant antinomianism.[112] Writing in *Harper's New Monthly Magazine* in 1869, a prominent American-born Unitarian, M. D. Conway, described the White Quaker community more kindly as a 'sort of free-love Quaker monastery'.[113] However, J. H. Blunt's, *Dictionary of Sects*, published in 1874, was extremely hostile, defining them as 'Antinomians of the worst description', cloaking villainy in the most sanctimonious language.[114]

Any assessment of the White Friends must take full account of Jacob's contradictory and, at times, dubious morality. The sect's founder remains an enigma. Contemporaries divided between those who thought Jacob was a charlatan and those who thought him a deluded fanatic. He was undoubtedly a bigot who had little time for the views of other dissenters, many of whom were members of his own family, or well-meaning critics.[115] The latter did not exaggerate the violence of the sect's own literature as these 'Publishers of the Truth' refused to temper their language. Jabob's judgement on backsliders before the schism and the disruption of church services were part of his desire to return to the purity of early Quakerism, but his other actions, most notably the rejection of his wife and 'marriage' to Abigail, suggest that he was not immune to the worldly temptations he scorned in others. Certainly it was his sexual

---

of Barmby see *Progress*, vol. 31, p. 27.

[111] Greer, *Quakerism*, p. 384.

[112] *Leinster Express*, 29 April 1843 stated that they adopted Owen's system 'in worldly concerns, rendering it more mischievous, under the false semblance of a spiritual guidance'.

[113] M. D. Conway, 'South coast saunterings in England', *Harper's New Monthly Magazine* (New York), 39 (August, 1869), p. 341. The sect's free-love reputation is noted in an article reprinted in *Littell's Living Age*, 149 (1922), pp. 170–6 (p. 175).

[114] J. H. Blunt, *Dictionary of Sects, Heresies, Ecclesiastical Parties, and Schools of Religious Thought* (London, 1874), p. 469.

[115] For response to well-meant criticisms by the Englishman, Richard Child, see *Progress*, vol. 28, pp. 60–5.

proclivities, alleged or actual, more than anything else which harmed the sect's public reputation. They sat awkwardly with a code of ethics which turned upon godly behaviour and following the Inner Light. The predominantly female households of the White Quaker communities suggest that Jacob exercised a strange and possibly unhealthy hold over female Quakers who sought a more simple life, while the male following proved more transient, especially after the communal way of life had been established.

The sect's immediate impact on Irish Quakerism outside afflicted families was stronger than later Quakers perhaps appreciated. The seceders, after all, were socially significant and 'steady' Friends whose exploits convulsed Irish Quakerism 'to such an extent that they formed the staple subject of the gossip at Quarterly Meetings, and all occasions when it is customary or proper for people to gossip at all'.[116] Decades afterwards, those involved in the dispute avoided all discussion of the unhappy affair.[117] As a later biography written by Jacob's great niece recalled, during her grandmother's childhood the White Quakers were never mentioned.[118] Their continued infamy is revealed in the correspondence of an early twentieth century Quaker historian, J. Ernest Grubb, suggesting that because of the White Quakers' 'loose views' on marriage, great care would have to be exercised in making any reference to the sect and their practices in the *Friends' Historical Journal*.[119] Greer claimed that the more rigorous discipline which was imposed on the Dublin Monthly Meeting outlasted the schism.[120] Yet later, Isabel Grubb stated that the experience may have helped to inculcate more tolerant attitudes to offenders. She noted that 'at least they attempted to live their religion, and not only to theorize about it'.[121] But it is still the case that resistance to 'constructive change' and the fear of open discussion remained a feature of the Society.[122] It is unlikely that the schism helped

---

[116] *National Anti-Slavery Standard*, 28 October 1847, p. 87.

[117] See M. Legg, *Alfred Webb. The autobiography of a Quaker nationalist* (Cork, 1999), pp. 21–2 in which it is noted the Quaker S. V. Peet's ambition to write the sect's history had been thwarted.

[118] L. M. Jacob, 'Memories of a Quaker Childhood in Ireland and Pennsylvania' (n.p., n.d.), p. 5 (copy in LSF).

[119] LSF, J. Ernest Grubb to Norman Penney, letter dated 2 September 1914, after index in notebook, pasted in front of first volume of the 3 volume copy of *Progress*.

[120] Greer, *Quakerism*, p. 385.

[121] I. Grubb, *Quakers in Ireland, 1654–1900* (London, 1927), p. 130.

[122] See R. S. Harrison, *Richard Davis Webb: Dublin Quaker printer, 1805–72* (Dublin, 1993), pp. 3, 39, and his 'Irish Perspectives on the Anti-Slavery

reform Irish Quakerism through the 'leaven' of plain living, as Jacob's great niece suggested, since extremism and notoriety made it a subject of shame.[123] Observers were mistaken when they identified the White Quakers with fashioning the 'new moral world' of the utopian socialists, for they set out to restore an old moral world. Unfortunately the reality of the White Quaker community was far removed from the godliness of the early Quakers.

Movement', *JFHS*, 56, 2 (1991), 106–25 (115–16). For details of the schism's negative impact see his *A Biographical Dictionary of Irish Quakers* (Dublin, 1997), p. 19.

[123] Jacob, 'Memories', p. 5.

CHAPTER EIGHT

'HIGH DAYS AND HOLY DAYS':
ST PATRICK'S DAY IN THE NORTH EAST
OF ENGLAND, C.1850–1900

JOAN ALLEN

Ever bless and defend the sweet land of our birth,
Where the shamrock still blooms as when thou wert on earth;
And our hearts shall yet burn, wheresoever we roam,
For God and St Patrick and our native home.[1]

The annual St Patrick's Day celebrations, in whatever part of the world
they are held, have been marked by some, if not all, of the same staple
features: masses and religious services, flagship processions, monster
meetings and demonstrations, concerts and variety shows, and a good deal
of festive eating and drinking. But this feast day has always functioned in
other ways too, not least as an annual opportunity for Irish migrants to
publicly proclaim and celebrate their birthright. The singing of 'Patrick-
hymns' were an important part of the ritual as the Irish called upon their
patron saint to save their faith and their country.[2] Beyond its religious
significance as the hymn of choice for exiled Irish Catholics, the above
few lines from *Hail Glorious St Patrick* offer some powerful insights into
the way that this occasion has traditionally been marked. It is the
inextricable nexus between faith and nation, so imaginatively articulated,
which invests the hymn with its patriotic message and, arguably, it is this
unequivocal 'call to arms' that has so often helped to dictate the form and

---

[1] *Hail Glorious St Patrick*: words by Sister Agnes; tune: Ancient Irish Melody.
[2] Leon V. Litvack, 'The psychology of song; the theology of hymn: songs and
hymns of the Irish migration', in Patrick O. Sullivan (ed.), *The Irish World Wide:
history, heritage, identity* (6 vols. Leicester, London and Washington, 1992–2000),
5: *Religion and Identity* (1996), p. 80.

content of the St Patrick's Day festivities.[3] While there is no doubt that devotional practices stood at the heart of the celebrations, and attendance at church services was regarded as an absolute requirement for Irish Catholics, this was only one element of a programme of cultural activities that blended a heady cocktail of religious and political loyalties.

The human cost of the Great Famine of 1847[4] has cast a long shadow over the history of the Irish in Britain and, until fairly recently, the grand narrative that has been constructed has focussed most upon the difficulties that enforced migration posed: poverty and ill-health, dislocation and resettlement, unemployment and, inevitably, discrimination.[5] This is not altogether surprising for these problems were not short-lived and their impact upon the vast majority of Irish migrants has been well documented. However, in the mid-1990s, historians such as Patrick O'Sullivan moved the agenda along from a close focus upon the 'culture of migration' to the effect that migration had upon creative activity and Irish cultural life.[6] To a large extent, this new dimension in Irish studies was eager to explore the Irish at play, to counterbalance a story weighed down by tales of loss and dispossession with one which began the process of acknowledging that this was far from the whole picture. Notwithstanding the difficulties they faced, or maybe because of them, Irish popular culture and the migrant's capacity for leisure and pleasure survived intact. And, as recent writers have observed, we can uncover just as much about the survival strategies of Irish migrants by looking at their celebrations and associational life as we can by picking over the Census returns and employment records.[7]

---

[3] Ibid., p. 78.
[4] For example, see Cecil Woodham-Smith, *The Great Hunger: Ireland, 1845–49* (London, 1962); Lynn Hollen Lees, *Exiles of Erin: Irish migrants in Victorian London* (New York, 1978); P. J. Waller, *Sectarianism and Democracy: a political and social history of Liverpool, 1868–1939* (Liverpool, 1981); Frances Finnegan, *Poverty and Prejudice: Irish immigrants in York, 1840–1875* (Cork, 1982); Christine Kinealy, *This Great Calamity: the Irish famine, 1845–1852* (Dublin, 1994).
[5] For example, see Donald MacRaild, *Irish Migrants in Modern Britain, 1750–1922* (Basingstoke, 1999); Roger Swift (ed.), *Irish Migrants in Britain, 1815–1914: a documentary history* (Cork, 2002); Paul O'Leary, *Irish Migrants in Modern Wales* (Liverpool, 2004); Terence McBride, *The Experience of Irish Migrants to Glasgow, Scotland, 1863–1891* (Lampeter, Queenstown and Lewiston, 2006).
[6] O'Sullivan (ed.), *Irish World Wide, 6: The Creative Migrant* (Leicester, 1994).
[7] Roger Swift and Sheridan Gilley (eds), *The Irish in Victorian Britain: the local dimension* (Dublin, 1999).

More than any other event in the Irish calendar the St Patrick's Day festival offers a unique prism through which to view the interaction between migrants and communities, and observe the religious, social and political priorities that came into play, differentially, in accordance with the prevailing regional or local influences. The study of St Patrick's Day is, of course, not new and this analysis is greatly indebted to Mike Cronin and Daryl Adair's landmark volume, *The Wearing of the Green*, which has surveyed the national holiday from its earliest listing as a saint's day in the Irish calendar in 1607 to its modern, commercially-driven and more mainstream four-day celebration.[8] By their own account, Cronin and Adair were 'principally concerned with Saint Patrick's Day as a theatre for the expression of community and negotiation of difference'.[9] Theirs is a remarkably rich and ambitious study which offers a comparative analysis of the way that St Patrick's Day was commemorated in different parts of the world, and the authors have demonstrated how the national festival could reconnect, albeit only in spirit, an Irish Diaspora scattered across three continents. In selecting how the feast was marked in major cities such as New York, Chicago and Boston; Toronto and Montreal; Sydney and Melbourne; Dublin and Belfast, and then considering its particular manifestation in major British settlements such as Liverpool and London, they provide a contrasting and nuanced reading of all that was distinctive about the festival in such diverse urban settings. Nonetheless, their expansive study still leaves much for other historians to discover and analyse; it is still possible to claim that what emerges may not be entirely representative. On the grounds of demography alone, the funding stream for the celebrations in these major American, Australian and Canadian conurbations was bound to be substantial and this has implications for the scale of such festivals. In cities like New York for example, with its melting pot of ethnically-diverse cultures, St Patrick's Day parades were perceived to have a key role to play in community building. The far greater numbers involved and the commercial opportunities associated with it must have made it easier to justify, and fund, the organisation of elaborate processions and displays. It is notable, too, that much of Cronin and Adair's attention is devoted to the street parade, its appearance and disappearance, and inevitably rather less attention is paid to other aspects of the St Patrick's Day festivities.[10]

---

[8] Mike Cronin and Daryl Adair, *The Wearing of the Green: a history of St Patrick's Day* (London and New York, 2002).

[9] Ibid., p. xvi.

[10] Ibid., p. xxiv. For a discussion of those other manifestations see T. G. Fraser (ed.), *The Irish Parading Tradition: following the drum* (Basingstoke, 2000).

This study aims to consider the extent to which the North East of
England, dominated by Newcastle as the regional capital but with the
majority of its Irish migrants living and working in small towns and
suburbs, conformed to the model which Cronin and Adair have so
carefully delineated. It will survey St Patrick's Day activity between the
mid-1850s, by which time Irish migrants in the North East had established
a strong network of religious and ethnic associations, and the turn of the
twentieth century when the national feast day is believed to have become
increasingly a vehicle for demonstrating 'compatible loyalties . . . rather
than hostility and challenges to the existing power structures'.[11] In doing
so, it will concern itself rather less with the trademark shamrock, green
ribbons and traditional Irish entertainment, although these patriotic
expressions were just as essential to the north-east celebrations. Formal
attendance at special feast day masses, too, may be taken as a given. The
symbiotic relationship between Roman Catholicism and Irish nationalism
is the crucial subtext here and this will be held to explain the aggressively
political character of the region's annual celebrations, not just in the
period under review but well into the twentieth century.[12]

In the past, and with the exception of work by Roger Cooter,[13] Frank
Neal,[14] Donald MacRaild[15] and Joan Allen,[16] the North East has not

---

[11] Cronin and Adair, *Wearing of the Green*, p. 60, quoting K. A. Miller, *Emigrants
and Exiles: Ireland and the Irish exodus to North America* (Oxford, 1985), p. 7.
[12] Joan Allen, ''Keeping the faith': the preservation of Celtic identity in Britain in
the late nineteenth century', in Richard C. Allen and Stephen Regan (eds), *Irelands
of the Mind: memory and identity in modern Irish culture* (Newcastle, 2008), pp.
32–49.
[13] Roger Cooter, *When Paddy Met Geordie. The Irish in County Durham and
Newcastle 1840–1880* (Sunderland, 2005). See also Caroline L. Scott, 'A
comparative re-examination of Anglo-Irish relations in nineteenth-century
Manchester, Liverpool, and Newcastle upon Tyne', unpublished University of
Durham, PhD thesis, 1998.
[14] Frank Neal, 'English-Irish conflict in the north-east of England', in John
Belchem and Patrick Buckland (eds), *The Irish in British Labour History*
(Liverpool, 1993), pp. 59–85; Frank Neal, 'Irish settlement in the north-west and
the north-east of England in the mid-nineteenth century', in Swift and Gilley (eds),
Irish in Victorian Britain, pp. 75–100.
[15] Donald M. MacRaild, *Faith, Fraternity and Fighting: the Orange Order and
Irish migrants in Northern England, c.1850–1920* (Liverpool, 2005); Donald M.
MacRaild, '"Abandon Hibernicisation": priests, Ribbonmen and an Irish street
fight in the north east of England in 1858', *Historical Research*, 76, 194 (2003),
557–73.

featured heavily in the vast literature on the Irish in Britain.[17] Historians of the Irish diaspora have tended to focus most of their attention upon the known concentrations in Lancashire, West Yorkshire and London, and upon 'cities of conflict' such as Liverpool, Manchester, Glasgow and London. Yet, while the Irish-born community in the North East of England may be considered small in comparison to these major settlements, Frank Neal has confirmed that in 1851 Northumberland and Durham had the 'fourth largest concentration of Irish-born' in England and Wales.[18] There were large Irish communities in Newcastle, Sunderland, Gateshead, Durham and Stockton as well as smaller clusters dispersed throughout the two north-east counties.[19] Inevitably, Newcastle's precocious industrial reputation as a place where skilled and unskilled work was plentiful acted as a magnet to those urgently in need of stable employment, and the regional capital absorbed the lion's share – more than 7,000 – of the incoming settlers.[20] However, as others have shown, density rather than numerical strength should be regarded as the more crucial determinant of the emigrant experience. It is on these grounds that Gateshead's Irish community, which has been estimated at a ratio of 1:4 in 1871,[21] can usefully be compared with that of Newcastle and even the small County Durham village of Ryhope, which the *Newcastle Daily Chronicle* likened to Connemara or Tipperary in 1873, warrants scrutiny.[22]

---

[16] Joan Allen, *Joseph Cowen and Popular Radicalism on Tyneside, 1829–1900* (London, 2007), ch. 4 and 6.

[17] For other recent work, see D. M. Jackson and D. M. MacRaild, '"The Conserving Crowd": Mass Unionist demonstrations in Liverpool and Tyneside, 1912–13', in D. George Boyce and Alan O'Day (eds), *The Ulster Crisis, 1885–1921* (Basingstoke, 2006), pp. 229–46; Joan Allen and Richard C. Allen, 'Competing Identities: Irish and Welsh migration and the North East of England', in Adrian Green and Anthony Pollard (eds), *Regional Identities in North East England, 1300–2000* (London, 2007), pp. 130–66.

[18] The Irish-born population has been estimated at 31,167 in 1851, some 4.4 per cent of the total population. See Neal, 'Irish settlement in the north-west and the north-east of England', p. 76. For further information see Roger Swift, 'The Irish in Britain', in O'Sullivan (ed.), *Irish World Wide, 2: The Irish in the New Communities* (Leicester, 1992), p. 57, who notes that 5.4 per cent of the population of Durham were Irish.

[19] Neal, 'Irish settlement in the north-west and the north-east of England', p. 78. See also, Allen and Allen, 'Competing Identities', pp. 137–8.

[20] See table 2 for detailed statistics drawn from the 1851 Census in Neal, 'Irish settlement in the north-west and the north-east of England', pp. 78–9.

[21] Ibid.

[22] *Newcastle Daily Chronicle*, 'Our Colliery Villages', 25 January 1873.

A small indigenous Catholic community of some 10,000 souls had survived the Reformation but after the Irish Famine a great upsurge in the numbers of Irish migrants dramatically transformed the religious profile of the region.[23] Even taking into account the flawed methodologies of gathering basic demographic data in the first half of the nineteenth century, the 1851 Religious Census offers a fair indication of how the region's Irish community grew. The Census set the Roman Catholic population of Northumberland and Durham at 26,000 and, in view of the fluctuating settlement patterns of the Irish in this period, this is likely to be a fairly conservative estimate. An ambitious church-building programme in the second half of the century established a raft of new parishes, especially in the colliery villages that were such a dominant feature of the landscape of the two counties, and extant parish records reveal that by 1914 the numbers of registered Roman Catholics had multiplied 'sevenfold' to approximately 190,000.[24] Even allowing for a modest conversion rate among the indigenous population this increase is mostly attributable to nineteenth-century Irish emigration to the two counties. Given that Irish settlers to the North East were overwhelmingly of the Roman Catholic faith[25] they suffered less from the internal divisions that were such a marked feature of other major areas of Irish settlement, especially those with a strong Orange Lodge tradition.[26] Community relations were, of course, occasionally disturbed by outbreaks of petty

---

[23] Cooter, *When Paddy Met Geordie*, p. 46.

[24] Ibid., pp. 50–1 offers two maps showing the distribution of churches and missions. For statistics, see Michael Morris and Leo Gooch, *Down Your Aisles. The Diocese of Hexham and Newcastle 1850–2000* (Hartlepool, 2000); R. J. Cooter, 'Hibernians and Geordies in the Nineteenth Century', *Northern Catholic History*, 4 (1976), 20–9; W. J. Nicholson, 'Irish Priests in the North East in the Nineteenth Century', *Northern Catholic History*, 21 (1985), 16–24.

[25] Allen, *Joseph Cowen and Popular Radicalism on Tyneside*, ch. 4. For a discussion of the close relationship between Roman Catholicism and Irish nationalism see Allen, 'Keeping the Faith', pp. 78–91.

[26] Steven Fielding, *Class and Ethnicity: Irish Catholics in England, 1880–1939* (Manchester, 1993), p. 34 compares Newcastle favourably with Manchester, noting that before 1880 sectarianism in Manchester was fuelled by Orangeism. On the impact of Orangeism elsewhere see Waller, *Sectarianism and Democracy*; Tom Gallagher, *Glasgow: the uneasy peace* (Manchester, 1987); Neal, 'English-Irish conflict in the North East of England'; Neal, 'Irish settlement in the north-west and the north-east of England'; MacRaild, 'Abandon Hibernicisation', 563, and his *Culture, Conflict and Migration: the Irish in Victorian Cumberland* (Liverpool, 1998). On Orangeism in the North East, see MacRaild, *Faith, Fraternity and Fighting*.

violence but these tended to be the exception rather than the rule, prompted by emotive events such as the Maynooth question in 1852,[27] the Garibaldi riots in Newcastle in 1866 which were sparked by anxieties over the Italian unification movement,[28] or the provocative speechmaking of William Murphy in 1867 which created mayhem in North Shields.[29] Such disturbances do not seem to have been connected to the St Patrick's Day parades which generally proceeded without incident.[30] The dispersed nature of the region's small Protestant Irish community meant that conflict was unusual and relatively small scale. The vibrancy of Catholic associational life was a positive force. It united the vast majority of Irish exiles in the two counties and served to militate against the erosion of faith that had been noted in Wales, for example, much to the concern of Catholic hierarchy. In the North East the Church's social ministry acted as an important bulwark not just against lapsation but assimilation; the Irish constituted a cohesive and tight-knit group whose first loyalties were to their homeland.[31] And, as Mary Hickman has cogently argued, tensions among the wider community in response to the revitalisation of Catholicism would simply have reinforced national and religious solidarities.[32]

Cronin and Adair have highlighted the financial constraints which determined that St Patrick's Day celebrations in Britain were mostly modest affairs in the first half of the nineteenth century. In the main, these earlier celebrations passed by with little newspaper comment unless they were accompanied by sectarian clashes.[33] In the immediate aftermath of the Irish Famine exuberant celebrating was roundly condemned by the *Liverpool Mercury* on the grounds that any spare resource should be spent on the poor, the sick and the homeless.[34] Evidence of St Patrick's Day celebrations in the North East in this period is very scarce, suggesting that

---

[27] Cooter, *When Paddy Met Geordie*, pp. 73–6.

[28] Dan Jackson, "'Garibaldi or the Pope!' Newcastle's Irish riot of 1866', *North East History*, 34 (2004), 49–82.

[29] *Newcastle Daily Chronicle*, 26 August 1867; MacRaild, *Culture, Conflict and Migration*, pp. 178–83.

[30] Cooter, *When Paddy Met Geordie*, p. 78.

[31] For example, see Raphael Samuel, 'The Roman Catholic Church and the Irish Poor', in Roger Swift and Sheridan Gilley (eds), *The Irish in the Victorian City* (London, 1985), pp. 267–99.

[32] Mary Hickman, *Religion, Class and Identity: the State, the Catholic Church and the education of the Irish in Britain* (Aldershot, 1995), p. 93.

[33] Cronin and Adair, *Wearing of the Green*, p. 32.

[34] *Liverpool Mercury*, March 1848, as cited in Ibid., p. 32.

the gatherings of Irish Catholics were either too small (in keeping with the demographics at that time) or too private to register an impact on the local press. The muted Orange Lodge presence has already been noted and the 'Glorious Twelfth' celebrations registered only rarely in the local press.[35] However, the eclectic diary of Richard Lowry, a clerk with the Newcastle and Carlisle Railway, reveals that the Newcastle Irish community were sufficiently large to warrant the celebration of St Patrick's Day in 1842 with a procession.[36] In 1846, too, the procession through the streets of Newcastle and Gateshead that year is said to have presented a 'brilliant spectacle'.[37] The decision to take to the streets may well reflect the important role of the procession in Tyneside popular culture at that time. It has been argued that the civic calendar of Newcastle Corporation was 'one of the most ceremonial in the country',[38] and by their very nature such exhibitions were opportunities for local dignitaries to display their wealth and superior status. The annual celebration of Ascension Day in May was the high point of the social calendar. In keeping with the river Tyne's commercial importance, it was customary for the mayor and the civic elite to lead a flotilla of decorated boats up river in a ceremony which displayed their power and, indeed, marked out the geographical boundaries of their authority for all to see. The response of those who were excluded from the ritual was to institute their own version of civic display and thus the flourishing craft guilds and friendly societies on Tyneside frequently processed with due pomp and plenty of 'flags, symbols and bands'.[39]

As the century progressed, the organisation of the St Patrick's Day events increasingly became contested territory for the Catholic Church was eager to counter the prevailing belief that the Irish were inherently hedonistic and debauched. The Church hierarchy was particularly anxious to refute the accusation that the Irish were all inveterate drinkers. The success of Father Mathew's Teetotall Crusade in Ireland in the 1840s suggested that a concerted campaign could yield results. In Ireland, St

[35] MacRaild, *Faith, Fraternity and Fighting*, p. 198.
[36] Norman McCord, 'Victorian Newcastle Observed: the diary of Richard Lowry', *Northern History*, XXXVII (2000), 252.
[37] *Gateshead Observer*, 21 March 1846.
[38] Bill Lancaster, 'Sociability and the City', in Robert Colls and Bill Lancaster (eds), *Newcastle upon Tyne: a modern history* (Chichester, 2001), p. 321.
[39] McCord, 'Victorian Newcastle Observed', 252–3; Lancaster, 'Sociability and the City', p. 322ff. For a discussion of ritual events as the occasion 'par excellence' for symbolic display see Dominic Bryan, 'Drumcree and "The Right to March": Orangeism, ritual and politics in Northern Ireland', in Fraser, *Irish Parading Tradition*, pp. 192–3.

Patrick's Day had been seized upon as an opportunity for the Mathewites to display their conversion to sobriety.[40] In Britain, temperance confraternities, endorsed by both the Catholic hierarchy and the Hibernian Society, sought to direct celebrants away from the excesses that had seen the Darlington anniversary condemned as 'one continual orgy'.[41] In 1854 the orderly nature of the Newcastle procession drew favourable comment from the local press which observed that the behaviour of the Irish had 'considerably improved' in recent times.[42] It was a similar picture in Newport, south Wales, in 1862 where Fr Richardson successfully implemented his 'Truce of God' – a three-day abstinence during the St Patrick's Day festival.[43] That same year, when the local Irish paraded through the streets of Gateshead and Newcastle on St Patrick's Day, the Newcastle Hibernian Society donated the proceeds of the day's events to the Newcastle Infirmary. Even so, they were still condemned as subversive Ribbonmen by the Church which actively sought to outlaw them by denying the sacraments to any known Hibernians.[44] In March 1865 Bishop Hogarth took personal charge of the Newcastle celebrations and dictated that rational and sober amusements were the order of the day.[45]

It is difficult to pinpoint exactly when public processions ceased to be the central feature of the festival in the region but nationally, as Cronin and Adair note, they became increasingly rare in the 1850s. Thereafter St Patrick's Day was typically observed by indoor activities: large meetings, celebratory dinners, musical soirees and balls.[46] As the rising tide of nationalist sentiment aroused the hostility and suspicion of the British

[40] H. F. Kearney, 'Fr. Matthew: Apostle of Modernisation', in Art Cosgrove and Donal McCartney (eds), *Studies in Irish History: presented to R. Dudley Edwards*, (Dublin, 1999), pp. 174–5.
[41] Cooter, *When Paddy met Geordie*, p. 32, quoting from the *Durham Chronicle*, 23 March 1866; Cronin and Adair, *Wearing of the Green*, pp. 46–50; Jacqueline Turton, 'The Irish poor in nineteenth century London', in Swift and Gilley (eds), *Irish in Victorian Britain*, p. 146.
[42] *Newcastle Chronicle*, 24 March 1854, as cited by Cooter, *When Paddy Met Geordie*, p. 79.
[43] Chris Williams, '"Decorous and Creditable": The Irish in Newport', in O'Leary (ed.), *Irish Migrants in Modern Wales*, p. 74.
[44] Ibid., pp. 35–6.
[45] *Newcastle Daily Chronicle*, 17 March 1865, and cited by Shane Cullen, *Fragmens Sur Les Institutions Republicaines IV (Panels 1–48)*, 1, 1 (Newcastle, 1996), p. 13. For a discussion of attempts elsewhere to steer the celebrations in a more respectable direction see MacRaild, *Culture, Conflict, and Migration*, p. 107.
[46] Cronin and Adair, *Wearing of the Green*, p. 32.

authorities in the latter half of the 1860s the celebrations came under closer official scrutiny. There were great fears that the St Patrick's Day events would exacerbate existing tensions and become a recruiting ground for nationalist activism. In March 1865, the Catholic hierarchy of Glasgow were at pains to counter the growing influence of the Irish National Association of Scotland which had taken charge of the festivities. Bishop Murdoch took the unusual step of sending a pastoral letter which virtually ordered the faithful to stay at home or be judged 'guilty of mortal sin'.[47] More focus was placed on *Corpus Christi* processions as a way of stressing the religiosity and respectability of the Glasgow Irish.[48] In the event, the Fenian rising of 1867 seemed to demonstrate that such worries were well founded. The Manchester Irish were an obvious target of police surveillance but it is notable that the North East was also considered to be a high risk area and in need of additional security forces. *The Times* was quick to claim that the iron and steel yards and coal mines of the North East, which employed large numbers of Irishmen, were the training ground for Fenian 'drillings and other such like movements'.[49] In the weeks and months which followed, the deployment of police and troops was stepped up and a number of false arrests were made in Durham, Weardale and Hartlepool following supposed 'sightings' of the Manchester escapees.[50] Newcastle's reputation as a hotbed of Fenian activity even prompted the local police force to secure powers to carry arms, and several hundreds of special constables were sworn in at North Shields.[51]

Rising tensions among Irish communities in Britain following the execution of the 'Manchester Martyrs' in November 1867, and the Clerkenwell explosion in December alarmed the Catholic Church almost as much as the government. Some of this tension was exacerbated by a hostile press which rejected the claim that the killing of Sergeant Brett was a political crime. Most newspapers, though notably not the *Newcastle Chronicle*, insisted that full weight of the law was warranted for what the *Daily Telegraph* described as a 'vulgar, dastardly murder'.[52] Irish

[47] McBride, *Experience of Irish Migrants to Glasgow*, p. 51.
[48] Elaine McFarland, 'Marching from the Margins: Twelfth July parades in Scotland, 1820–1914', in Fraser (ed.), *Irish Parading Tradition*, p. 67.
[49] As cited in Cooter, *When Paddie Met Geordie*, p. 149.
[50] *Newcastle Daily Chronicle*, 26 September 1867, 28 September 1867.
[51] Ibid., 10 October 1867, 16 October 1867, 8 November 1867.
[52] *Daily Telegraph*, 2 November 1867, as cited by Michael de Nie, *The Eternal Paddy: Irish identity and the British press, 1798–1882* (Wisconsin and London,

communities were outraged, and insisted that the three men had been executed 'solely because they were Irishmen'.[53] In most of the major areas of settlement the Irish began to organise protest marches and mock funerals. While the Glasgow authorities were naturally reluctant to allow any display of Fenian solidarity in 1867 they were even more fearful that the proposed march would prompt the city's 4,000 Orangemen to retaliate and cause serious public disorder.[54] In Newcastle, conflict over a planned 'funeral' procession in memory of the Manchester Martyrs was only averted by the intervention of the Bishop of Hexham and Newcastle who calmed the situation and persuaded the Irish population that it was in their best interest to avoid any provocative public displays.[55] With so much of the St Patrick's Day events given over to celebrating and memorialising Irish heroes such as Robert Emmett and Theobald Wolfe Tone it is hardly surprising that homage to the executed Manchester Martyrs should thereafter become an essential element of the ritual. The Manchester Martyrs assumed iconic status and images of William Allen, Philip Larkin and Michael O'Brien were regularly emblazoned on the colourful St Patrick's Day banners and other festival literature.[56]

Friction between Irish nationalists and Orangemen was a thorny issue for the authorities in conflict cities such as Glasgow where the confessional divide was more evenly balanced, especially in July when the Twelfth parades were customarily held. The Grand Lodge in that city abandoned their parade in July 1868 in a bid to demonstrate their willingness to avoid confrontation. This proved to be a shrewd tactic in the long term and, as Elaine McFarland notes, such restraint was well rewarded after 1872. The wider public were increasingly disinclined to see public processions embargoed on the grounds that any unruly behaviour could be punished in the usual way.[57] As in Ireland in the late-1870s, careful surveillance, not prohibition, was judged to be a more judicious strategy by the authorities. Yet, even after the Party Processions Act was repealed in 1872, street parades continued to be very rare in north-east England. The procession of 400 who marched through the streets of

---

2004), p. 163. For the sympathetic response of the Newcastle press see Allen, *Joseph Cowen and Popular Radicalism on Tyneside*, ch. 4.
[53] de Nie, *Eternal Paddy*, p. 162.
[54] McFarland, 'Marching from the Margins', p. 66.
[55] *Newcastle Journal*, 16 December 1867.
[56] Cronin and Adair, *Wearing of the Green*, p. 61; Alvin Jackson, *Ireland 1798–1998* (Oxford, 1999), pp. 103–5; Graham Davis, *The Irish in Britain, 1815–1914* (Dublin, 1991), p. 198.
[57] McFarland, 'Marching from the Margins', p. 67.

Wallsend and Willington Quay in 1875, carrying green banners and accompanied by the local brass band, scarce compare with the 60,680 Irishmen who paraded through Ulster in 1874.[58]

The success of the indoor political meeting in the North East which dominated the annual festival throughout the 1870s and 1880s can be linked to the active involvement of several prominent Irish nationalists. As Roger Cooter has noted, the St Patrick's Day celebrations 'lost much of their former sentimentality [and] . . . became occasions for hard-core political rallies'.[59] John Barry, who had played a key role in promoting Isaac Butt's Home Rule initiative in the 1870s, before securing election as a nationalist MP, had spent his childhood and formative years in the North East. Other Irish nationalists, such as Joseph Biggar, Edward Savage, Timothy Healy and John Walsh, had equally significant local connections which helped to ensure that the region was never short of high profile nationalist speakers. This was especially helpful for the competition for 'big names' during the St Patrick's Day celebrations was often fierce.

It was largely due to their good offices that in March 1875 the services of John Martin MP were secured to chair the meeting. He presided over a national concert in Newcastle Town Hall at which all proceeds and profits were dedicated to the relief of Irish political prisoners and their families. In the same way, a concert held that same day in the Newcastle Mechanics' Institute donated all profits to the Home Rule Confederation of Great Britain.[60] In Sunderland, A. M. Sullivan, MP for Louth, addressed a gathering in the Victoria Hall and seized the opportunity to chastise those whose ideal festive entertainment entailed large quantities of alcohol. They were, he said, 'a disgrace to the national name' for Irishmen in England had a responsibility to 'win respect from the community around them'.[61] In the mid-1870s the temperance lobby was still battling to reform the habits of Irish citizens by providing a counter culture to the drunken excesses associated with many celebrations.[62] Moreover, the need to encourage sobriety and, by extension, self-discipline was prioritised by the Church hierarchy who, with Cardinal Manning's express endorsement,

---

[58] *Newcastle Daily Chronicle*, 18 March 1875. See also Cronin and Adair, *Wearing of the Green*, pp. 54, 56.
[59] Cooter, *When Paddy Met Geordie*, p. 162.
[60] *Newcastle Daily Chronicle*, 18 March 1875.
[61] Ibid.
[62] Davis, *Irish in Britain*, pp. 117, 158. See also Cronin and Adair, *Wearing of the Green*, pp. 47–50, 60; Gerard Moran, 'The National Brotherhood of St Patrick', pp. 212–35, in Swift and Gilley (eds), *Irish in Victorian Britain*, pp. 212–35 (p. 218).

advocated the establishment of temperance groups such as the League of the Cross and, in the mid-1880s, the Catholic Young Men's Society (CYSM).[63]

In the late-nineteenth century, as the popularity of the St Patrick's Day festivities grew apace, organising major events required careful coordination and some delicate negotiation with the various parish and associational committees to ensure a good turnout at all events; an army of volunteers was needed to provide entertainment and refreshments. In some measure this role was taken on by the Irish literary societies which had sprung up in and around most of the region's towns and villages. As might be expected, the Newcastle Irish Literary Institute acted as a kind of regional headquarters for associational life of all kinds: political, social and cultural. The idea of establishing a dedicated meeting house had first been proposed at a gathering of influential Irishmen in the Portland Arms Inn in April 1871. Its founding members included the infamous Fenian Michael Kelly, John Walsh, a senior officer of the IRB Supreme Council, and Edward Savage and Tim Healy who were both employed by the North East Railway Company.[64] As with the establishment of similar institutes in the region, the preferred location was close to the parish church. In this instance, suitable premises – a fine three story house which had once been the residence of a prosperous Newcastle merchant – were found in Clayton Street, not far from St Mary's Catholic Cathedral which had been founded in 1844.[65] Within a short space of time, the Institute was offering a range of social activities, including the meetings of the Reading and Debating Society,[66] supper dances and balls[67] and annual excursions during Race Week.[68] By the mid-1880s such thriving centres of cultural recreation could be found in Sunderland, Newcastle, South Shields and North Shields.[69] The Irish Institutes in London were held to be 'non-sectarian and non-political' by the Victorian social commentator George Sims but

---

[63] Allen and Allen, 'Competing Identities', p. 142.

[64] Joseph Keating, 'The History of the Tyneside Irish Brigade', in Felix Lavery (ed.), *Irish Heroes in the War* (London, 1917), p. 58. Michael Kelly was the Principal of the Newcastle Catholic High School.

[65] Ibid., p. 57.

[66] *Irish Tribune*, 29 January 1887.

[67] Ibid., 14 February 1885, 20 April 1887.

[68] Ibid., 7 May 1887.

[69] Ibid., various dates including 14 February 1885, 19 February 1887, 2 July 1887, 16 July 1887.

this was certainly not the case in north-east towns.[70] Beyond their
immediate social and confessional functions these institutes became a
focal point for political activities too: as a secure meeting space for the
expression of more radical opinions; a safe haven where nationalist
campaigns could be planned, financed and coordinated. As the *Irish
Tribune* reported in February 1885, the North Shields Literary Institute
was active

> not only in diffusing literature, but by providing a regular meeting place,
> for the National League has done much for the success of that body . . . the
> organisation of the Irish people enabled them at a recent election to return
> a candidate to the council, pledged to work in Irish affairs.[71]

Much later, in 1917, one leading member of the Newcastle Institute
recalled how 'political felons, John Daly, O'Donovan Rossa, Davitt and
more had been visitors to the Institute . . . for thirty-seven years the
Institute had been the Irish storm centre'.[72]

The Newcastle Institute and others that were set up in the mid-1880s in
North and South Shields and Sunderland became the preferred meeting
place for the Irish National League [INL], and it was the branch
committees of the League and the Home Rule Association (HRA) which
usually took the lead in organising the St Patrick's Day events in the
region. Inevitably, this gave the festival its strong political focus. From its
inception, the Home Rule movement quickly garnered support in the main
centres of settlement and the presence of an influential local man was
often a key factor in its success. In Glasgow, the Home Rule cause is held
to have suffered because the local Liberal, Robert Dalglish, was 'cautious
rather than overtly sympathetic'.[73] Newcastle, on the other hand, was
uniquely advantaged in having the backing of Joseph Cowen MP, the
renowned local radical and newspaper entrepreneur. In 1872, Alex
Sullivan of the *Nation* singled Cowen out for special praise at a public
meeting in Newcastle while his pro-Irish sympathies were more formally
endorsed when Isaac Butt selected the town as the optimum venue for
convening the first meeting of the Home Rulers in August 1873.[74] This

---

[70] George R. Sims (ed.), *Living London* (London, 1902), and cited in Swift, *Irish Migrants in Britain*, p. 191.
[71] *Irish Tribune*, 14 February 1885.
[72] Keating, 'History of the Tyneside Irish Brigade', p. 77.
[73] McBride, *Experience of Irish Migrants to Glasgow*, p. 57.
[74] For Cowen's political career and pro-Irish sympathies see Allen, *Joseph Cowen and Tyneside Radicalism*, pp. 92–3.

rallying call proved to be a great success and local branches of the HRA soon proliferated, earning the region a reputation as an important stronghold of the INL.[75] Most typically, the Tyneside celebrations were marked by a large gathering in Newcastle Town Hall presided over by Councillor Bernard McAnulty. In 1876, Major O'Gorman MP was in attendance to pay tribute to the late John Martin,[76] while the 1877 meeting had secured Richard Power MP as guest speaker to rally the crowd. McAnulty, who was an executive member of the Home Rule Confederation, had been elected in 1874 as Town Councillor for the All Saints ward, a constituency with a large Irish population.[77] Power's stirring speech on that occasion electrified the revellers, though he was careful to avoid direct criticism of the British government. Irish independence was his theme and he was at pains to claim that this was not just desirable but inevitable:

> her institutions are not our institutions, her language is not ours, her religion is not ours, our customs are different, our traditions are not the same, we live differently . . . my friends it is this difference of habits, characters, and tastes that makes it impossible for them to reconcile their laws to our inclinations or approach.[78]

In Barrow where the 1876 celebrations had been marred by drunken and violent excess, the local HRA were determined to reassert their control. Charles Stewart Parnell was invited as keynote speaker in 1877 and he seized the opportunity to press for the immediate release of the Fenian prisoners.[79]

Most historians agree that the tempo of Irish nationalism grew apace in the 1880s in the wake of the 1881 Coercion Act and the imprisonment of Parnell and other leading Nationalist MPs. When news broke of the Phoenix Park murders, the newfound *detente* between Gladstone and Parnell in 1882 was undermined, though not derailed. Gladstone's position on Irish Home Rule had shifted significantly by the mid-1880s and the propagandist potential of the St Patrick's Day celebrations in 1885 and 1886 was not lost on the INL leadership as they sought to strengthen the

---

[75] Ibid., p. 99.
[76] *Newcastle Daily Journal*, 18 March 1876.
[77] T. P. McDermott, 'Irish workers on Tyneside in the 19th Century', in Norman McCord (ed.), *Essays in Tyneside Labour History* (Newcastle, 1977) p. 167. McAnulty was the first Irishman to sit on an English Town Council.
[78] *Newcastle Weekly Chronicle*, 24 March 1877.
[79] MacRaild, *Culture, Conflict and Migration*, p. 116.

case for independence. Careful planning was crucial if the opportunity was
not to be wasted. The proprietor of the weekly *Irish Tribune* and an
executive member of the Newcastle INL, Charles Diamond,[80] sought to
rally the troops on to greater efforts: 'What are the Newcastle Irishmen
doing about St Patrick's Day? Time is passing and they must bestir
themselves if the grand old festival is to be kept with the *éclat* that has
characterised the Newcastle demonstration in times past.' He was
concerned that the Newcastle festivities tended to 'overshadow other
districts' and that this had a negative impact on political activity. He was
keen to encourage North and South Shields, Hebburn, Jarrow, Walker and
Gateshead to hold their own separate events as he thought this would
maximise the impact of the political message: 'Self-reliance and self-
government needs to be developed', he insisted, as he called upon local
priests to get involved in the League. If they did, he argued, this would be
to the advantage of the Church: '"Priests and people" should be the motto.
Let St Patrick's Day inaugurate its practice.'[81]

   With preparations underway at such an early stage the 1885 St
Patrick's Day demonstration was set to be bigger and better than previous
meetings. Members of the INL throughout the region, well schooled by the
Diamond press, busily agitated the cause of Home Rule at every
opportunity. At a meeting of the John Bryson Branch in Cowpen Village
on 1 February the gathered members sarcastically proposed that Joseph
Chamberlain 'should put a piece of paper around his head with the
inscription 'Apartments to Let' and praised Gladstone 'our illustrious
leader'.[82] In this buoyant climate not one, but two, members of the Irish
Parliamentary party agreed to attend the Newcastle demonstration. John
O'Connor MP (Tipperary) and P. J. Power MP (Waterford) added their
weight to the proceedings organised under the auspices of the No 1 branch
of the INL. The pricing structure which ranged from a gallery view at 3d.,
back seats 6d., front seats 1s. and platform seats at 2s. was carefully
calibrated to enable the widest possible cross section of Irish society to
attend.[83] Mr Power drew attention to the fact that Newcastle was so well
served by its representative, Joseph Cowen MP, who was 'one of the
truest, one of the staunchest friends Ireland ever had'.[84] On this occasion,

---

[80] For Diamond's early career in Newcastle see Allen, 'Keeping the faith'; See also
Joan Allen, 'Charles Diamond', in Laurel Brake and Marysa Demoor et al. (eds),
Dictionary of Nineteenth-Century Journalism (Gent and London, 2009), p. 166.
[81] *Irish Tribune*, 14 February 1885.
[82] Ibid., 7 February 1885.
[83] Ibid., 26 February 1885.
[84] Ibid., Special Supplement, 21 March 1885.

the surplus funds raised at the event were committed to the INL National Executive. Other regional meetings also managed to secure big name speakers. Large crowds gathered in the Mechanics' Hall in Darlington, for example, to hear W. Redmond MP call upon them 'to exhaust every possible means to win their country's liberty'.[85]

In 1886, organisation for St Patrick's Day began in earnest in early January with some preparations already underway at Annitsford, Cowpen, and other places. The INL meeting in Cowpen referred to their recent local election success. Members formally approved the proposal to set up a Parliamentary fund and to launch the subscription on St Patrick's Day.[86] Similar calls had been made in Glasgow and other places, and again the chief sponsor of the fund raising strategy was the Diamond press which was, by then, circulating widely throughout England and Scotland.[87] At a meeting in the Newcastle Irish Literary Institute Diamond set up an organising committee of twenty-five to plan a major demonstration. He was determined to 'prove to our American brethren that though not so well favoured in worldly goods, the Irishmen here are as ready and willing to respond to the call of duty as they themselves are'; he was confident that 'a couple of thousand pounds' could be raised.[88] Across the region, branches of the INL in Bedlington, Blyth, Willington, Sunderland and Bishop Auckland began to put their plans in place and invite prominent nationalists. David Crilly MP (North Mayo) was the chosen speaker for the Newcastle meeting while Spennymoor INL was intent upon securing the good offices of J.F.X. O'Brien, 'one of the men of '67'.[89]

Unfortunately, despite the months of planning, the St Patrick's Day demonstrations proved to be 'unsatisfactory in the extreme', because many of the region's invited speakers, with very little notice, had reneged on their promises to attend.[90] Writing in the *Irish Tribune*, Diamond complained bitterly that the National League organisation was too centralised and that this was becoming obstructive. The national executive of the INL exerted great influence over the movements of Irish MPs and it would appear that its organisation was shambolic; three letters from the Newcastle Committee requesting political speakers had all gone unanswered. As the *Irish Tribune* reported 'From similar causes' the Manchester and Leeds demonstrations had fallen through and the entire

[85] Ibid.
[86] Ibid., 2 January 1886.
[87] Ibid., 9 January 1886.
[88] Ibid., 16 January 1886.
[89] Ibid., 13 March 1886.
[90] Ibid., 20 March 1886.

system badly needed revision; it was this kind of 'carelessness' which wasted the fundraising efforts of the people.[91] As one of the principal organisers, Diamond was naturally anxious to confirm that the collapse of the planned programme was outside of their control. No doubt he was fearful that some would demand a full refund on the grounds that tickets had been sold under false pretences. Initially, it was thought that David Crilly had failed to turn up because of prior commitments in the House but his letter to the Newcastle INL soon revealed that this was not the case: the Irish members, he explained, had been 'absolutely commanded to remain here' and prevented from attending the meetings.[92] Nor was this to be the only occasion when local organisers were let down. Similar problems surfaced in 1887 when James Carew, MP for Kildare, failed to turn up to address the Willington celebrations and worse still, sent an eleventh hour telegram cancelling the arrangements. If the INL were incensed by this cavalier attitude, on this occasion there was nothing in the *Irish Tribune* to suggest that that the arrangements had gone badly awry. The *Tribune* merely reported that the procession that had been organised in his honour still went ahead.[93] Even allowing for the fact that the debate on Home Rule was then approaching a critical stage, the decision by the executive to require members to remain at Westminster seems foolhardy. Their political success depended upon the mass platform and the annual St Patrick's Day events represented a vital opportunity for the Irish Parliamentary Party to exert its influence. It is tempting to speculate on the impact this had upon the nationalist project and it is clear that this is an instance where a study of St Patrick's Day organisation in other parts of Britain might prove illuminating.[94]

At the end of the 1880s, local Irish people were galvanised by the coercive policies of the Government and the continuing failure to secure Home Rule. Although there is little indication that the Irish were organising on the same scale as in 1885 and 1886, nationalist arguments were just as aggressively expounded as this St Patrick's Day poem printed in the *Irish Tribune* on the eve of the feast day in 1889 indicates:

> And bid them at their country's call be up to work like men,
> That Faith and Freedom, hand in hand, may bless our land again.

---

[91] Ibid.

[92] Ibid.

[93] Ibid., 26 March 1887.

[94] McBride, *Experience of Irish Migrants to Glasgow*, pp. 153–4 details some of the conflict that arose over the festival organisation in Glasgow and the impact that visiting speakers had upon the democratic agenda.

And, honest men of every creed will aid that holy cause,
Till foul Coercion Acts give place to honest Irish laws.[95]

The 1889 Tyneside demonstration was held in Bath Lane Hall, a smaller and less prestigious venue than the Town Hall but still filled to capacity to hear to T. D. Sullivan MP (Dublin) belittle Balfour's futile attempt to 'subdue' the Irish.[96] Elsewhere the Irish were showing their mettle. A major St Patrick's Day demonstration in Manchester's Free Trade Hall saw John Redmond MP address a crowd of some 7,000 people and condemn the 'unconstitutional and oppressive policy of the Government, and the scandalous treatment of Irish political prisoners', while in America $15,000 was raised for the Parnell Defence fund.[97] In 1890, there was standing room only at the demonstration in the Town Hall. The platform banner 'God Save Ireland' set the agenda and the walls were handsomely decorated with portraits of Irish politicians and patriots. However, the proceedings were marred by the problem of securing suitable speakers. Apologies were read out from Michael Davitt and Dr Charles Tanner MP (County Cork Mid) for it seemed that the Irish members were once again 'under authority' and only 'went whither they were sent', this time to more prestigious meetings elsewhere.[98]

It is noticeable that as the new century dawned, the celebrations began to change and, in part, this reflected the loss of key personnel to the local movement. The death of activists such as Bernard McAnulty who had exercised great influence on Irish affairs in his role as town councillor and Joseph Cowen MP who had supported Irish Home Rule long before it became Gladstonian orthodoxy, and fought a succession of Coercion bills in the House of Commons, left a vacuum in local politics that was seemingly impossible to fill. On the eve of the feast day in 1906, John O'Connor MP spoke warmly of their contribution and mourned their loss to the 'cradle city of the Home Rule movement in England'.[99] The change did not pass by unremarked by the *Newcastle Daily Chronicle* either and its Editorial commented upon the improved relations between England and Ireland.[100] Instead of 'being a sign of revolt', the wearing of shamrock had

---

[95] Poem penned by James Lynch, a schoolteacher from Coatbridge, published in the *Irish Tribune*, 16 March 1889.
[96] Ibid., 23 March 1889.
[97] Ibid.
[98] *Newcastle Daily Chronicle*, 18 March 1890.
[99] Ibid., 17 March 1906.
[100] Ibid.

become socially acceptable, and among London Society it had become seasonably 'fashionable'.[101]

In conclusion, evidence suggests that the political agenda dominated the celebrations in the North East to an unusual degree. In 1911 Joseph Devlin was presented with a donation of £70 for the Irish parliamentary fund at a St Patrick's Day reception in the County Hotel, Newcastle.[102] While not all of the events held to mark the national feast day were as successful as the planners would have wished, they do not appear to have contemplated abandoning their view that this was the premier occasion for protesting their difference and not, as some have claimed, an opportunity for demonstrating compatible loyalties.[103] And, of course, any emphasis in this study on the political dimension should not be taken to suggest that the region's Irish settlers always took themselves, or the cause of Irish nationalism, too seriously. The political part of the proceedings undoubtedly assumed precedence, for all the reasons indicated above, but there was always time for revelry too. When the serious business of the evening was concluded, the carpets were rolled back and the Newcastle INL executive and their compatriots danced the night way, often until four in the morning.[104]

---

[101] Ibid., 'London Lights' column. Wider public acceptance and participation in the festival was noticeable in other British cities by the turn of the century. See Cronin and Adair, *Wearing of the Green*, p. 61.
[102] *Newcastle Illustrated Chronicle*, 18 March 1911.
[103] Cronin and Adair, *Wearing of the Green*, p. xiv.
[104] *Irish Tribune*, 19 March 1887.

CHAPTER NINE

'EXPLOITED WITH FURY ON A THOUSAND PLATFORMS': WOMEN, UNIONISM AND THE *NE TEMERE* DECREE IN IRELAND, 1908–1913

D. A. J. MACPHERSON

The Protestants of Belfast were a formidable social and economic force at the beginning of the twentieth century. As the Catholic population of the city declined, Belfast became a stronghold of Irish Protestantism, so that by 1911 over three-quarters of the city's inhabitants professed the Protestant faith.[1] Yet despite their demographic dominance, the Protestants of Belfast were insecure. The strength of the Catholic population of Ireland outside of Belfast, the disestablishment of the Church of Ireland in 1869, and the strength of Home Rule politics all served to convince Ulster Protestants that 'they were facing a Catholic-inspired nationalist threat to their entire way of life'.[2] Protestant fears of Catholic Ireland came to a head at the beginning of 1911 with the conjunction of three events: Asquith's introduction of the third Home Rule Bill in the House of Commons; the foundation of the Ulster Women's Unionist Association to fight Home Rule; and the publicizing of an alleged application of the Papal decree invalidating mixed marriages, the decree *Ne Temere*, which insisted that children born of a mixed marriage should be brought up as

---

[1] A. C. Hepburn, *A Past Apart. Studies in the history of Catholic Belfast 1850–1950* (Belfast, 1996), p. 4.

[2] D. Hempton and M. Hill, *Evangelical Protestantism in Ulster Society 1740–1890* (London, 1992), p. 167. For statistics on the strength of the Catholic population of Ireland during the nineteenth century see W. E. Vaughan and A. J. Fitzpatrick, *Irish Historical Statistics: Population 1821–1971* (Dublin, 1978), p. 49.

Catholics. Hinging on the extraordinary McCann marriage case in which
Unionist politicians claimed that a Belfast Presbyterian, Agnes McCann,
had her children removed from her care by the father's Catholic priest,
women became involved in Unionist politics in order to preserve the
safety and sanctity of Ulster Protestant home life against the threat of
Home Rule. Ulster Unionist women saw their domesticity as affording
them a role in public life, which they exploited to the full, becoming
enthusiastic participants in the campaign against Home Rule. As a
resolution of the executive committee of the Ulster Women's Unionist
Council (UWUC) in 1911 argued, a Dublin-based, Catholic-dominated
parliament was seen as a threat to the 'civil and religious liberty of the
women of Ireland and the security of their homes'.[3] This chapter examines
the intersection of gender, politics, national culture and popular beliefs in
the heated moment of the McCann marriage case, and demonstrates the
importance of religious principles to Ulster Unionists at the time of the
third Home Rule Bill crisis.

Much historical writing on the hardening of Ulster Unionist attitudes
during 1911–12 is guilty of a double omission, ignoring the role of women
in promoting opposition to Home Rule and neglecting the centrality of
religion and anti-Catholic sentiment to the galvanisation of Unionism at
this time.[4] Paul Bew's admirable study of Unionism and Nationalism at
this time focuses on the political aspects of the McCann marriage case,
neatly drawing out how the incident was played out on the floor of the
House of Commons as a Unionist attack on the looming imposition of
Home Rule on Ireland, and how the issue of mixed marriage insinuated its
way into the final version of the bill. Yet he does not adequately
demonstrate the importance of religion and the impetus the McCann case
gave to female Unionist political action.[5] One of the few specific studies

---

[3] Public Record Office Northern Ireland (PRONI), D.1098/1/1, Minute Book of the
Executive Committee of the Ulster Women's Unionist Council, 16 June 1911.
[4] For recent work that seeks to redress these problems, see Alan Megahey, '"God
will defend the right". The Protestant Churches and opposition to home rule', in D.
George Boyce and Alan O'Day (eds), *Defenders of the Union. A survey of British
and Irish Unionism since 1801* (London, 2001), pp. 159–75; Graham Walker, 'The
Irish Presbyterian anti-Home Rule Convention of 1912', *Studies*, 86, 341 (1997),
71–7; Diane Urquhart, *Women in Ulster Politics 1890–1940. A history not yet told*
(Dublin, 2000); D. A. J. MacPherson, 'Women, Home and Irish Identity:
Discourses of Domesticity in Ireland, *c*.1890–1922', unpublished University of
London, PhD thesis, 2004, ch. 6.
[5] Paul Bew, *Ideology and the Irish Question. Ulster Unionism and Irish
Nationalism 1912–1916* (Oxford, 1994), pp. 31–4. Bew's analysis is echoed by
Tony Hepburn's recent analysis of northern Nationalism, See A. C. Hepburn,

of mixed marriages in Ireland, R. M. Lee's account of the *Ne Temere* decree, omits much of the political and religious implications of the McCann case, instead offering a sociological analysis of the event based on Stanley Cohen's notion of 'moral panic'.[6] Diane Urquhart's study of women's participation in Ulster politics briefly mentions the *Ne Temere* decree but neglects to analyse its centrality to the emergence of the UWUC in 1911.[7] However, the timing and manner in which Unionist women's opposition to Home Rule intensified suggests that the McCann marriage case acted as a vital spur to action in the Protestant community of Ulster.

The McCann marriage case came at a moment of great insecurity for Ireland's Protestant minority. In terms of demography, apart from the exceptional case of Belfast, Catholics were the dominant confession of Ireland, comprising seventy-four per cent of the population in 1911.[8] Despite a marginal decline in the Catholic population in Ireland during the nineteenth century, the Protestant community was most alarmed by the numbers of Catholics entering middle-class, professional life. Between 1861 and 1911, the proportion of Catholic barristers in Ireland grew from thirty-four to forty-four per cent. Over the same period, the numbers of Catholic doctors rose from thirty-five to forty-eight per cent and the Catholic share of senior civil service posts in the newly enlarged Irish administration leapt from thirty-nine to sixty-one per cent.[9]

Confidence in the ability of the Union to endure, shaken by the first two Home Rule bills in 1886 and 1892 and the disestablishment of the Church of Ireland in 1869, was further undermined by political developments during the first decade of the twentieth century. Constructive unionism, the term used to describe the Tory government's efforts to mollify the cause of Home Rule from 1895 to 1905 ('kill it with kindness' in Gerald Balfour's impromptu characterisation of this policy), may have been welcomed by some of Catholic Ireland, but many in the Protestant community interpreted it as further evidence of the withering

---

Catholic Belfast and Nationalist Ireland in the Era of Joe Devlin, 1871–1934 (Oxford, 2008), pp. 129–31.

[6] Raymond M. Lee, 'Intermarriage, Conflict and Social Control in Ireland: The Decree "*Ne Temere*", *Economic and Social Review*, 17, 1 (1985), 11–27; Stanley Cohen, *Folk Devils and Moral Panics: the creation of Mods and Rockers* (London, 1972).

[7] Urquhart, *Women in Ulster Politics*, p. 62.

[8] Vaughan and Fitzpatrick, *Irish Historical Statistics*, p. 49. For Belfast exceptionalism see Hepburn, *A Past Apart*, p. 34.

[9] John Hutchinson, *The Dynamics of Cultural Nationalism* (London, 1987), pp. 261–2.

away of the bonds between Ireland and mainland Britain.[10] R. L.
Crawford's journal, the *Irish Protestant*, founded in 1901, described this
policy as the 'Romanisation of Ireland by the Balfour brothers', capturing
the feelings of many Ulster Protestants at the beginning of the twentieth
century.[11]

The resurgence of Irish nationalist politics contributed to Protestant
feelings of unease. Following the disarray of the 1890s, the formation of
the United Irish League (UIL) in 1898 and the reorganization in 1904 of
the Ancient Order of Hibernians (AOH) under the Belfast West
Nationalist MP, Joe Devlin, galvanised Irish constitutional nationalism as
a mass-movement. Within two years of its foundation, the UIL claimed
almost 35,000 members spread throughout 180 branches in Ireland.[12] The
AOH, benefiting from what Bew has described as Devlin's masterstroke in
registering the organisation as a friendly society under the terms of the
1911 National Insurance Act, grew to a membership of almost 170,000 in
Ireland and Britain by 1913.[13] Such Irish nationalist advances were
interpreted fearfully by the Unionist community in Ireland, who avidly
devoured the anti-Catholic outpourings of activists such as M.J.F.
McCarthy and saw the AOH in particular as a sinister manifestation of
Catholic secret society culture which would impose a Roman Catholic
ascendancy on Ireland under a Home Rule parliament.[14]

Irish Protestants viewed developments in the Catholic Church from the
same negative perspective. In the decade leading up to the *Ne Temere*
decree, Protestants had been irked by Catholics being deterred by the
Church hierarchy from attending memorial services for Queen Victoria in
1901, an increasingly voluble Catholic participation in street processions,

---

[10] Andrew Gailey, *Ireland and the Death of Kindness: the experience of
constructive Unionism, 1890–1905* (Cork, 1987), p. 65; Megahey, "God will
defend the right", p. 164. See also Andrew Gailey, 'The destructiveness of
constructive unionism. Theories and practice, 1890s–1960s', in Boyce and O'Day
(eds), *Defenders of the Union*, pp. 227–50.

[11] Quoted in Megahey, "God will defend the right", p. 165.

[12] Conal Thomas, *The Land for the People. The United Irish League and land
reform in north Galway, 1898–1912* (Corrandulla, 1999), pp. v, 13; Patrick
Maume, *The Long Gestation. Irish nationalist life 1891–1918* (Dublin, 1999), p.
30.

[13] *The Weekly Freeman*, 15 March 1913, p. 64; Hepburn, *A Past Apart*, p. 167;
Bew, *Ideology and the Irish Question*, p. 75.

[14] Megahey, "God will defend the right", p. 165. For examples of Protestant
attitudes towards the AOH, see the speech of Thomas Sinclair at the Presbyterian
Anti-Home Rule Convention in Belfast, 1 February 1912, reported in *Belfast
Weekly News*, 8 February 1912.

and the demands for the provision of a Catholic university.[15] The promulgation of *Ne Temere* in 1908, despite attracting the condemnation of the Protestant Churches, was not initially interpreted as a taste of the religious persecution to come under a Home Rule parliament.[16] This may have been because the requirement to baptise children of mixed marriages as Catholic had existed since the eighteenth century; *Ne Temere* simply reinforced and codified existing practice.[17] Moreover, mixed marriages had long been settled by the convention, in Belfast at least, of religious endogamy, and since the middle of the nineteenth century, Protestants had viewed mixed marriages as Catholic and, therefore, as having no place in their communities.[18] Indeed, as 'An Ulster Presbyterian' wrote in 1912, such a prohibition on mixed marriages was not unknown in the Protestant faith, and that it 'had been conveniently forgotten that as late as 1844 the Church of Ireland held that a marriage of an Episcopalian and a Presbyterian by a Presbyterian clergyman was not legally binding'.[19]

What roused Protestant opinion against *Ne Temere* was the publicizing of the McCann marriage case at the end of 1910. William Corkey, Minister of Townsend Street Presbyterian Church in Belfast, wrote to the local press to draw the public's attention to the plight of one of his flock, Mrs Agnes McCann.[20] Agnes had been married in a Presbyterian church to Alexander McCann, a Catholic, before the promulgation of the *Ne Temere* decree in 1908, and they each worshipped at their own church.[21] However, in 1910 Corkey alleged that Alexander McCann's parish priest visited their house to inform the McCanns that their marriage was invalid unless

---

[15] Megahey, "God will defend the right", p. 165.

[16] Lee, 'Intermarriage, Conflict and Social Control in Ireland', 16.

[17] Ibid., 14.

[18] As Hepburn argues 'a sample of over 5,000 Belfast households in 1901 revealed no more than a dozen mixed marriages'. See Hepburn, *A Past Apart*, pp. 241–2.

[19] An Ulster Presbyterian, *Ulster on its Own; or An Easy Way with Ireland. Being a proposal of self-government for the five counties round Lough Neagh* (Belfast, 1912), p. 9.

[20] The Rev. William Corkey, *Glad did I live* (Belfast, 1961), p. 151.

[21] Lee, 'Intermarriage, conflict and social control in Ireland', 16. An article in the *Londonderry Sentinel*, a Unionist paper, dates their marriage to May 1908, *after* the *Ne Temere* decree came into effect, which would dispute Lee's assertion that the McCanns married 'some years before'. This dating is confirmed by a letter to *The Times* from the Rev. Dudley Fletcher, a Church of Ireland minister who gave his support to Mrs McCann, see 'The McCann Marriage', *The Times*, 9 February 1911, p. 6. The decree was promulgated on 2 August 1907 and was enforced from 19 April 1908. See 'Mixed Marriages in Ireland. The McCann Case', *Londonderry Sentinel*, 9 February 1911, p. 7.

they re-married in a Catholic ceremony. Agnes refused to follow the priest's and her husband's wishes, leading to a breakdown in the marriage and the subsequent flight of Alexander McCann with their two children. Corkey claimed that when Mrs McCann attempted to discover where her children had gone, the Catholic priest withheld information regarding their whereabouts.[22]

Corkey's letter caused uproar amongst the Protestant community of Ireland. They had long feared that any measure of Home Rule would lead to such restrictions on their religious freedom, and that the Catholic Church would have an overbearing influence in the new Ireland, acting almost outside of the law of the land.[23] If such an outrage as the McCann case could occur while Ulster was under the full protection of the British parliament, Unionists argued, then what fate awaited them under a Dublin-based, Catholic-dominated Home Rule assembly? 'Rome Rule', as Unionists characterised this measure of Irish self-government, would mean that they would be under the heels of 'the emissaries of a foreign potentate'.[24] As Mrs Moore, one of the leading organisers of the Ulster Women's Unionist Association (UWUA) and wife of the MP for North Armagh, William Moore, asked at a meeting on Lurgan Town Hall on 5 May 1911, 'if our homes are not sacred from the priest under existing laws, what can we expect from a priest-governed Ireland?'[25]

Protestant outrage manifested itself first through public meetings, held throughout Ireland and Britain, and then on the floor of Parliament. Agnes McCann had been advised by the Belfast Presbytery to petition the Lord Lieutenant of Ireland, Lord Aberdeen, in order to enlist the help of the police in discovering the whereabouts of her children.[26] Lord Aberdeen replied that there was nothing to warrant his intervention or the interference of the police, and that the matter should be pursued through

---

[22] Corkey, *Glad did I live*, p. 151.
[23] R. F. G. Holmes, '"Ulster will fight and Ulster will be right": The Protestant Churches and Ulster's resistance to Home Rule, 1912–14', in William J. Sheils (ed.), *Studies in Church History, 20: the Church and war* (Oxford, 1983), pp. 321–35.
[24] 'Home Rule Menace. Formation of Women's Unionist Association', *Londonderry Sentinel*, 24 January 1911. For the extent to which religious feeling entered political debate over Unionist opposition to Home Rule see Thomas C. Kennedy, '"The gravest situation of our lives": Conservatives, Ulster and the Home Rule crisis, 1911–14', *Eire-Ireland* 36, 3–4 (2001), 67–82.
[25] Public Record Office Northern Ireland (PRONI), D.3790/4, Lurgan Women's Unionist Association, Minute Book 1911–1921, 26 April 1911.
[26] Lee, 'Intermarriage, Conflict and Social Control in Ireland', 17; 'The Decree "Ne Temere"', *The Times*, 1 February 1911, p. 9.

the civil courts.[27] The McCann case was then taken up in the House of Commons by the Unionist member for Dublin University, J. H. Campbell. After rehearsing the details of the alleged abduction of Agnes McCann's children on the instigation of her husband's Catholic priest, Campbell remarked on the fear this case inspired amongst the Unionist community, assuring Parliament that

> it had strengthened the unalterable determination of the loyalists and Protestants in that country – that at any sacrifice and cost they would struggle to retain what they believed to be the only guarantee for the continued enjoyment of their civil and religious rights, to live under the laws that had received the sanction of that Imperial Parliament.[28]

The Nationalist response, led by Joe Devlin and John Dillon, followed a two-pronged strategy: Dillon's job was to calm Unionist fears about a Home Rule parliament; Devlin's to divert attention from the question of religious and civil liberty, and instead expose the McCann case as a fabrication designed purely as a political stick with which to beat the Nationalist community of Belfast. Dillon denied that the Catholic Church had any right 'to impose conditions of its own in addition to the conditions required by the law of the land'.[29] It was, in Dillon's view, a case of a priest intervening not in a happy home, but in a bickering household. For the Nationalists, the law of the land took priority over any religious decree, and the coming of Home Rule for Ireland would not alter that. Dillon attempted to soothe Unionist concerns, arguing that 'I do not believe that there is the slightest risk of any alteration of the law of Ireland which would make the smallest atom of injustice or civil disability on anyone because he was not a member of our Church'. His description of the Catholic Church as 'our Church', however, would have done little to assuage Unionist fears.[30] John Redmond, the leader of the Irish Parliamentary Party, summed up the Nationalist position on the McCann case in a speech in March 1911, arguing that 'the *Ne Temere* Decree has not pretended, and does not pretend, to overrule [sic] the ordinary civil

---

[27] 'Lord Aberdeen and the Mixed Marriages Case', *The Times*, 9 January 1911, p. 6.
[28] 'The Case of Mrs McCann', *The Times*, 8 February 1911, p. 12. See also *Hansard*, 5th series, xxii, p. 174 (7 February 1911).
[29] 'The Case of Mrs McCann', *The Times*, 8 February 1911, p. 12.
[30] 'Belfast Marriage Case. A Conclusive Debate in the House of Commons', *Weekly Freeman*, 11 February 1911, p. 3.

laws of the land'.[31] Redmond concluded that Home Rule would act as a safeguard for Protestants in Ireland; under the terms of a Dublin Parliament, 'no law causing oppression to men because of religious beliefs would ever be allowed to become enacted, because the Imperial Parliament would be there to prevent it'.[32]

Devlin, MP for Belfast West, eschewed Dillon's mollifying tone and portrayed the incident as a piece of opportunistic politicking on the part of the Unionists:

> Why was the woman's [Mrs McCann] statement made public five days before the West Belfast election? The fact was the whole matter arose out of a wretched domestic quarrel of the lowest meanest kind . . . Placards were printed with the words 'Will you vote for Devlin and have Protestant children taken up by priests?' The incident had been one of the greatest assets for the Ulster Tory Party since William III.[33]

Devlin went on to give an account of the genesis of the incident, describing how it had started as a dispute in a Catholic church when Mr McCann was attempting to have his son baptised, following the convention for children of mixed marriages that a son would take his father's religion and a daughter her mother's.[34] It was, according to a letter from the friends of Mr McCann received by Devlin, a story of 'domestic misery, with which the priest had nothing to do'.[35] Devlin denounced the tactics of the Unionists in trying to use the McCann case to influence the outcome of an election: 'the incident occurred in October, and the miserable story was dragged into the political arena for party purposes on the eve of the election by the leaders of the Ulster Unionist Party'.[36] Patrick Little, a member of the Young Ireland Branch of the United Irish League, confirmed Nationalist suspicions that religious freedom had little to do with the Unionist's championing of Agnes McCann:

> Why were these cases made matters of *Haute Politique*, when they were matters for the Police Court? This muck-raking reflects very little honour on the Unionist Crusaders. If these cases prove anything, they prove the

---

[31] 'The National Festival. With our Kith and Kin Abroad', *Weekly Freeman*, 25 March 1911, p. 2.
[32] Ibid.
[33] 'The Case of Mrs McCann', *The Times*, 8 February 1911, p. 12; 'Belfast "Kidnapping" Case', *Irish News*, 8 February 1911, p. 6.
[34] Lee, 'Intermarriage, Conflict and Social Control in Ireland', 15.
[35] 'The Case of Mrs McCann', *The Times*, 8 February 1911, p. 12.
[36] Ibid.

inadvisability of mixed marriages. But there is a high premium on dirty Irish linen just at present.[37]

Devlin, however, did not simply take the side of the husband in the McCann case, arguing instead that it was the economic plight of women in Belfast, and not the perceived wrongs of the *Ne Temere* decree against them, that was of greater significance for the female population of the city.[38] Devlin criticised the clergy of Belfast for their lack of support for a recent meeting of women to protest against sweatshop conditions in some of the textile factories when they had been all too keen to leap on to platforms to fight for Mrs McCann. At this mostly Protestant gathering 'not a single voice was raised on behalf of the toiling women who were doing so much to build up the greatness of the city and advance the material interests of their masters'.[39] Devlin, Dillon and the rest of the Irish Parliamentary Party interpreted the McCann case as a political stunt, designed to bolster the Protestant community of Ireland against the imminent threat of Home Rule.

Political stunt or not, the McCann case and the affront to Protestant religious liberty it represented spurred the Unionists into action at the beginning of the debate over the third Home Rule Bill in 1911. The role of women at this important stage of Unionist political development was vital and helped yoke together fears for the future sanctity of the Protestant home with Unionist opposition to Home Rule. Religion, and women's determination to uphold Protestantism in the home, therefore, were central to the emergence of the UWUA throughout Ulster during 1911. The first meeting of the UWUC was held in January 1911, during the McCann crisis, and by 1912, between 40,000 and 50,000 women had become members of the thirty-two UWUAs throughout Ulster.[40] The domestic rhetoric employed by women to explain their reasons for involvement in the UWUA confirms the centrality of the mixed marriage issue to the emergence of female Unionist political activism.

The McCann case was the catalyst, to a large extent, for women's opposition to Home Rule. Edith Mercier Clements, one of the leading members of the UWUA, argued at a meeting in Lurgan Town Hall in May 1911 that the McCann case made Home Rule a central concern for Ulster women: 'when it was possible for one of their sex, a poor woman, to be bereft of her husband and children, of all that made home life dear . . . then

---

[37] Patrick J. Little, *Rome Rule* (Dublin, 1912), pp. 19–20.

[38] 'Belfast "Kidnapping" Case', *Irish News*, 8 February 1911, p. 6.

[39] Ibid.

[40] Urquhart, *Women in Ulster Politics*, p. 61.

it was undoubtedly a woman's question'.[41] Mrs Lowry declared at a
meeting of the Comber Branch of the Women's Unionist Association in
March 1912 that 'the Ne Temere decree was a woman's question, and they
were going to get up a petition against it'.[42] Mrs M. Sinclair, the honorary
secretary of the North Tyrone UWUA, stressed the fear of 'Rome Rule'
that the McCann case appeared to confirm: 'under a Nationalist
Government the Ne Temere Decree would be strictly enforced, and the
sanctity of Home Life violated'.[43] The Rev. T. R. C. Hughes, chairman of
the North Antrim Women's Association concurred, arguing that the *Ne
Temere* decree interfered with family life and urged 'every man and
woman in Ulster' to oppose Home Rule, for the whole question was
'bound up with religion and family life'.[44]

The intimate connection between an Ulster woman's duty to protect
the life of her home and the perceived threat presented by Home Rule was
made very clear in Mrs W. J. Allen's speech at the inaugural meeting of
the Lurgan Women's Unionist Association in January 1911.[45] Mrs Allen
stated that the McCann case had produced a state of 'uproar' in Ulster
because of the 'kidnapping of two Presbyterian children by a
representative of the Pope of Rome'. Women's ability to defend their
home, in Allen's opinion, would be tested by a Home Rule parliament:

> What was the use of preaching healthy homes for themselves and their
> children if the laws of the King were flouted, a happy home broken up, a
> wife and mother flung on the streets, the children torn from her breast, her
> very clothes and furniture taken and the door of her house shut in her face?
> What was the use of preaching healthy homes if those who had control
> under Home Rule were permitted to do such things under British law,
> while the representative of the King [the Lord Lieutenant, Lord Aberdeen]
> refused to exert his full influence and power to restore that home and those
> dear children? . . . The women of Ireland should appeal to her Majesty the
> Queen in the sacred name of wife and mother, to take such steps as would
> restore that home . . . 'By a great price we purchased this freedom' and let
> them tell all who would dare filch it from them that the only Home Rule

---

[41] PRONI, D.3790/4, Lurgan Women's Unionist Association, Minute Book 1911–
1921, 26 April 1911.
[42] 'Women's Unionist Association. Meeting of the Comber Branch', *Northern
Whig*, 1 March 1912, p. 9.
[43] 'Women's Unionist Association', *Fermanagh Times*, 9 November 1911, p. 2.
[44] 'North Antrim Women's Association', *Belfast News-Letter*, 16 August 1911, p.
7.
[45] 'Unionism in Lurgan. Women's Association Formed', *Lurgan Mail*, 14 January
1911, p. 5.

they desired was in that sacred spot, that home where woman's duty lay as queen.[46]

The connection between the defence of Ulster homes against the threat of Home Rule and religious freedom is made clear in the wording of the petition against the *Ne Temere* decree organised by the UWUC in January 1912.[47] The petition, signed by 104,301 women, set out the grounds on which Home Rule would specifically affect women, and indicates the importance of religion to Ulster women's defence of their homes against Home Rule:[48]

a) Serious dangers would arise to our social and domestic liberties from intrusting [sic] legislative functions to a body of which a large permanent majority would be under ecclesiastical control.
b) No legislative safeguards would avail to protect us against such dangers, as the Roman Catholic Church refuses to recognise the binding effect of any agreements which curtail her prerogatives and claims an uncontrolled jurisdiction in the provinces of education and the marriage laws, a claim which has been recognised in practice by the Irish Parliamentary Party.
c) The late iniquitous enforcement of the *Ne Temere* Decree – a decree which specifically affects the women of Ireland – and the slavish acquiescence of the Irish Nationalist members of Parliament in its operation, demonstrate that in an Irish Parliament the natural instincts of humanity would be of no avail against the dictates of the Roman Church.
d) The dominating power of ecclesiastics over education in Ireland, which is already excessive, would be largely increased and schools and colleges under the control of religious orders would be state favoured institutions under an Irish Parliament.
e) There would be no prospect of beneficent legislation to ameliorate the conditions of life of unprotected women engaged in industrial work in many conventual institutions, as the Irish Nationalist members of Parliament steadfastly oppose any such legislation.
f) No valid reason has been advanced for depriving Irish women of the rights and priviliges [sic] which they now enjoy.[49]

---

[46] Ibid.
[47] Diane Urquhart, ''The female of the species is more deadlier than the male'? The Ulster Women's Unionist Council, 1911–40', in Janice Holmes and Diane Urquhart (eds), *Coming into the Light. The work, politics and religion of women in Ulster 1840–1940* (Belfast, 1994), p. 99; PRONI, D.1098/1/1, 28 March 1912.
[48] PRONI, D.2688/1/9, Ulster Women's Unionist Council Year Books, 'Annual Report for 1912', p. 7. The report goes on to say that the number signing the petition would have been much higher 'had time permitted'.
[49] Ibid.

Each point of this petition invoked the attack of Home Rule on Protestantism. Women's defence of the home life of Ulster was also a defence of its religion; the home was a site of identity in female Unionist politics in which women would defend religious freedom.

Protestant reaction to the *Ne Temere* decree, therefore, acted as the inspiration for the founding of Ulster Women's Unionist Associations throughout the province. The bulk of female Unionist rhetoric concerned itself with the defence of their Ulster, Protestant homes from the imposition of Home Rule. From the very beginning, inspired by the McCann case, the UWUA placed the protection of home life at the centre of its arguments against the dissolution of the Union. A resolution passed at a meeting of the Executive Committee of the UWUC in 1911 outlined the importance of the Union to the preservation of Ulster home life:

> That the Ulster Women's Unionist Council protest in the strongest manner against the passing of any Home Rule Bill for Ireland, as they know that the civil and religious liberty of the women of Ireland and the security of their homes can only be guaranteed under the Legislative and Administrative Union of Great Britain and Ireland.[50]

An almost identical plea was sent in a letter to Bonar Law in the spring of 1913 welcoming him to Ulster on his first visit as leader of the opposition.[51]

The connection between preserving their homes and maintaining the Union was affirmed at a meeting of the Lurgan Women's Unionist Association on 5 May 1911 in Lurgan Town Hall. Mrs W. J. Allen once again proposed a resolution at the meeting similar to that made at the central meeting in Belfast:

> We call upon all Irish Unionist women to do their utmost and put forth every effort to enlighten all true friends of the empire as to the grave dangers which the granting of Home Rule would mean to our country and our homes, and to assist the English and Scottish electors to a better understanding of the Irish question.[52]

Mrs Allen went on to suggest that they should 'support their menfolk in every way' to safeguard the Union, which embodied everything of

---

[50] PRONI, D. 1098/1/1, Minute Book of the Executive Committee of the Ulster Women's Unionist Council, 16 June 1911.
[51] PRONI, D. 1098/1/1, Sub-Committee re. Easter Demonstration, 28 March 1912.
[52] PRONI, D. 3790/4, Lurgan Women's Unionist Association, Minute Book 1911–1921, 26 April 1911.

importance to women, from their civil and religious liberty to their homes and their children: 'Home was a woman's first consideration, or should be, and they should remember that in the event of Home Rule being granted, the sanctity and happiness of home life in Ulster would be permanently destroyed.'[53] Mrs Allen's speech confirmed the intimate connection between women's domestic role ('her first consideration') and the fight against Home Rule that the UWUA would wage in the public sphere.

Such a connection was made time and again in speeches and demonstrations organised under the auspices of the UWUA. At a meeting of the association in November 1911 in Ballinamallard, County Fermanagh, Mrs Sinclair, one of the leading figures on the UWUC, gave a speech eliding the preservation of home life with the maintenance of the Union. Mrs Sinclair described Home Rule as a 'great danger that threatened their country and their homes'. She had come to speak to them not because she was 'a suffragist or anything like that', but because 'she took an interest in her home'.[54] Earlier a meeting of the UWUA in Portadown had heard similar opinions voiced. Mrs Moore addressed the gathering in May 1911, arguing that 'their homes and their country were once more in danger' and that they should support their menfolk in their opposition to Home Rule: 'That whatever the men of Ulster determined to do in defence of their liberties and homes the women of Ulster were with them.'[55] This identification of male involvement in the defence of the home suggests that men as well as women could defend the home, and it was only because the home was perceived as the proper sphere of female endeavour that female Unionism employed domestic rhetoric.

The connection between female Unionism and defence of the domestic sphere was reiterated in an article in the *Ballymoney Free Press* from 1911.[56] The newspaper welcomed the Ballycastle Women's Unionist Association as the 'beginning of female efforts in public affairs' and that women should be involved in the fight against Home Rule because 'the woman knows where the shoe pinches in the household'; a woman's role in the home, so the newspaper article argued, gave women an interest and responsibility in political affairs.[57] At a meeting of the Lurgan Women's

---

[53] Ibid.
[54] 'Women's Unionist Association', *Fermanagh Times*, 9 November 1911, p. 2.
[55] 'Ulster Women's Unionist Council. Meeting in Portadown', *Northern Whig*, 11 May 1911, p. 10.
[56] PRONI, D. 2688/5/1, Ballycastle Branch of the North Antrim Women's Unionist Association, Minutes 1911–1934. A newspaper cutting from *Ballymoney Free Press* (n.d.), c.1911.
[57] Ibid.

Unionist Association in May 1911, Mrs Moore outlined the threat of
Home Rule to the home life of Ulster Unionists and the necessity of doing
political work in England. Women could do this work because of their
domestic influence:

> Women had great influence in their own homes, not because of their
> cleverness or capability as housewives, but because their hearts were in
> their homes, and she wanted every woman she saw present to put her
> whole heart into that movement until the impending crisis was over.[58]

Ulster women's contribution to the defence of the Union was based, then,
not on their skills in housewifery or childcare, but on their emotional
commitment to the home; there was nothing women could do *as
housewives* to combat Home Rule.[59]

Women's defence of the home was tied closely to their safeguarding
religion. Already we have seen how, as in the UWUC's resolution in June
1911 against Home Rule, the formula of female Unionist protest often
married the 'security of the home' with 'civil and religious liberty'.[60]
Despite Lady Londonderry's plea at the second meeting of the UWUC that
the case against Home Rule should be made on 'social, economic and
financial grounds' in order to avoid the charge of 'Ulster bigotry', such a
religious identification was, in practice, hard to avoid as Protestantism was
one of the defining features of Ulster identity.[61] An editorial that appeared
in the *Belfast News-Letter* commenting on Ulster Day at the end of
September 1912 stressed the importance of religion and the threat posed to
it by Home Rule.[62] The newspaper paid tribute to the meeting held by the
UWUA in Ulster Hall in Belfast, yet argued that the matter was not
political: 'the women of the Unionism of Ulster are not in politics . . . For
them Home Rule is a matter, as Mrs Murland [one of the speakers at
Ulster Hall] put it last night, of their religion, their homes and their
children.'[63] Referring to a speech by the Dowager Marchioness of
Dufferin and Ava, the editorial concluded that women opposed Home
Rule because it would 'endanger their religious liberties and well-being'.[64]

---

[58] PRONI, D. 3790/4, 26 April 1911.
[59] 'Women's Unionist Association. Successful Meeting in Lurgan', *Lurgan Mail*,
29 April 1911, p. 6.
[60] PRONI, D. 1098/1/1, 16 June 1911.
[61] Ibid., 30 January 1911.
[62] *Belfast News-Letter*, 1 October 1912, p. 5.
[63] Ibid.
[64] Ibid.

Exactly how did Ulsterwomen hope to combat the third Home Rule Bill? Despite the constant pleas that Ulster women were not interested in politics, the practical efforts of the UWUA to combat Home Rule concentrated on the established political activities of canvassing and education work. The political nature of the type of work Unionist women could undertake was outlined by Lady Londonderry at the inaugural meeting of the UWUA at the beginning of 1911.[65] Londonderry appealed to 'Loyalist women all over Ireland' to 'canvass voters, to trace removals, and to endeavour to bring every single voter to the poll during elections, so that every seat in Ulster shall be won for the Union'.[66] Women, to borrow Alvin Jackson's tart phraseology, were to defend the Union by immersing themselves in the 'geegaws of Edwardian electioneering'.[67] Yet most of this work was to be carried out not in Ireland, but in mainland Britain, attempting to convince the electorate of England and Scotland to vote for the preservation of the Union. Unionist women were to achieve this by writing letters, sending out Unionist literature, and by visiting the British mainland to organise meetings during elections and by-elections, and to canvass door-to-door.[68]

A meeting of the Executive Committee of the UWUC in March 1911 discussed a proposal from the London-based Women's Amalgamated Unionist and Tariff Reform Association to receive 'Irish Unionist workers' in England to arrange meetings and canvass the vote.[69] A letter from Mrs Graham Hope, 'Organizing Secretary' of this Association, explained that the women involved should be

> of two classes: First, ladies capable of speaking at small cottage meetings, in village schools, or in ladies' drawing rooms, possibly even at larger meetings; Second, women of any class who will be content to go from house to house talking to each individual occupier and explaining all the facts.[70]

---

[65] PRONI, D. 2846/1/2/3, Londonderry Papers, Women's Unionist Association, 'The Fight Against Home Rule. Nationalist Hatred of England' (n.p., n.d.), and reprinted from the *Belfast News-Letter*, 24 January 1911, pp. 2–5.

[66] Ibid., p. 4.

[67] Alvin Jackson, 'Unionist Myths', *Past and Present*, 136 (1992), 170.

[68] At this time Wales was a stronghold of nonconformity, Liberal politics and the nascent Labour movement. It was unlikely to respond favourably to overtures from Unionism and Conservatism.

[69] PRONI, D. 1098/1/1, 3 March 1911.

[70] Ibid.

The role of women was not to speak at large political meetings, but instead to address small, informal, domestic gatherings, though it is interesting to note the class-differentiation outlined in the letter, which reflects the dominance of upper-class women in the higher echelons of female Unionism.

The work of the Lurgan Women's Unionist Association demonstrated further the political activism of the women's Unionist movement. At a meeting of the Association held in May 1911, Mrs Moore detailed the activities of some of the branch's women in England: 'the ladies of Lurgan district had taken a part in elections in two English constituencies by sending Irish papers and literature on the Irish question, and with most satisfactory results'.[71] The UWUC Report for 1911 detailed their 'campaign in Great Britain', in which 'six ladies were sent to work for the Unionist candidate at the Haddington Bye-Election in April, and one of your members worked in Cambridgeshire for almost a month, and in the neighbourhood of Gloucester for about a week'.[72] Furthermore, in July 1913 seven female Unionist workers were sent to Walthamstow, East London, to canvass for the Unionist cause.[73]

At the annual meeting of the Lurgan Women Unionists, the details of Unionist work in sending literature to English and Scottish voters were discussed.[74] The meeting described their links with the Women's Unionist Association in England, and how they had sent over two thousand leaflets to the mainland. Miss Crawford announced that she had undertaken to 'send literature to working men's clubs in West Bromwich, Staffordshire, and Suffolk'.[75] The annual meeting of the Portadown Branch focused on similar activities with the President, Mrs Dougan, stating that they sent 'about 120 newspapers in the week to voters across the channel'.[76] A similar story was told at the East Down Women's Unionist Association's annual meeting at the beginning of 1912. According to a report in the *Belfast News-Letter*, the association devoted its energies to electioneering:

[71] PRONI, D. 3790/4, 13 May 1911.
[72] PRONI, D. 2688/1/9, Ulster Women's Unionist Council Year Books, 'Report for 1911', p. 3.
[73] PRONI, D. 2688/1/1, Ulster Women's Unionist Council, Minutes of Standing Committee re: Active Workers 1911–1916, 16 July 1913.
[74] 'Lurgan Women Unionists. Annual Meeting of the Association', *Lurgan Mail*, 10 February 1912, p. 6.
[75] Ibid.
[76] 'Women's Unionist Association. Annual Meeting of Portadown Branch', *Lurgan Mail*, 18 May 1912, p. 7.

There are also almost 100 members in different parts of the constituency sending Unionist papers and literature to Radical voters in England and Scotland, and several members, as well as sending papers, write personal letters advocating the maintenance of the Legislative Union. There have been a few public meetings, but so far the association has devoted itself more exclusively to collecting funds to send speakers to England and Scotland.[77]

Thus we can see how the work of the UWUA, motivated by the McCann case and the desire to preserve the religious liberty of their Ulster homes, was almost entirely political and devoted to electioneering in England and Scotland.

The largely political nature of female Unionist activism may be seen in the discussions held by the UWUC about whether or not to broaden out its activities beyond campaigning in British elections. This debate arose in 1913 as Unionism teetered on the brink of armed resistance to the imposition of Home Rule. An Ulster Volunteer Force (UVF) had been formed early in 1913 for the purpose of drilling and training an indigenous armed force, with a significant cache of arms provided by the Larne gun-run of April 1914.[78] In the UWUC, a difference of opinion arose over whether or not to reduce their electioneering and concentrate instead upon giving ancillary support to the UVF. At a meeting of the UWUC Advisory Committee in June 1914, some of the committee members expressed dissatisfaction with their political work:

Some of the Committee urge that constitutional methods of resisting Home Rule have proved useless, that force alone can decide the issue and that therefore all funds should be applied to the equipment of the UVF. They consider that by raising money to send to speakers and canvassers to Great Britain and distribute literature, and especially by spending such a large sum on such work at a General Election, the Council is allowing itself to be made the fool of the English Conservative party, who have no regard for Ulster except as a lever for securing their own return to power.[79]

However, the committee came to the conclusion that it would be more productive to continue with their purely political work: 'the funds of the

---

[77] 'East Down Women's Unionist Association. Annual Meeting in Downpatrick', *Belfast News-Letter*, 10 January 1912, p. 6.
[78] Patrick Buckland, 'Irish Unionism and the New Ireland', in D. G. Boyce (ed.), *The Revolution in Ireland, 1879–1923* (London, 1988), p. 77.
[79] PRONI, D. 2688/1/5, Ulster Women's Unionist Council Advisory Committee Minutes 1913–1914, 15 June 1914, 'Memorandum for Submission to Sir Edward Carson'.

council should therefore be devoted to the extension and vigorous
presecution [sic] of a campaign by speakers, canvassers and distribution of
literature in order to rouse public opinion in England and Scotland'.[80]
Thus, the UWUC was committed to campaigning and electioneering in
mainland Britain in order to defend the Union. Despite this overtly
political work, the rhetoric behind the political actions of the UWUC
framed the defence of Ulster religious life within the language of separate
spheres to justify their involvement in Irish public life. Female Unionists
intervened in Ulster politics by referring to the educative and domestic
roles of women.

The educative role of women was delineated at the first meeting of the
UWUA in January 1911. Mrs Mercier Clements, the honorary secretary of
the movement, described the 'valuable work women had done at elections
and bye-elections' in the past and how the UWUA sought to formalise this
work.[81] She went on to describe the utility of canvassing in bye-elections,
arguing that it was a means of 'educat[ing] the working classes'.[82] Mercier
Clements promoted the notion that women should fulfil an educative role
in society, an idea which gained ground in Victorian Ireland through the
course of the nineteenth century, and which sought to define women as
responsible for the education of Irish children and wider society. This idea
was discussed at the inaugural meeting of the Carrickfergus Women's
Unionist Association in May 1911, in which Mrs McCalmont outlined the
work women could do, and stated that by sending speakers over to
England they could 'educate the public there as to their fears in regard to
Home Rule'.[83] Ulsterwomen's educative role was emphasised at the
annual meeting of the East Down Women's Unionist Association. Mrs
James Craig, wife of the leading Ulster politician, argued that 'the English
and Scotch voters were . . . ignorant of the Irish question' and that by
'personally writing letters, sending marked newspapers and suitable
leaflets across the water' women could educate the British voters.[84]

Ulsterwomen were assigned the role of educating the British electorate
because of the notion prevalent in late-nineteenth and early-twentieth
century Britain and Ireland that women were the innate repositories and
guardians of all that was virtuous and good in society. Such an idea

---

[80] Ibid.
[81] PRONI, D. 2846/1/2/3, WUA, 'The Fight Against Home Rule', p. 5.
[82] Ibid., p. 6.
[83] 'Women's Unionist Association. Branch formed at Carrickfergus', *Northern Whig*, 5 May 1911, p. 12.
[84] 'East Down Women's Unionist Association', *Belfast News-Letter*, 10 January 1912, p. 6.

appeared in a speech by the Duchess of Abercorn at a meeting of the UWUC in Ulster Hall, Belfast, early in 1912. The Duchess argued that women had great influence in society that should be used to promote the Union: she told her audience that they were 'all aware that women were able to do a great amount of good with gentleness, tact and quiet influence when they were organised and worked well together'.[85] An editorial in the *Northern Whig* from January 1911 made clear this connection between a woman's supposed virtues and her influence on public life.[86] Arguing that the 'women of Ulster have as much at stake in the maintenance of the Union of the United Kingdom as have its men', the editorial asserted that women should be responsible for the virtue and standards of public life:

> To uphold civil and religious liberty, to testify on behalf of justice and honour and righteousness in public as well as in private life, to protest undivided loyalty to the Throne, and to withstand the forces that make for corruption and tyranny – these are the duties which every good woman is ready to fulfil in as far as in her lies.[87]

The *Northern Whig* promulgated the notion that women should bring their private virtue into the public sphere in the defence of Ulster against Home Rule. Women, because of their domestic qualities, could play a role in public life, defending the civil and religious liberties of Protestant Ulster.

Female unionist involvement in the campaigns against the third Home Rule Bill was inspired, therefore, by the close connection of religion, politics and domesticity in Ulster. On 28 September 1912 over half a million Unionist men and women descended on City Hall in Belfast to sign a 'Covenant' and a 'Declaration' documenting their opposition to the British government's proposal for a measure of Home Rule in Ireland.[88] It marked the culmination of a political campaign involving the participation of thousands of Ulster women in what Alvin Jackson has described as 'the first truly popular mobilization of Unionism'.[89] The alleged child-abduction of the McCann case gave concrete form to popular Protestant beliefs about the impact of Home Rule on their community, inspiring tens of thousands of female Unionists to take up the political fight for the defence of the Union and their Protestant homes.

---

[85] 'Ulster Women and Home Rule. Speech by the Duchess of Abercorn', *Londonderry Sentinel*, 20 January 1912, p. 7.
[86] 'The Rallying of Ulster Womanhood', *Northern Whig*, 24 January 1911, p. 6.
[87] Ibid.
[88] Alice Stopford Green, *Ourselves Alone in Ulster* (Dublin and London, 1918), p. 6; PRONI, D. 1098/1/1, 16 January 1913.
[89] Jackson, 'Unionist Myths', 184.

CHAPTER TEN

'WHAT HAS BEEN STARTED IN THE CINEMA HAS ENDED IN MATERNITY HOMES FOR SINGLE GIRLS': THE CHURCH OF ENGLAND AND POPULAR CULTURE IN THE INDUSTRIAL DIOCESE, DURHAM *c.*1860 – *c.*1930

ROBERT LEE

In March 1791, troubled for too long by a stye on his right eye-lid that conventional medicine could not relieve, the clergyman-diarist James Woodforde decided to experiment with a popular remedy:

> As it is commonly said that the Eye-lid being rubbed by the tail of a black Cat would do much good if not entirely cure it, and having a black Cat, a little before dinner I made a trial of it, and very soon after dinner I found my Eye-lid much abated of the swelling and almost free from Pain. I cannot therefore but conclude it to be of the greatest service to a Stiony on the Eye-lid. Any other Cats Tail may have the above effect in all probability – but I did my Eye-lid with my own black Tom Cat's Tail.[1]

Woodforde's experiment seems innocuous enough, but it is not possible to imagine a Church of England clergyman attempting to repeat it a hundred years later. Clergymen had by then placed themselves in the front line of the 'reformation of manners' and part of their mission was to replace the muddled, semi-pagan thinking that was felt to characterise much contemporary popular culture with the new, clean lines of self-help, dignity and duty.

---

[1] The Rev. James Woodforde (ed. J. Beresford), *The Diary of a Country Parson 1758– 1802* (Oxford, 1978), pp. 395–6 (diary entry for Friday, 11 March 1791).

From the moment of his arrival in his Norfolk parish, James Woodforde not only *accepted* but actively *sponsored* the local culture that he found there, even though it was very different from the culture of his previous parish in Somerset. The various examples of largesse and customary doles, as well as the annual parish perambulation, were all readily embraced by Woodforde. His diaries recorded a world that was cyclical and in developmental terms largely static, and popular culture during this early part of the nineteenth century demonstrated a constituency that extended well beyond the labouring class. Much of it was tolerated and indulged, if not actually participated in, by elites.

The subsequent attack upon, and elite distancing from, popular culture has been attributed by writers like Alun Howkins to socio-economic motives. Describing the assault on traditions such as the Whitsuntide holiday, Howkins discerns 'the need to impose the time and work disciplines of developing capitalist society on an essentially pre-industrial labouring population'.[2] Alongside this campaign another, much more subtle, process was at work, one that Howkins has described as 'cultural incorporation', by which means elites adopted and adapted elements of popular culture until it served *their* social, economic and political objectives.[3] Of course, these are issues that encircle the encounters between the Church of England and popular culture in a *rural* setting. The purpose of this chapter is to examine whether a similar set of encounters might be discerned in an *industrial* environment and, in particular, whether the relationship between Church and popular culture described the same trajectory of change in the very specific setting of the Durham coalfield.

Certain pressure points in this relationship might be presumed to be similar, whatever the location or economic circumstances of the diocese or parish. Firstly, for many new incumbents, the dislocation from their Oxbridge cloister – whether it was to village green or to mining community – frequently came as a considerable culture shock. Suddenly detached from a support network of colleagues from similar backgrounds, outlooks and cultural tastes it was frequently difficult for clergymen to settle themselves *personally*, a crisis that transcended issues of religious belief and pastoral care.

Secondly, to the frustration of many clergymen, elements of popular culture had become conflated with Christian teaching to produce a hybridised belief system that hovered somewhere between picturesque

---

[2] Alun Howkins, 'The taming of Whitsun: the changing face of a nineteenth-century rural holiday', in E. and S. Yeo (eds), *Popular Culture and Class Conflict, 1590 –1914* (Brighton, 1981), p. 187.

[3] Ibid., p. 205.

ignorance, political radicalism and outright blasphemy. Arguably, a popular religion that demonstrated intuitive understanding of the links that bound together past, present, future, nature and supernature had the potential to offer a challenge to initiatives for change, as well as offering alternative modes of social and political expression. Demonstrations of effigy-burning and 'rough music' continued to be reported well into the twentieth century, and the tone of the reports generally exuded disbelief, shock and outrage, especially when the targets appeared to be strike-breaking miners, or representatives of social authority like police officers, magistrates and clergymen.

Thirdly, even when its expression was not overtly political, popular culture and its associated knowledge-system posed a threat because it evoked a time when the lot of the working-class had supposedly been rather better. Intertwined with traditional ways of working were traditional ways of thinking and doing, which the emerging industrial economies of mid-nineteenth century Britain began increasingly to disrupt. Hitherto, social and economic relationships had tended to rest on the twin pillars of popular culture and popular custom, and had at their heart a dialogue of rights and responsibilities from which society took much of its sense of cohesion. The political dimension of this was described by E. P. Thompson as a 'plebeian culture', an important weapon in the arsenal of the poor, and 'a defence against the intrusions of gentry or clergy'.[4] At the same time it must be acknowledged that it was not only the value systems of elites that 'plebeian culture' challenged, for 'it was increasingly viewed by socialists as dulling the senses of the proletariat and as a cataract preventing the perception of the reality of exploitation'.[5] Recognition of this fact has led influential writers like Gareth Stedman Jones to question whether notions of social authority and cultural incorporation have been allowed to intrude too far into the debate. As Jones puts it:

> Far more attention has been paid to the ways in which entrepreneurs or the propertied classes attempted to change popular uses of leisure time than to the ways in which craftsmen, artisans or working-class activists attempted to organize their non-work time or sought to reorientate the use of non-work time by others.[6]

---

[4] E. P. Thompson, *Customs in Common* (London, 1993), p. 12.
[5] J. M. Golby and A. W. Purdue, *The Civilisation of the Crowd: popular culture in England, 1750–1900* (Stroud, 1999), p. 12.
[6] G. Stedman Jones, 'Class expression versus social control? A critique of recent trends in the social history of "leisure"', in G. Stedman Jones, *Languages of Class: studies in English working-class history 1832–1982* (Cambridge, 1983) p. 77.

Even so, it cannot be denied that many mid-nineteenth century clergymen – the new generation who were increasingly occupying the pulpits vacated by the James Woodfordes of this world – believed the task of liberating the uneducated mind from the fallacies of popular culture fell to *them*, and was straightforwardly an issue of parochial leadership. What, then, were the particular circumstances of the relationship between the Church of England and popular culture in the Durham coalfield between 1860 and 1930; how far was the Church's association with the 'reformation of manners' in conflict with its need to retain relevance and accessibility within the coalfield community; and to what extent was the requisite level of parochial leadership possible? As demonstrated elsewhere, the central strategy of the Durham diocese after 1860 was increasingly to recruit, train and deploy local men as part of a unified and targeted campaign to re-establish the Church of England in the communities on the coalfield. Durham University was instrumental in this strategy, and the enthusiastic recruitment of lower-middle class men who were given ministries in the mining parishes from whence many of them had come – their training thus unaffected and unmediated by the potentially alienating influence of Oxbridge – can clearly be seen in the latter decades of the nineteenth and the first two decades of the twentieth centuries.[7] This is the essence of the Church of England's mission into the Durham coalfield, its terms of engagement having been established at a public meeting held in Newcastle in January 1860.[8]

The mission immediately encountered aspects of popular culture that were either unameliorated by any prior contact with organised religion or had been mediated in advance of the Church of England's arrival by Nonconformist religion in general and Primitive Methodism in particular. In the preceding half century or so, while James Woodforde was immersing himself in the culture of his Norfolk parish and brushing a cat's tail against his inflamed eye-lid, the Church of England in the North-East coalfield had been facing an expression of popular culture that can be traced through the songs, ballads, poems and dialogues that had been widely disseminated in print since the seventeenth century. The best-known and most enduring of these included *The Collier's Wedding* (c.1720), *The Colliers' Rant* (already old when first printed in 1793) and *Bob Crankey's 'Size Sunday'* (1804). These frequently celebrated the wild,

---

[7] Robert Lee, *The Church of England and the Durham Coalfield, 1810–1926: clergymen, capitalists and colliers* (Woodbridge, 2007).
[8] Anon, *Statement Illustrative of the Amount of Spiritual Destitution in the Diocese of Durham* (Durham, 1859).

untamed spirit of pitmen, a spirit in which rowdiness and disrespect was endemic, even among the elderly, and even in church:

> . . . The gates fly open, all rush in,
> The church is full with folks and din;
> And all the crew, both great and small,
> Behave as in a common hall:
> For some perhaps that were threescore,
> Were never twice in church before;
> They scamper, climb and break the pews,
> To see the couple make their vows . . .[9]

This was a form of popular culture that some elite figures held responsible for the poor standards of morality and sobriety they perceived among the poor. Again, this was not a perception that emanated solely from an Anglican/elite point of view. Other popular entertainments that centred on foot-racing, cock-fighting, poaching and gambling at cards were felt to demonstrate the same potential to degenerate into drunkenness, brawling and criminality, and socialist chroniclers of the coalfield scene, like Sidney Webb, were certain that the moral tone had been raised only by the arrival of trade unionism and Primitive Methodism.[10]

Strikingly, however, after a period during which so many interest groups seemed to be working to secure its demise, the decline of popular culture became a cause for anxiety and regret. The antiquarian movement, with clergymen prominent, began to prize old superstitions, customs and dialects, seeing in them the vanishing core of a type of knowledge that was 'other' and valuable. Of course, there was nothing new in the phenomenon of the clergyman-historian, but the later nineteenth-century spirit of antiquarianism seemed to reflect a widespread mood that some indefinable quality of life was being lost.

One means of tracking the antiquarian awakening among clergymen in the North East is to analyse the weight of their contributions to *Archaeologia Aeliana*, a journal of local history and archaeology publ-

---

[9] Edward Chicken, *The Collier's Wedding* (c.1720; Newcastle, 1829 edn). D. Harker, *Songs and Verse of the North-East Pitmen, c.1780–1844* (Gateshead, 1999) has more on many of these, and their significance is discussed in M. Vicinus, *The Industrial Muse: a study of nineteenth-century working-class literature* (London, 1974) and R. Colls, *The Colliers' Rant: song and culture in the industrial village* (London, 1977).
[10] S. Webb, *The Story of the Durham Miners, 1662–1921* (London, 1921), pp. 17–21.

ished by the Newcastle Society of Antiquaries.[11] The highest percentage of clerical contributions to this journal occurred during the 1820s but there are nevertheless clear signs that their antiquarian involvement held up strongly during the peak years of industrialisation, before declining rapidly in the early twentieth century. For at least some of these clergymen, contributions were motivated by regret at the depredations wrought by the coal industry on the local landscape:

> Alas, the glories of Bearpark have departed! Its trees are attenuated, its green meadows are smirched with coal-dust, its river is polluted. Eighty years ago it was the chief asset in the gift made by the dean and chapter for the endowment of the University of Durham, and is today the scene of the activities of the Bearpark Colliery Company.[12]

Industrial destruction of the countryside and its culture was a theme also endorsed by the pitman poet Alexander Barrass:

> High on this bank sweet-sloping to the shore,
> And mantled by a verdure-tinted grace . . .
> The ravished eye of admiration sees,
> Built, as if yearning for the wood's embrace,
> A mean, brick row, half hid behind the trees.[13]

This first, symbolic penetration into the trees by the pit row would later become the wholesale rape of the landscape, forever transformed under the grid-iron plan of new townships. Soon it was felt that 'the pit hovers around the miner and the pit village like a sparrow-hawk over its victim'.[14] Many clergymen were concerned that spirituality could not thrive in these circumstances, still less when economic decline struck in these single-industry communities.

This concern partly motivated the 1928 visitation of Bishop Hensley Henson, who asked his clergymen to assess the impact of unemployment upon spirituality.[15] Over two-thirds of them (67.2 per cent) recorded that it had had either a moderately or a severely detrimental effect. Unemployment

---

[11] Lee, *Church of England and the Durham Coalfield*, pp. 242–5.

[12] The Rev. Henry Gee, 'A sixteenth-century journey to Durham', *Archaeologia Aeliana*, 3, series xiii (1916), 110.

[13] A. Barrass, *The Derwent Valley and Other Poems* (Newcastle, 1887), p. 95.

[14] J. McCutcheon, *Troubled Seams: the story of a pit and its people* (Durham, 1955), foreword.

[15] Durham University Library Palace Green [henceforth DUL PG], AUC 4/14. Visitation Returns, 1928.

'produces an atmosphere of apathy and disheartenment, sullenness and suspicion'; 'the people become embittered against institutions', particularly 'against religion' where it 'fosters a spirit of discontent'. 'It is', said one clergyman, simply 'the saddest feature of my work'.[16] What made these emotionally brutalised, economically vulnerable communities even more fragile was the fact that many of those suffering the effects of economic decline were themselves relative newcomers to the Durham coalfield. The population growth that had so wrong-footed the Church of England in the decades before the launch of its mission was almost entirely fuelled by immigration and, whether they came from near or far, many immigrants were ill-prepared for the economic and social landscapes they encountered on the coalfield:

> The day my mother and our family travelled from Flimby to Boldon Colliery, in Durham, I felt instinctively the great difference between an agricultural county and one which is purely industrial . . . When one who has spent his years in the country and by the sea finds himself amongst great aggregations of steel erections and chimnies, something closes up within . . . When we came to Boldon Colliery that sense of closed-in-ness increased, for I had lived my life up to this time in little more than single-street communities where there was always not far off the sea and wide-stretching country, woods, and distant mountains. We now found ourselves in streets which seemed to my childish eyes miles long, an endless number of streets, every house and every street alike . . . Barracks, barracks everywhere, and noisy, bustling life.[17]

There was a recognition, too, that the sense of dislocation and anomie brought on by industrialisation could bring moral danger. After decades during which the principal threat to decency seemed to stem from an established popular culture, the perception dawned that the communal spirit it reflected had probably been less morally destructive than the artificial, alienating, mammon-worshipping pastimes that had replaced it in migrant communities which lacked the same level of cultural association. 'If innocent pleasures are not indulged in,' warned one clergyman, 'the tendency is to seek for gratification in amusements that are not innocent or wholesome'.[18]

While many clergymen saw in these circumstances their most exciting and worthwhile challenge, others saw in them an assault on the human

---

[16] Ibid. Responses of the Rev. E. Pestle (Tanfield); the Rev. R. Ellison (Lumley); the Rev. H. J. Cheeseman (Deptford St Andrew); the Rev. C. Morgan (Ebchester).

[17] J. Lawson, *A Man's Life* (London, 1944), pp. 27–8.

[18] The Rev. P. H. Ditchfield, *Vanishing England* (London, 1910), p. 375.

spirit, and one that they had neither the strength nor the energy to face down. Whether he personally felt inspiration or desperation, however, the clergyman's mission to preserve a spiritual context for life had to negotiate a path around the paradox that lay at the heart of Church-coalfield relations throughout the nineteenth century: the notion that the clergyman should be 'close to' the community but not 'of' it. He might be from a background that enabled him to understand and communicate with them, but he was there to lead his parishioners towards higher things rather than to lose himself in *their* ways and problems, and a certain detachment and 'otherness' was inevitable and desirable. In spite of this guiding principle, census returns from the urban parishes repeatedly suggest curates and incumbents who had become very much 'of' their communities and were now more or less embedded, living in the toughest working-class districts in modest rectories or in shared accommodation and humble lodging-houses. These were men that the Durham diocese had recruited to lead its mission into the coalfield but for whom the realities of working-class life had never been intended to be so immediate, constant and acutely felt.

The church building was itself often physically remote from the collier's world, as well as being spiritually remote because colliers seldom went there. Even so, the most optimistic clergymen believed that the parish church would continue to exercise a kind of visceral hold upon the conscience of its community because it was between its four walls that the great rites of passage of the coalminer's life were played out. As one clergyman wrote:

> . . . [the miner] has always been accustomed to regard it as in a peculiar sense his own Church. It is a sentiment analogous to that of the love of country in the bosom of the patriot. The Church is not an ephemeral and transitory Institution, which came up in a night and may perish in a night. It has come down to him as an inheritance . . . [and] he will not give up the inheritance of his fathers.[19]

Whether such a deep sense of connection could be sustained in the decades of mass migration is another matter, and it seems that at least part of the motivation for the post-1860 mission in the Durham coalfield was a recognition that it could not. Migration that was at once on a massive scale and *continuous* may have been an economic necessity, but it did terrible damage to the Church's project for spreading spiritual calm. By the 1840s the coalfield was populated by a people who were 'exceedingly unsettled

---

[19] The Rev. J. Davies, *The Working Man in Relation to the Church of England* (London, 1861), pp. 17–18.

and fond of change'.[20] In April 1844 Bishop Edward Maltby shared his fears of social and political strife with the Home Office:

> The whole county from Durham to Hartlepool on the one hand, and to West Auckland on the other is one of vast excavation; teeming with a numerous and ignorant population; under the influence of Chartists and other artful men and easily stimulated by liquor.[21]

Clergymen had to minister in 'constructed communities', hastily and cheaply thrown together by the colliery companies and displaying minimal affinity with the landscapes they occupied. In theory, at least, the Church of England should have been well-placed to bind these disparate communities together. As an organisation it encouraged labour mobility while at the same time offering a symbolic rock of stability to which migrants could cling. Its clergymen were expected to feel the pulse of each parish as they made their regular round of domestic visits, and the reports that they made – in the form of quadrennial visitation returns – provide an excellent source for analysing their encounters with popular culture. What emerges from them is a clear sense that the climate of rapid, continuous change in the mining districts was making the clergyman's job much more difficult. Established, long-term incumbents who had been inducted in a pre-industrial era found that the ground had shifted beneath their feet and presented them with a teeming new population with whom they felt no affinity. The forces of migration and constant parish boundary changes combined to wreck fragile 'mental maps' and nascent senses of belonging among potential congregations, almost as soon as they had formed. Bishop Henson showed sensitivity to this, and urged incoming clergymen neither to be the 'new broom' nor to be too demanding when they took over their new parishes. 'The really essential thing in going into a new parish is to win the trust of the people', he wrote to one, and to another: 'You must make allowance for the lax tradition in which these people have grown up . . . [rather than] impose arbitrarily a higher rule than . . . their consciences acknowledge.'[22]

---

[20] Parliamentary Papers XVI: *Children's Employment in Mines*, 1842. Evidence of Mr Green, governor of Durham Gaol, to the Children's Employment Commission, 1842.

[21] National Archive, HO/45/644, Bishop Maltby to Sir James Graham, Home Office, 15 April 1844.

[22] E. F. Braley (ed.), *Letters of Herbert Hensley Henson* (London, 1954), p. 31 (Henson to the Rev. J. E. Perry, 24 August 1924) and p. 43 (Henson to the Rev. T. L. Lomax, 9 October 1925).

All of which is not intended to suggest that genuine connection could not be achieved. A tangible sense of fellow-feeling can be detected in the pastoral letter sent by Joseph Roscamp in December 1893 to his ex-parishioners at Stanley Crook in the week following the fire that had destroyed their church:

> Many of you, like myself, will feel that associations of the past have been broken, and that we who had watched its growth from its foundations up to its completion have reason to mourn its destruction . . . [but] although the fabric has gone, there still remains the spiritual church and life in the hearts of the worshippers. The truths we learnt and the blessings we received cannot be destroyed by fire.[23]

Roscamp's empathy may have had a good deal to do with the fact that he was the son of a miner, but his subtle way of blending a shared identity in the past with a spiritual concern for the future effectively transcended connections based purely on sociological or political compatibility. It was of its time, too. Connection that was posited on a spiritual yearning for a lost Eden, rapidly vanishing before the relentless firestorm of industrialisation, informed an antiquarian sense of awareness among certain clergymen that reached something of a peak at around the time Roscamp was writing. This regret at the visible and social changes being wrought by industrialisation was something that, for a few decades, transcended party political differences and established a fellow-feeling (if not common cause) between Conservative-inclined clergymen, pitmen poets and socialist thinkers like Robert Blatchford and William Morris.

Whether this fellow-feeling was exemplified or negated by the process of cultural incorporation is a matter very much in the eye of the beholder. Certainly, the didactic quality of ceremony was well understood in the nineteenth century. As one clergyman wrote, 'It is not . . . by what the Lord Mayor feels in his coach, but by what the apprentice feels who gazes at him, that the public is served.'[24] Something of this mentality informed the 'parish entertainments' that were an increasing feature of the parochial scene in the late-nineteenth and early-twentieth centuries. More participatory than the Lord Mayor's procession, certainly, they nevertheless revolved around the same abstractions of hierarchy, authority

---

[23] Durham County Record Office (henceforth DCRO), EP/Sta 39, *Stanley Crook Parish Magazine*, December 1893.
[24] The Rev. William Paley, Archdeacon of Carlisle, writing in 1825, and cited in A. M. C Waterman, 'The ideological alliance of political economy and Christian theology, 1798–1833', *Journal of Ecclesiastical History*, 34 (April, 1983), 238.

and deference, and were designed to give them a similar visible
embodiment in ritual and pageant. Newspaper accounts of the various
Coronation, Jubilee and Empire Day celebrations reveal a striking
unanimity in the conduct of these occasions throughout the county. Taken
together they amount to an expression of high-paternalism, organised in
such a way as to make them a celebration of the power of local landowners
and industrialists *and* the power and glory of the British Empire. As one
contemporary observer wrote,

> What a revolution of taste . . . has taken place in the English people . . . the
> times and the spirit of the times are changed – we are become a sober
> people. England is no longer Merry England but busy England; England
> full of wealth and poverty, extravagance and care.[25]

A single edition of the *Durham Chronicle* during the miner's strike of
1892 nevertheless quickly dispels any suggestion that 'busy England' had
entirely usurped the role and significance of popular culture in people's
political lives. On 25 March there are reports of the bank inspector at the
Marquess of Londonderry's Rainton pit being rough-musicked on his
return home from work; tin pans and kettles being rattled outside the home
of a working miner in Brandon; the rattling of tin pans at the home of a
man who looked after the pit horses at Littleburn; a crowd of women and
children attacking pit officials at Haswell; the 'tin-panning' of blacklegs at
South Hetton; hissing, hooting, yelling and stone-throwing at the
brakesman of New Herrington Colliery; a 'horrible din' and the 'throwing
of sods of grass' at two miners in Pelton Fell; mobbing and missile-
throwing at a strike-breaker in Silksworth; and the accompaniment of tins
and pans inflicted on pit officials at Tow Law. Rough music could turn
dangerously violent, too: the Silksworth incident led to the discharge of a
fire-arm and the maiming of John Urwin, the fore-overman at the pit.[26]
    A generation later, rough-music was still playing a prominent role in
political confrontation. During the 1925 strike, miners at Chopwell – a
community so radical that it had come to be known as 'Little Moscow' –
meted out a humiliating punishment to the vicar's son, who had taken it
upon himself to go to work in the local pit as a strike-breaker. Tin-panned,
rough-musicked and garlanded with wreaths from the churchyard – all to
the raucous accompaniment of 'Lead kindly light' and 'Rock of ages' –
the vicar's son was paraded around for all to see. A nervous breakdown

---

[25] William Howitt (1840), and cited in R. Bushaway, *By Rite: custom, ceremony
and community in England, 1700–1800* (London, 1982), p. 239.
[26] *Durham Chronicle*, 25 March 1892.

brought an end to the young man's brief career in the coalmines.[27] This was popular culture red in tooth and claw, the political manifestation of a working-class psyche that had always tended – in the elite view – towards the 'annoying, wasteful, immoral . . . threatening and dangerous'.[28] Of course, popular culture was not always politicised, but it was seldom without some shade of deeper social significance and it was something with which the Church of England had either to wrestle or find an accommodation.

This was a task made harder by the fact that aspects of popular culture were partly shaped by a diffusive Christianity. Consequently, the average nineteenth-century coalminer could never be dismissed as 'Bob Crankey', nor stereotyped as the bawdy, boozy adherent of the world of *The Collier's Wedding*. Because of the influence of trade unionism and Primitive Methodism – as celebrated by Sidney Webb – clergymen encountered many parishioners who were sober, industrious and serious about religion and politics, and above all unlikely to bend to the wishes of the Church simply through a reflex of deference. 'Are the clergy themselves capable or willing to adapt to life in the communities?' asked one parish priest, concluding that 'Much depends on the individual priest, his personality, his willingness "to get alongside" his people, and understand the changes that have taken place in their community.'[29] This observation was actually made in 1982, but it would have resounded with equal relevance to the coalmining communities at any time during the preceding one hundred years. The idea that the Church should be a responsive, adaptable organisation, capable of changing in accordance with local circumstances, had come to be seen as a desirable – if difficult to achieve – aim, and its essence informed Bishop Henson's 1928 advice to new incumbents, cited earlier. Arguably such an aim would not have commended itself so strongly to the pre-1860 diocese, where *stability* seemed to be more highly prized than flexibility.

By favouring adaptability over stability and flexibility over rigidity, the Durham diocese was attempting to respond realistically to the evidence provided by its own visitation returns during the late-nineteenth and early twentieth-centuries, in which clergymen reported that their parishioners were being exposed to more troublesome cultural influences than ever

---

[27] L. Turnbull, *Chopwell's Story* (Newcastle, *c*.1978).

[28] R. D. Storch, 'Persistence and change in nineteenth century popular culture', in R. D. Storch (ed.), *Popular Culture and Custom in Nineteenth-Century England* (London, 1982), pp. 1–20.

[29] The Rev. James Hargreave, Trimdon, in *'When the Pit Closed'*: *a report on the ministry in former mining villages* (Bishop Auckland, 1982), p. 27.

before. An increase in disposable income and enhanced access to travel meant that miners and their families enjoyed a host of new entertainment possibilities, many of which took place on a Sunday where they represented an irresistible counter-attraction to churchgoing. In 1928, Bishop Henson asked his clergymen to make an assessment of the secularising impact of this new world of leisure. In their responses, sixty-eight per cent of the clergy thought that they faced a more secular Sunday than hitherto and that the religious quality of Sundays had been substantially eroded; seventy-one per cent believed that this was due to the wider availability of travel opportunities, with many parishioners using buses to travel to the seaside or to visit relatives on Sundays rather than going to church; thirty-eight per cent thought cinemas and dances were to blame; and sixteen per cent thought that the recent introduction of Sunday broadcasting was having a negative effect, although the majority saw this innovation as a boon to the sick and elderly who could not get to church.[30] Those that regretted it saw in religious broadcasting a diminution of the 'corporate character of church membership' and an encouragement towards increasingly individualistic approaches to worship.[31]

Clerical fears about travel were not entirely new. In 1847 the Rev. John Davies of Gateshead had warned against 'the various modes of steam conveyance, by land and water . . . which bear with awful and melancholy effect on the observance of the Sabbath'.[32] Some communities in 1928, like Jarrow St Mark and Hamsteels, had parish populations that were, in any case, too poor to take advantage of whatever new travel opportunities might be on offer.[33] Other parishes with a slightly broader economic mix faced a two-pronged pressure on church attendance, with the poorest parishioners becoming disillusioned and apathetic about religion while slightly more prosperous parishioners headed-off every Sunday on cycle, car, charabanc and train outings.[34] What perhaps *was* new in the 1928 responses was a recognition that people needed and deserved a break: a chance to 'get away from themselves'.[35] This desire for escapism was satisfied by the cinema. 'In a drab district and in poor homes the desire for

---

[30] DUL PG, AUC 4/14, Visitation Returns, 1928.

[31] Ibid., response of the Rev. Bertram Spencer, Firtree.

[32] The Rev. J. Davies, *An Address of the Clergy to the Inhabitants of the Parish of Gateshead* (Gateshead, 1847), p. 6.

[33] DUL PG, AUC 4/14, Visitation Returns, 1928, response of the Rev. J. Wallace, Jarrow St Mark, and the Rev. John Hewish, Hamsteels.

[34] Ibid,. response of the Rev. Charles Morgan, Ebchester.

[35] Ibid., response of the Rev. Robert Rudd, Trimdon Grange.

brightness finds an answer in cinema & dancing', said one clergyman,[36] and another acknowledged that 'the cinema is more exciting . . . [than] . . . the organisations on which churches have relied in the past such as Scouts, Girl Guides, etc.'[37] Cinema could even be 'a great blessing . . . wholesome . . . educative . . . a factor in increased sobriety'.[38] These responses were, however, untypically positive. Behind most clerical attitudes to popular entertainment there persisted the view that to allow popular culture to flourish without a controlling hand from the Church was a recipe for the moral dissipation that would inevitably follow. The Rev. Henry MacKenzie of Benfieldside was unequivocal in this respect. 'What has been started in the Cinema', he wrote, 'has ended in Maternity Homes for single girls'.[39]

Of all aspects of popular culture confronted by the Church, the most ubiquitous was that of alcohol. Drink had become embedded in the life and labour of the North East as an integral part of the annual bindings, at which ale traditionally flowed to seal the employment contract.[40] By 1861 it was seen by at least one clergyman as 'the besetting sin . . . of the whole north'.[41] Throughout the nineteenth century, the diocesan authorities conducted surveys of drunkenness, and in visitation returns clergymen were regularly asked to comment on its prevalence and impact in their own parishes.[42]

At the 1861 visitation, for instance, the Durham clergy were asked whether they detected an improvement or deterioration in levels of drunkenness.[43] Their response gives no sense of incipient crisis. One-third

---

[36] Ibid., response of the Rev. J. Hawke, St Peter, Monkwearmouth.

[37] Ibid., response of the Rev. O. Mordaunt Burrows, Venerable Bede, Monkwearmouth.

[38] Ibid., response of the Rev. F. S. Myers, South Moor.

[39] Ibid., response of the Rev. H. MacKenzie, Benfieldside.

[40] R. Colls, *Pitmen of the Northern Coalfield: work, culture and protest 1790–1850* (Manchester, 1987), p. 104.

[41] DUL PG, AUC 4/1, Visitation Returns, 1861. Response of the Rev. A. Duncombe Shafto, Brancepeth.

[42] Much of the discussion which follows is based upon the visitation surveys of 1861, 1882 and 1904. Footnotes which follow the formula 'Response of [clergy name], [parish], [date]' originate from the following sources: DUL PG, AUC 4/1 Visitation Returns 1861; DUL PG, AUC 4/5, (1882); DUL PG, AUC 4/10, (1904). See also D. Butler, 'Defeating the demon drink: the 1904 Licensing Act and its implementation in Durham City, 1906–1939', *Durham County Local History Society Bulletin*, 54 (May 1995), 52–65; and DCRO, D/X984/1, 8 Sons of Temperance Society Minute Books, 1866–1917.

[43] DUL PG, AUC 4/1, Visitation Returns, 1861.

of them (43) did not trouble to reply at all, and only fourteen expressed deep concern about the situation. What they *did* frequently comment upon was the linkage between drunkenness and migrant labour. The itinerant pit-sinkers working the east Durham coalfield were singled out by some,[44] and Catholics by others,[45] but few troubled to conceal their conviction that the problem was made incalculably worse by the presence of the Irish. 'Drunkenness [is] very prevalent among the Irish', declared the Rev. Henry Peters of Sunderland St John and his verdict was almost directly echoed by the Rev. Benjamin Kennicott of All Saints, Monkwearmouth ('Among the Irish much drunkenness prevails') – Kennicott here giving no sign that his parish ministry was itself in crisis because of *his own* drinking.[46]

Analysis of *why* people turned to drink was patchy. The Rev. G. J. Fox of St. Nicholas, Durham, thought it was inevitable, given the presence of '39 Drunkeries in my parish',[47] and the theory that drunkenness was simply the consequence of having too many pubs was one that had plenty of support. There were other suspects, too. Ninety-three per cent of respondents in 1904 thought that working men's clubs had had a particularly bad influence on drinking habits. There was, nevertheless, a well-developed strand of opinion which held that the availability of drink could not alone account for its excessive consumption. Many clergymen attributed drunkenness to a general sense of dissipation in the working population, and thought that it might be countered by thrift,[48] more brass bands,[49] or a sharp economic downturn.[50] But there was also a recognition that people turned to drink – like the cinema – as a means of escape. The Rev. Canon Body spoke with regret of the impoverished urban masses who had 'nothing to make their lives bright or happy or pleasant, and whose only happiness in the amelioration of their hard life was when they

---

[44] For instance, the response of the Rev. W. Wilson, Ryhope (1861).

[45] Response of the Rev. J. M. Hick, Trimdon (1904).

[46] DUL PG, AUC 4/1, Visitation Returns, 1861. See also the response of the Rev. J. Todd, Shincliffe. For Kennicott's eventual dismissal from his living because of his drinking, see DUL PG, DDR/EJ/CLD/2, Clergy discipline cases. The alleged drunkenness of Irish migrants in the area is explored in F. McDonnell, 'The Irish in Durham City', *Durham County Local History Society Bulletin*, 47 (December 1991), 68–82.

[47] Response of the Rev. G. J. Fox, St. Nicholas, Durham (1861).

[48] Response of the Rev. S. Atkinson, Eighton Banks (1882).

[49] Response of the Rev. W. Reeman, Fairfield (1882).

[50] Response of the Rev. J. Law, South Hylton (1861), who saw drinking decline and behaviour improve during an economic recession.

lay in the grip of intoxication'.[51] Consequently, some argued that the temperance-minded clergyman had done only half a job if he steered members of his flock away from the pub. They had to be offered some other 'innocent and improving recreation for the winter evenings', otherwise they would be sure to drift back there.[52]

Surprisingly, perhaps, very few clergymen made a direct link between drunkenness and aggravated criminality. This was in spite of the fact that drink-related cases represented anything between thirty-six and fifty-one per cent of the local magistrates' workload between 1856 and 1896.[53] These figures are, of course, at the mercy of historic attitudes to crime and criminality and the extent to which certain misdemeanours were thought to be worth prosecuting. It nevertheless illustrates an interesting trend. Drunkenness combined with criminality reached a peak somewhere in the 1860s and 1870s. Thereafter the figures described a sharp decline. This may or may not have been due to the work of the various temperance organisations: what cannot be denied is that the statistical downturn coincided with the heyday of the temperance movement in the coalfield parishes.

Visitation enquiries in 1882 and 1904 posed specific questions about temperance organisation, and the responses indicate high and increasing levels of provision: around half of all parishes in 1882 and almost two-thirds by 1904 had some kind of temperance organisation.[54] The Church of England Temperance Society and the Band of Hope were the most widespread, but prominent among the rest were the Good Templars, the Temperance Guild and the Blue Ribbon movement.[55] Many parishes had more than one temperance group, to the extent that some clergymen feared they could become rivals. At Heighington, for instance, the Rev. Charles Dyson resisted the temptation to start his own society because the Wesleyans already had one, and 'to have another . . . would only take away from the one already in existence'.[56] Of the 146 clergymen in 1904 who recorded a temperance organisation in their parish, seventy-nine

---

[51] Speech to the Framwellgate Mission. See *Durham Chronicle*, 6 May 1887.

[52] *Newcastle Weekly Chronicle*, 26 October 1872.

[53] DCRO, PD/Du 1, 3, 7, 14: Durham City Petty Sessions Court Registers, 1856–1917.

[54] DUL PG, AUC 4/5, Visitation Returns 1882; DUL PG, AUC 4/10, Visitation Returns 1904.

[55] This pattern is described on a national scale in a slightly earlier era by J. F. C. Harrison, *Drink and the Victorians: the temperance question in England 1815–1872* (London, 1971).

[56] Response of the Rev. C. Dyson, Heighington (1904).

(54.1%) said that they were actively involved in its running. Others were deliberately *not* involved, for a number of reasons. The Rev. William Chapman of Holmside was simply not wanted by his local Lodge of Good Templars.[57] There were also those who thought that temperance work should be a matter of example rather than formal organisation. 'Our Temperance movement is simply the involvement of the whole tenor of Church Life,' wrote one, 'just like missionary work'.[58]

Significantly, however, there was also a thread of active *hostility* towards the temperance organisations, and at Sunderland St. John, Tow Law and Westgate the clergymen did all they could to keep them out of their parishes.[59] There was a feeling that 'a parish may be over-organised';[60] that 'too many organisations exhaust the workers';[61] even that workers might be driven to drink out of an oppositional spirit towards over-zealous temperance groups.[62] Clerical antipathy towards temperance organisations may have stemmed, in part, from the way in which they symbolised what Hugh McLeod has described as 'the transition from a religion of faith to a religion of works'.[63] Although there were many exceptions, these were groups that appealed most strongly to the nonconformist and evangelical mind, and many of the clergymen who shied away from them undoubtedly came from the High Church tradition. Above all, temperance campaigners were sometimes felt to carry about them the whiff of extremism. As the Rev. Frederick Cory put it in 1904, 'the Intemperance movement is marred by a very fanatical spirit'.[64] Particular suspicion was reserved for teetotalers, long regarded in some quarters as an 'anti-Christian sect'[65] and treated with disdain in the twentieth century by those who, like Bishop Henson, thought their strictures could only lead to the unworkable madness of Prohibition.[66]

---

[57] Response of the Rev. W. Chapman, Holmside (1904).

[58] Response of the Rev. H. C. Windley, Bensham St Chad (1904).

[59] Responses of the Rev. F. A. Leake, Sunderland St John; the Rev. T. H. E. C. Espin, Tow Law; the Rev. E. Johnson, Westgate.

[60] Response of the Rev. H. Birtley, St Paul West Hartlepool (1904).

[61] Response of the Rev. W. White, Esh (1904).

[62] Response of the Rev. T. H. E. C. Espin, Tow Law (1904).

[63] H. McLeod, *Religion and the Working Class in Nineteenth-Century Britain* (London, 1984), p. 34.

[64] Response of the Rev. F. Cory, Frosterley (1904).

[65] A. Hays, 'The Band of Hope and the Christian churches c.1847–1914', unpublished University of Durham, MA thesis, 2003, p. 3.

[66] E. F. Bradley (ed.), *Letters of Herbert Hensley Henson* (London, 1950), p. 35. Henson to the Rev. W. Bothamley, 6 December 1924.

The view expressed by Brian Harrison, among others, that temperance had had a brief association with radical politics, Chartism and early socialism but by the 1860s was essentially a religious movement,[67] is subjected to a severe test by some early-twentieth century visitation returns from Durham. It is clear that some clergymen believed the fanaticism and eccentricity they detected in the temperance movement operated alongside the even more pernicious influence of political radicalism. In fact temperance and radicalism had a relationship of considerable – even contradictory – complexity. The Rev. J. J. Brown of Coniscliffe and the Rev. G. Firth of Dalton-le-Dale had found their local temperance movements to be, respectively, too political and too anti-Church to join. Their perception was flatly contradicted by that of the Rev. George Ross-Lewin of Benfieldside, who thought that temperance groups had *failed* to get off the ground in his parish because 'radical politicians' had used their influence against them.[68] This apparent contradiction adheres to a pattern which can be read again and again in visitation returns over the years. Links made between temperance and trade unionism existed side-by-side with those made between temperance and anti-radicalism, with Methodism frequently a factor common to both sides.

In this respect Harrison's other principal argument – that a later generation of radical secularists disliked the temperance movement's religious leadership, wanting a sober working class but seeing temperance as a 'cloak for religious proselytism'[69] – is borne out by the sources. It is clear that it was not only from an elite direction that this aspect of popular culture was coming under attack. Movements like Methodism and trade unionism were also playing a significant role in the transformation of popular attitudes. Both urged temperance and teetotalism as a route to working-class independence and self-respect: as one trade union leader wrote to his brother trade unionists in 1880, labourers should 'unite for mutual intercourse, instruction and information. Knowledge is power. Leave off smoking and tippling and get to reading, thinking and acting.'[70]

It could be argued that, if James Woodforde's world was one in which popular culture was understood, tolerated and even sponsored by elites, and a later world one in which ultimately only respectable, elite-driven culture would do, much of the intervening period was one of transition,

---

[67] B. Harrison, 'Religion and Recreation in Nineteenth-Century England', *Past and Present*, 38 (December, 1967), 98–125.

[68] Responses of the Rev. J. J. Brown, Coniscliffe, the Rev. G. Firth, Dalton-le-Dale and the Rev. G. Ross-Lewin, Benfieldside (1904).

[69] Harrison, 'Religion and Recreation', 113.

[70] George Rix, and cited in Howkins, 'The taming of Whitsun', p. 188.

during which – for a time – industrial dioceses, like that of Durham, had
worked hard to reach some kind of accommodation with popular culture
before eventually coming to see it as running counter to the mission of
reform. Popular culture and custom in the early nineteenth century was, as
Thompson says and as *The Collier's Wedding* demonstrates, neither
revolutionary nor deferential.[71] It was, however, of profound importance to
the social cohesion of the local community, and customary rituals
sanctioned by the church were essential as a means of establishing senses
of identity and belonging.

By the end of the nineteenth century it could also be argued that the
process of cultural incorporation was well advanced, and the church's
legitimation of popular culture had been transformed into something paler,
emptier, and stripped of its meaning. The church – building, calendar and
incumbent – that had once been an integral part of (or at the very least not
overtly hostile to) popular culture, became an institution with which
parishioners felt altogether less at ease. It is no mere coincidence that at
the same time as a number of respondents to the 1928 visitation in Durham
acknowledged that many parishioners no longer attended church because
poverty and unemployment had left them with a 'lack of nice clothes',
some clergymen were also noting rather bitterly that there seemed to be
plenty of money for 'dancing, cinema, excursions &c.'[72]

As the two drifted ever further out of touch, popular culture began to
frame its own stereotypical portrait of the Anglican clergyman. While
James Woodforde came to be seen as a literary rather than a historic
character, an iconic personification of a dimly-understood 'world we have
lost', twentieth-century literary depictions of the clergymen that had
succeeded him frequently settled on the image of a withdrawn, buttoned-
up character, symbolically lost in the echoing corridors of a too-big
rectory, demonstrating by word and deed that he was ill-at-ease with his
parishioners, his family and his job:

> It's not easy . . . the English are not a deeply religious people. Even many
> of those who attend divine service do so from habit. Their acceptance of
> the sacrament is perfunctory: I have yet to meet the man whose hair rose at
> the nape of his neck because he was about to taste the blood of his dying
> Lord. Even when they visit their church in large numbers, at Harvest
> Thanksgiving or the Christmas Midnight Mass, it is no more than a pagan

---

[71] E. P. Thompson, *Customs in Common* (London, 1993), p. 64.
[72] DUL PG, AUC4/14, Visitation returns, 1928. See, for instance, the responses of
the Rev. Gibson Salisbury, Chester-le-Street, and the Rev. N. Burgess,
Waterhouses.

salute to the passing seasons. They do not need me. I come in useful at baptisms, weddings, funerals. Chiefly funerals.[73]

Readings of the fracture between Anglicanism and popular culture that are sympathetic to the notion of 'cultural incorporation' rely on an equation between 'mission' of the kind undertaken in nineteenth-century Durham and a broad interpretation of the term 'restoration'. In such an interpretation, the replacement of crumbling masonry, collapsing floors, rotten and disorderly pews, the building of new churches and the development of new parishes was much more than an ecclesiastical refurbishment: it was deeply symbolic of an ongoing drive for '*spiritual restoration*'. A church that many felt had become tolerant, lazy, effete, even corrupt in the late-eighteenth and early-nineteenth centuries, and had drifted below the radar of consciousness of many migrants into the Durham coalfield, was now attempting to re-assert itself as a force in the community. In its fullest form the restoration mission came complete with elite-driven festivities, usually celebrated on days of significance for the political establishment and designed, essentially, to replace popular festivals with a church service and tea on the rectory lawn. Like them, the restored or newly-built church in the paternalistic diorama of the nineteenth-century community made a statement, a 'direct assertion' on the part of landed and industrial interests 'of wealth and local paramountcy'.[74]

Many historians now argue that notions of 'social control', 'hegemony', 'appropriation' and 'cultural incorporation' go too far when seeking to explain what Victorian reformers of popular culture were up to. Here, for instance, is Stedman Jones on the issue:

The very fact that so little verbal defence was made of traditional popular recreation, is not merely because rational recreationists monopolized the means of communication. It was because workers themselves were very divided on whether traditional forms of recreation were worthy of defence . . . Leisure institutions which remained essential to workers – pubs for example – were strongly defended. But others were given up with little resistance, because they had ceased to have a point. It is really dangerous

---

[73] J. L. Carr's literary portrait of the fictional clergyman, the Rev. J. G. Keach, in *A Month in the Country* (London, 1980), pp. 97–8. The novel is set in 1920.
[74] C. Brooks, 'Building the rural church: Money, power and the country parish', in C. Brooks and A. Saint (eds), *The Victorian Church: architecture and society* (Manchester, 1995), p. 66.

to interpret the disappearance of pre-industrial recreations simply as a huge defeat.[75]

It could even be argued that 'defeat' was actually experienced by elites, and that a response to popular culture that tacked between hostility, sympathy, antiquarian understanding and rigid opposition epitomised the awkward journey undergone by the Church of England during the nineteenth and early-twentieth centuries. In the Durham coalfield, as elsewhere, the transformation of popular culture embraced elements of religious conviction, political belief, paternalism, radicalism, conservatism and Methodism, all demonstrating their own internal conflicts but each moving the process forward by increments. Increasingly influenced by the ethics of temperance, moderation, self-help and self-discipline, North East pitmen began to put more and more distance between themselves and the 'Bob Crankey' stereotype of old. Even though the transformation of popular culture was far from being an exclusively Anglican project, clerical involvement with popular culture was more often marked by tension and disputation than by ecumenical harmony and in their encounters with a culture to which they themselves did not subscribe, clergymen sometimes lapsed into the language of suppression.

Before the reformers had got to work in earnest, the advice of some influential voices was to leave popular culture well alone. As one eighteenth-century tract advised, clergymen should remember the maxim: 'He is a meek and humble man who meddleth not himself in temporal concerns.'[76] By the mid-nineteenth century John Buddle, the managerial and administrative power behind the throne of Lord Londonderry's coal interest, was pointing out to anyone who would listen that popular culture posed no particular threat, so long as it did not become too politicised. The entertainments of miners, were concerned chiefly with having 'fought our Cocks, drank our Yell & chewed our Backy quietly and on a pay Night amused ourselves with a canny bit on a fight, nobit to ken whee was the best hewer'.[77] But, by the early-twentieth century, there were signs that the elimination of 'Bob Crankey' was close. If the evidence suggests that this elimination was the result of numerous political and religious

---

[75] G. Stedman Jones, 'Class expression versus social control', p. 88.

[76] Norfolk Record Office, FEL 813, 555 x 8: *Considerations on the Poor Laws* (1775).

[77] John Buddle to Ralph Iveson, 8 October 1819, and cited in R. Colls, '"Oh Happy English Children!" Coal, class and education in the North East', *Past and Present*, 73 (1976), 92.

initiatives, including many that originated within the working class, there were clearly those within the Church of England who felt that it had been the intention of their denomination all along, and that with them lay the credit for Crankey's demise. As the Rev. R. T. Heselton of West Rainton indicated, control of popular culture and 'social control' remained indivisible concepts in the minds of some:

> There are no Cinemas – I have rebuilt the Church Hall & made it the most attractive Hall in the district. By this I am beginning to have control over all the social functions in the neighbourhood.[78]

---

[78] DUL PG, AUC 4/14, Visitation Returns, 1928. Response of the Rev. R. T. Heselton, West Rainton.

NOTES ON CONTRIBUTORS

Joan Allen is a Senior Lecturer in Modern British History at Newcastle University and an editor of *Labour History Review*. Her research interests are in nineteenth-century radical politics, the Irish in Britain and the history of the popular press. Among other things, she is the author of *Joseph Cowen and Popular Radicalism on Tyneside* (London, 2007) and (with Owen R. Ashton) the co-edited volume, *Papers for the People: a study of the Chartist press* (London, 2005). She is currently writing a biography of the Catholic Press baron and Irish nationalist, Charles Diamond.

Richard C. Allen is Reader in Early Modern Cultural History and Head of History at the University of Wales, Newport. He was formerly the Fulbright-Robertson Visiting Professor of British History (2006–7) at Westminster College, Missouri. He has published widely on many aspects of Quakerism in Wales and elsewhere, and on migration and identity. His most recent works are *Quaker Communities in Early Modern Wales: from resistance to respectability* (Cardiff, 2007) and the co-edited *Irelands of the Mind: memory and identity in modern Irish culture* (Newcastle, 2008). He is currently writing a study of Quaker migration entitled, *Transatlantic Connections: Welsh Quaker emigrants and Colonial Pennsylvania*, as well as co-authoring, *Quaker Networks and Moral Reform in the North East of England*.

Madeleine Gray is a Senior Lecturer in History in the University of Wales, Newport, and one of the editors of the *Gwent County History* published by the University of Wales Press. She has a long-standing interest in pilgrimages and saints' cults and in the visual imagery of medieval religion. Her book *Images of Piety*, on the iconography of late medieval religion in Wales, was published by BAR in 2000. More recently, she has published articles on the Last Judgement in medieval Welsh art and on the medieval tombs in Llandaff Cathedral. She is currently rewriting and re-visioning medieval saints' cults.

James Gregory is a Lecturer in Modern History at the University of Bradford. He is currently completing a biography of William Cowper-

Temple (Lord Mount Temple) and his second wife Georgina, two prominent figures in Victorian philanthropy and religious reform. He has researched and published chapters and articles on 'eccentricity' in British culture c.1760–1901 and recently published *Of Victorians and Vegetarians. The vegetarian movement in nineteenth-century Britain* (London, 2007).

David Ceri Jones is a Lecturer in History at Aberystwyth University. He is the author of *A Glorious Work in the World: Welsh Methodism and the International Evangelical Revival, 1735–50* (Cardiff, 2004). He has also written widely on the Enlightenment and Romanticism, particularly in a Welsh context. He is one of the editors of the *The Correspondence of Iolo Morganwg* (3 vols. Cardiff, 2007). He is currently writing a history of Calvinistic Methodism in England and Wales during the eighteenth century which will be published by the University of Wales Press in early 2010.

Clark Lawlor is Reader in English Literature at the University of Northumbria and Director of the Northumbria Academy of English Language and Literature. He is also Co-Director of the Leverhulme Trust-funded three year project entitled 'Before Depression: the representation and culture of "the English malady", 1660–1800'. His recent publications include *Consumption and Literature: the making of the romantic disease* (Basingstoke, 2006), which was shortlisted for the European Society for the Study of English Book Prize in English Literature, 2006–8. His research interests include literature and medicine, and representations of the body in literature and art.

Robert Lee is a Lecturer in Modern British History at the University of Teesside, specialising in nineteenth and twentieth-century social history. Much of his research in recent years has been concerned with the interaction between institutional religion and local society, resulting in two publications: *Rural Society and the Anglican Clergy, 1815–1914: encountering and managing the poor* (London, 2006) and *The Church of England and the Durham Coalfield, 1810–1926: clergymen, capitalists and colliers* (London, 2007). Wider research interests embracing the plight of the rural poor and the nature of political activism in the nineteenth-century countryside resulted in a further book, *Unquiet Country: voices of the rural poor, 1820–1880* (Bollington, 2005). He is currently preparing a comparative regional study examining the relationship between land-ownership and political dissent.

D. A. James MacPherson is a Teaching Fellow at the University of Bristol. He was formerly an AHRC Fellow at the University of Warwick where he worked on the 'Women in Modern Irish culture, 1800–2005' project. He has published on the associational life of Irish women, notably (with Donald M. MacRaild), 'Sisters of the brotherhood: Female Orangeism on Tyneside in the late-19th and early-20th centuries', *Irish Historical Studies*, 137 (2006), and (with David Renton), 'Immigrant Politics and North-East Identity, 1907–1973', in A. F. Pollard and A. G. Green (eds), *The North East and Regional Identity* (Woodbridge, 2007). He is currently working on a study of female Orange lodges in England and Scotland, 1850–1950.

Edward Royle is Emeritus Professor of History at the University of York. He has published extensively on the social history of Britain since the eighteenth century, with particular interests in radical politics, religion and the history of Yorkshire. His most recent works include an edition (with Ruth M. Larsen) of Archbishop Thomson's Visitation Returns for the Diocese of York, 1865, and his is currently working on a parallel volume of Bishop Bickersteth's Visitation Returns for the Archdeaconry of Craven, Diocese of Ripon, 1858.

Eryn White is a Senior Lecturer in the Department of History and Welsh History at Aberystwyth University. Her research concentrates on aspects of religion and culture in eighteenth-century Wales. She is the author of *'Praidd Bach y Bugail Mawr'*: *seiadau Methodistaidd de-orllewin Cymru 1737–50* (Llandysul, 1995), *The Welsh Bible* (Stroud, 2007), and co-author of *Calendar of the Trevecka Letters* (Aberystwyth, 2003). She also serves on the editorial board of the *Studies in Welsh History* published by the University of Wales Press.

INDEX

Abercorn, Duchess of 175
Aberdeen, Lord 162–3
absentees, church 46–7, 188
Acomb, Yorkshire 85, 92
Adair, Daryl 139, 143
Airedale 83
alcohol consumption
    Durham coalmining
        communities 10, 180, 189–
        93
    Quaker views on 53, 54, 57, 66,
        67, 73
Allen, Joan 8–9, 137–56
Allen, Richard 123
Allen, Richard C. 7, 8, 52–74
Allen, Mrs W. J. 166–7, 168–9
Allen, William 147
Almondbury, Yorkshire 78, 89–90
altars 12
America
    Hicksite schism 127
    Parnell Defence fund 155
    religious revival 75, 76, 79, 99,
        107
    St Patrick's Day celebrations
        139
    see also Georgia
Ancient Order of Hibernians (AOH)
    160
Anglican Church *see* Church of
    England
Angus, Betty 114
anti-Catholicism 113, 158, 160
anti-Methodism, Welsh 40, 110–12
anticlericalism 3, 126
antinomianism 127, 134
antiquarian movement 180–1

*Apology for the True Christian
    Divinity* (Barclay) 72–3
Apostolic Church 114
apprenticeships, Quakers 59
Aquinas, Thomas 15–16
Archaeologia Aeliana 180–1
Archer, Isaac 23–4, 25
Aretaeus 26, 32
Arminians 77, 86, 114
Ars Moriendi 5, 28, 36, 37
Ascension Day celebrations 144
Asquith, Herbert 157
Atkinson, Christopher 77, 81
Atkinson, Miles 81
Australia 139

Balfour, Gerald 159
ballads 179
Ballycastle Women's Unionist
    Association 169
Ballymoney Free Press 169
Bancroft, Richard, Bishop of
    London 19
Band of Hope 191
Bangor, diocese of 40, 41, 47
bankruptcy 63, 73
baptism 4, 15–16, 42
    Calvinist tradition 17, 18
    Luther's view of 16–17
    by women 15, 16, 18, 19
    see also unbaptized
Baptists 21, 83, 87, 88, 93
Barclay, John 123
Barclay, Robert 126
    *Apology for the True Christian
        Divinity* 72–3
Barkley, John 49
Barmby, J. Goodwin 130, 133

and Lloyd family of Dolobran
63, 69
poetry 61, 67
on sexual impropriety 68
teaching positions 56, 59
on vanity and foolish pastimes
63, 64
The Faithful Monitor 66
Kelsall, John Snr 53
Kelsall, John, son of John Jnr 62
Kennicott, Benjamin 190
Kent, John 79
Ker, Walter 76
Kidwelly, Carmarthenshire 50
Kippax, Yorkshire 81
Kirkby Wharfe, Yorkshire 91–2
Kirkpatrick, William B. 127
Knox, John 20

Lambston, Pembrokeshire 41
Lancashire 82 n., 141
Larkin, Philip 147
Latitudinarianism 78
Laugharne, Carmarthenshire 41
Law, Andrew Bonar 168
Law, William 77
law and burial practices 14–15, 18–
19
Lawlor, Clark 5–6, 26–38
League of the Cross 149
Ledsham, Yorkshire 78, 81, 84
Lee, Raymond M. 159
Lee, Robert 9–10, 176–97
Leeds, Yorkshire 81, 85, 87, 153
Leigh, Dr George 82
Leinster Express 134
Lenton, John 83
letter-writing networks, Methodist
6, 99, 100–3, 105–10
Lewis, George 70, 71
Lewis, John 99, 100, 102, 105, 114
Lewis, Richard 63
Lewis, Thomas 50–1
licences for dissenting meetings 92–
3

literacy 53
literary representation of disease 28,
29–30, 34–
Little, Patrick 164–5
Littleburn, County Durham 186
'lived religion' 95
Liverpool 139, 141
Liverpool Mercury 143
Llandaff, diocese of 40, 47
Llandeilo Fawr, Carmarthenshire 47
Llandovery, Carmarthenshire 21
Llandysul, Cardiganshire 45
Llanfyllin, Montgomeryshire 66–7
Llangadog, Carmarthenshire 49
Llangan, Carmarthenshire 24, 41
Llangatwg Lingoed,
Monmouthshire 43
Llanishen, Glamorgan 50–1
Llanwenog, Cardiganshire 45
Llanycrwys, Carmarthenshire 42
Lloyd family of Dolobran 63, 69
Llyswyrny, Glamorgan 49
Locke, John 104
London
Irish diaspora 141
Irish Institutes 149
Methodism 77, 102, 114
St Patrick's Day celebrations
139, 156
Londonderry, Lady 170, 171
Londonderry, Lord 196
Lowe, John 82–3
Lowry, Mrs 166
Lowry, Richard 144
Lurgan Women's Unionist
Association 166, 168, 169–70,
172
Luther, Martin 16–17
Lutheran Church 76

McAnulty, Bernard 151, 155
McCann marriage case (c.1909) 9,
158–9, 161–8
McCarthy, M. J. F. 160
McCulloch, William 99